Do It
Yourself
HEBREW
AND
GREEK

Do It Yourself

HEBREW AND GREEK

Everybody's Guide to the Language Tools

Edward W. Goodrick

ZONDERVAN
PUBLISHING HOUSE
OF THE ZONDERVAN CORPORATION
GRAND RAPIDS, MICHIGAN 49506

MULTNOMAH PRESS
PORTLAND, OREGON 97266

© Multnomah Press, 1976, 1980
Printed in the United States of America

Second Edition

Third printing 1981

Library of Congress Cataloging in Publication Data

Goodrick, Edward W   1913-
    Do it yourself Hebrew and Greek.

    1. Greek language, Biblical--Grammar.
2. Primers, Hebrew. I. Title.
PA817.G6 1980   488'.0076   79-25463
Multnomah: ISBN 0-930014-35-9
Zondervan: ISBN 0-310-41741-4

To John Brown of Haddington

TABLE OF CONTENTS

INTRODUCTION

LESSON 1 . . . . THE GREEK ALPHABET

LESSON 2 . . . . THE GREEK PARTS OF SPEECH

LESSON 3 . . . . THE GREEK CASE SYSTEM

LESSON 4 . . . . .THE GREEK VERB

LESSON 5 . . . . SYNTAX

LESSON 6 . . . . .HOW TO FIND THE GREEK WORD

LESSON 7 . . . . .IDENTIFYING THE FORM

LESSON 8 . . . . INTERPRETING THE FORM

LESSON 9 . . . . HOW TO DO A WORD STUDY

LESSON 10 . . . . HOW TO DO A WORD STUDY: CONTINUED

LESSON 11 . . . . USE OF THE GREEK LEXICON

LESSON 12 . . . . COMMON SENSE RULES FOR INTERPRETATION

LESSON 13 . . . . .THE USE OF COMMENTARIES

LESSON 14 . . . . THE HEBREW ALPHABET

LESSON 15 . . . . .HEBREW GRAMMAR

LESSON 16 . . . . HOW TO ANALYZE THE HEBREW WORD

LESSON 17 . . . . THE HEBREW LEXICON

LESSON 18 . . . . THE EXTERNAL CONTEXT: GEOGRAPHY

LESSON 19 . . . . .THE EXTERNAL CONTEXT: CULTURE

LESSON 20 . . . . .THE EXTERNAL CONTEXT: HISTORY

LESSON 21 . . . . .THE ROLE OF THE EXEGETE

LESSON 22 . . . . INTERPRETING IDIOMS

GLOSSARY OF TERMS

DETACHABLE WORKSHEETS AND ANSWER KEY

NEED

The slopes of the mountain are littered with the dead and dying. 90% of those who begin to study Greek in an effort to master the pinnacles of Bible knowledge do not continue with their language studies after completing their formal training. And the same holds true for 99% of those studying Hebrew. The mortality rate for those studying original Bible languages is horrendous!

Students spend enormous segments of time and energy memorizing vocabulary lists, declensions and conjugations, only to forget them in a few years through lack of use.

They burden themselves with these sizable memory projects just when their study time is at a premium; for, if they are not going to use this information, it is better that they use this time in other learning endeavors.

Now, such time spent is never a total loss. The individual student will always know how to use concordances, lexicons and commentaries based upon the original languages, for these have been his tools. But if only there had been a course of study which would have provided him these benefits without those demanding memory assignments.

Even the student who wants to persevere up the mountain needs a halfway house to serve as an immediate goal. Once there, he can contemplate his progress and determine whether he wants to complete his climb. This way, he avoids the total exhaustion of the uninterrupted climb as well as the catastrophe of total failure.

This manual will also serve the bright, mature Christian who loves Bible study so much he would give almost anything if he could break the "language barrier," but who would not dare mount so formidable an enterprise as a frontal approach on Hebrew and Greek.

Something must be done for him so that he can get at least a glimpse of the structure of these languages. He needs a manual which will give him guidance in the use of Bible study tools and which will unfold to him the mysteries of the elementary terminology involved in their use.

So this introduction to the Biblical Languages is designed to meet the needs of three groups of people.

1) The student who would not otherwise take Greek or Hebrew will gain understanding that will take him considerably beyond his English potential. He will be able to use the original language tools that are ordinarily limited to the "professionals."

2) This same result can be realized by the layperson who, though not having had the advantage of formal training in languages, can raise the standard of his Biblical study by the employment of much superior tools.

3) Finally, there is the student already committed to the language program or seriously considering it. His course of study is designed to provide him with a thorough knowledge of the language tools that he will be using all his life. Further, he will be getting his feet wet and his mind exposed to the practicality of the course he is pursuing.

> However, under no circumstance should this course be thought of as a substitute for the diligent study of grammar, vocabulary and exegesis. There must be no confusion in anyone's mind which is the "low road" and which is the "high road." It is our hope that once a person completes this course, having tested his competence on the "low road," he will see the value of further study and thus embark on the "high road."

PURPOSE

After consideration of needs, it is easy to spell out the purpose for this course of study. This course intends to provide the student with enough assistance so that he will have a basic understanding of the structures, primarily of Greek, but also of Hebrew. He will also develop an understanding of the basic vocabulary of exegesis. And, finally, he will employ this information, practicing the actual use of those tools of Bible study which are based on the original languages of the Bible, enough so that he will be able to continue on his own.

Such a course requires the following objectives:

1. Memory:
   a. The Greek alphabet
   b. The Hebrew alphabet
   c. The declension of the Greek article
   d. Greek prepositions

2. Understanding:
   a. The basic structure of Greek and Hebrew
   b. The elementary vocabulary of exegesis
   c. The purpose for the various Bible study tools

3. Skill:
   a. Sounding out Greek and Hebrew words
   b. Use of Greek and Hebrew alphabets in lexical study
   c. Selection of and use of appropriate Biblical study tools

PROCEDURES

Because the Bible was first written in Hebrew, Aramaic and Greek, the Bible student seeks to learn as much as he can about the languages themselves. The serious Bible student seeks to discover precisely what the Bible meant in these languages. In order to do this he must develop skills in the use of study tools which are based on the original languages.

This course provides an introduction into these areas. It also provides detailed guidance for the student as he begins to practice using the tools.

First, he will take a brief look at the structure of Greek, learn the alphabet and sounds, plus a very limited vocabulary, and practice using each tool by itself. Then he will use all the tools plus all his knowledge together in solving New Testament problems. He will then follow the same pattern with the Hebrew language. And finally, he will seek to solve Biblical problems which require research in both the Old and New Testaments.

What about Aramaic? We are not going to do anything special about the Aramaic language because the alphabet is identical to the Hebrew, and the tools we will be using include both the Hebrew and Aramaic parts. Furthermore, we will not be learning enough about Hebrew grammar to distinguish it from Aramaic. This is for the "high roaders."

Lectures will describe and demonstrate techniques of study. A worksheet form is supplied for each assignment. The paragraphs entitled "Purpose and Goals" before each assignment are very important

and should be read before starting the work on the
assigned problem. Without this page, the student
will not understand what his goals are and will not
be prepared for any quizzes in class that might
cover the purposes of the assignment. Any blanks in
these pre-assignment paragraphs should be filled in.
Understanding the goals and purposes of an assignment is an absolute "must" for meaningful learning
in these lab sessions.

However, the lessons and the worksheets are
designed so that a person may complete the study
without a teacher or help in his assignment sheets.

When the student runs across exegetical terms
he does not understand, he should look them up in
the glossary prepared for this in the back of the
book. If he doesn't know what the English terms
mean, he'll not be able to understand their usage
in Greek or Hebrew!

Do not try to master all of the data contained
in this book! Read it over, understand it, and then
try to remember where it is located. You will be
referring back to various pages time and time again.
Limit your memory efforts to the memory assignments.
Then devote your energies to understanding what the
principles are, what the problems are, and what the
techniques are to solve them and why it works that
way.

YOU ARE NOT SUPPOSED TO MEMORIZE THE DATA
GIVEN IN THIS BOOK. To do so is to try to negotiate
the "high road" using the wrong text.

LIMITATIONS

And this brings us to the next point. As has
already been said, this is the "low road" you are on.
The student will not learn Hebrew or Greek, will not
be able to translate, and will not become qualified
to do independent exegesis.

Pope might well have had this very course in
mind when he rhymed:

A little learning is a dangerous thing;
Drink deep, or taste not the Pierian spring.

The master exegete, knowing only too well the
lurking pitfalls caused by the languages' subtleties,
complexities, and exceptions, could ask, "Can it
really be done? Would not such a smattering of knowledge do more harm than good? Would it not give a
false feeling of confidence, tempting a person beyond

his depth? Would it not be better scholarship for
those who do not master the original languages to
confine their research to the English tools which are
many, excellent and ample?"

Unless these objections can be answered, this
course of study cannot be justified. Two observations
serve as rebuttal. First, one should not censure
this course because it falls so short of the ideal,
but rather commend it if it is any improvement over
current practice. Too often the church is abused by
some self-appointed authority, a Greek *Testament* in
one hand and a Bagster's *Analytical* in the other,
pontificating preposterous exegesis. How difficult
it is to remain charitable with one who, having discovered the Greek and Hebrew "gimmicks" in Strong's
Concordance, beclouds his witness with mispronuncia-
tions of Greek and Hebrew words and undermines good
translations by playing fast and loose with corrections based on the meager definitions of words found
there.

The second observation is that a person wants
his physician to know a lot of things, including the
limitations of his competence. If building this
insight is not in the curriculum of the medical
schools, it ought to be! This course is designed to
teach the student his limitations, which is an
advance over current procedures. For the argument
stated against this course also applies to the
ninety percent and the ninety-nine percent who,
though starting down the traditional route, do not
continue on. Thomas Huxley added an important
corollary to Pope. He asked:

> *If a little knowledge is dangerous, where is the man*
> *who has so much as to be out of danger?*

True, the ninety and the ninety-nine percent
will possess a better understanding of the complexities of the languages and will thus be better fore-
warned. But the continuous cautions offered in this
course can also forewarn the student who chooses to
follow only the "low road."

ENGLISH TOOLS

Before advancing to the Bible study tools
based upon the Hebrew and Greek, the student must be
familiar with tools available in the English language.
These tools are classified into nine categories:
concordances, commentaries, introductions, reference
Bibles, center column references, topical text books,
versions, atlases and dictionaries.

Concordances

For English use, the best concordance is an "exhaustive" or complete one. It is only available in the King James Version, and there is a choice of two: Strong's or Young's. The one done by Mr. Strong is much easier to use. There are concordances that are almost exhaustive for both the American Standard Version and the Revised Standard Version.

A concordance serves two functions. First, it can help to find a passage which you know, when you cannot remember the reference. Secondly, it can help find a new passage. Let's look at an example of each.

Suppose you remember the verse, ". . . if so be ye have tasted that the Lord is gracious," but you can't find it in the Bible. Take the most unusual word in the verse and look it up in the main section of Strong's *Concordance*. In this case, the best word to pick is "tasted" because it will appear less often that the other words. You will find the word "tasted" on page 999 and there are eight passages listed under it. This means that "tasted" is used only eight times in the entire King James Version. The reference is listed first and then the phrase in which the word appears in that verse is written out. Run your eye down each of the phrases until you find ". . . ye have t. that the Lord is gracious." Now glance to the left to find the reference, and you see it is in I Peter 2:3. The lost passage has been found!

But you can also find new passages. Now that you have found I Peter 2:3, you wonder if the Bible speaks about "tasting the Lord" in any other place. You will need to look, not only under the word "tasted," but also under the simple verb, "taste," and any other similar forms listed nearby. Looking under "taste," you find that there are twenty references. Your eye runs down the column until you notice "O t. and see that the Lord is good," and it is found in Psalm 34:8. Looking further, you will find two more phrases in Hebrews 6 which you will also want to look up.

Generally speaking, however, the latter method is not the most practical for studying specific subjects because you will be confronted with too many pages of references. For example, if you want to study the subject of "God," you would find that the list of passages under "God" covers twelve pages and it would be an unending job to sort out the various verses. Also, it is possible to miss important passages if the word under consideration is not mentioned in the text. While studying "forgiveness," the concordance would not lead you to the story of the prodigal son in Luke 15:11-32 simply because the word does not occur in the text.

Good commentaries explain the meaning of Scripture, verse by verse. Single volume commentaries on the whole Bible prove unsatisfactory because they are not large enough to comment that extensively. It is best to have either multi-volume commentaries over the whole Bible or have commentaries on individual books.

There are various types of commentaries. They may be devotional, homiletical, expositional, exegetical and/or critical.

Devotional: direct application of Biblical statements to one's spiritual need.

Homiletical: includes the above with illustrative materials and sermon outlines added.

Expositional: explanation of the whole text with attention to the flow of thought through the book.

Exegetical: minute analysis of the Greek and Hebrew texts.

Critical: historical, literary and textual criticism, with attention to controversial problems, and with lengthy introductions.

Commentaries tend to polarize themselves into two kinds: those that feature the aspects of the last two, and those that only present the first three. A knowledge of Hebrew and Greek is usually necessary to properly understand the exegetical-critical commentary. Much is already developed in the devotional, homiletical kind. The discerning, Spirit-led Bible teacher ought to be able to make his own applications, discover his own illustrations, and make up his own outlines.

One of the best commentaries, efficient in all five aspects, within the reach of the English reader, and serving as an example of what a non-Greek or non-Hebrew based commentary ought to be, is done by H. C. G. Moule on *Romans, Colossians, Philemon, and Ephesians.* (He is not to be confused with C. F. D. Moule.) Perhaps the best multi-volume set for the English reader is *The Tyndale Old and New Testament Commentaries.* See also Zondervan's *Expositor's Bible Commentary.*

The better introductions are limited to a single Testament. One must have at least one for each. They are the basic and best sources for background materials of individual books. They treat the canonicity, integrity, authenticity, authorship, destination, date, occasion, etc. of each book. At present the two best are: R. K.

Harrison, *Introduction to the Old Testament*, Eerdmans
Publishing, Grand Rapids, 1969 (1325 pp.), and
Donald Guthrie, *New Testament Introduction*, Inter-
Varsity Press, Chicago, 1970 (1054 pp.).

Reference Bibles

Reference Bibles contain study helps, mini-
introductions to books, a mini-concordance, often
a mini-commentary on difficult or significant verses,
and a mini-set of references directing the reader to
other scriptures which deal with the same theme.
These are excellent and to be recommended to the
beginning Bible student. However the advancing
Bible student soon out-grows his reference Bible
as he finds the inadequacy of its helps more and
more frustrating and as he adds full-grown helps to
his library. But the question is: How much of your
library do you wish to pack around with you everywhere you go?

Probably the best reference Bible is the
New Scofield, containing a text which moderately
improves on the King James Version. The *Holman
Study Bible* is a good Revised Standard Version
reference Bible done by conservative scholars.

**Center Column
References**

One does not progress very far as a Bible
student before discovering the value of the center
column references. *The Treasury of Scripture
Knowledge* (Revell) is a book-size enlargement of the
center column reference and replaces the one in a
reference Bible. This is an essential Biblical tool.

**Topical Text
Books**

References listed according to topics compose
the *New Topical Text Book* (Revell), also a very
handy tool.

Versions

One simply must have several versions of the
Bible for comparative study. My suggestions would
be: New American Standard Version, Revised Standard
Version, Jerusalem Bible, Phillip's and the New
International Version. One must never launch out
on an interpretation which requires a translation
which is not the consensus of the various versions.

Atlases

Because geography of the Holy Land is important in understanding the Bible, the Bible student
should have and use a good Bible atlas. My recom-
mendation is *The Macmillan Bible Atlas* by Yohanan
Aharoni and Michael Avi-Yonah, published by Macmillan
in 1977.

Dictionaries

The Bible student needs a good Bible dictionary
which is a quick, handy reference to almost any subject found in the Bible. I would recommend *The New
Bible Dictionary,* edited by J. D. Douglas, published

by Eerdmans in 1962.

You will notice the effort made to match up
the exercises with the subject content of the
accompanying lesson. That is, after the principle
is described and demonstrated during the lesson,
the student will go to the library and practice
putting those principles into practice. Furthermore,
as the student progresses, he will be asked to combine the skills he is gathering for the solving of
specific problems.

So if you are tempted to change the material
around, you will appreciate this warning about
getting the material out of sequence.

The 22 lessons are quite arbitrary, however.
I have been using this material for a class which
meets about 30 times. You might wish to take a day
or two before plunging in, and I strongly advise you
to take at least a day each for memorizing the alphabets and one each for the Greek article and the Greek
prepositions.

You will further note how, toward the end, the
lessons "peeter out," whereas the exercises come on
strong. I could fill them out artificially for cos-
metic reasons, I guess. But I wouldn't have any
pedagogical grounds for doing it.

I have taken this extra time myself for going
over the problems in the exercises after they have
been completed by the class, for practice reading in
Greek and Hebrew, for lectures on hermeneutics and
for exegetical lectures in the first chapters of
Genesis and John.

The answer key that is provided is detachable.
If the teacher should so desire, this may be handed
in at the first class session so that it may not be
a source of temptation for the student.

PRACTICE READING

If the student is going to work with the
original languages, he should learn how to sound out
the words. Therefore, a cassette tape with Hebrew
on one side and Greek on the other is available
through Multnomah Press, Portland, Oregon 97266.

Also, the first 47 verses of the Gospel of
John are printed on pages 1:9-11 for you to practice
on. Try to sound out each Greek word. Listen to the
Greek side of the cassette tape while following along
with your eyes.

When the tape leaves an interval between the
words, repeat the word out loud that has been sounded
out on the tape.

After you can follow along easily with your
eyes, then try to pronounce each Greek word as it is
being pronounced on the tape. The reading recorded
on the tape gets progressively faster. This is done
in order to help you gain speed in sounding out Greek
words.

If you devote considerable time to this
practice, it will pay you rich dividends later on.

SECOND EDITION

Besides minor corrections, up-dating, and clari-
fications here and there, Lessons Seventeen, Eighteen,
Nineteen, Twenty, and half of Lesson Sixteen have been
entirely rewritten. The content in the answer sheets
has been doubled.

ACKNOWLEDGEMENTS

I have received a lot of help from my friends,
whose contributions have made this study manual a much
better work than I could have produced alone. Though
there were more I want to mention the names of three:
Barbara Handt, Barry Keiser and especially John
Kohlenberger III who, in the first edition, wrote much
of the Hebrew material, made up the answer sheet and typ
the whole manuscript for the camera, and in this second
edition expanded the answer sheets and rewrote Lessons
Sixteen and Seventeen.

The 5,000 or so different languages we have in the world have not been properly classified. So far, two major groups have been identified. The largest contains the original language of the New Testament and the second largest, the two languages of the Old Testament. (See charts on pages 1:2 and 1:3.)

THE FAMILY OF NEW TESTAMENT GREEK

They call the largest group "Indo-European" (some prefer "Indo-Germanic"). It has been broken down into six major families. Our English is a combination of two of them, the basic Germanic affected later by the Italic. Greek is another one of the six.

Like all other languages, Greek is dynamic, always in a state of change. In historic progression, you go from its primitive state to Classical Greek to Hellenistic Greek to Byzantine Greek and finally to Modern Greek.

Our interest lies in Hellenistic Greek which identifies the kind of Greek used roughly in number of years as the number of the Antichrist and split equally between AD and BC.

The vernacular Hellenistic, the popular "street" Greek, the "lingua franca" of the period is called Koine Greek.

Biblical Greek is the Koine spoken by people in areas where Aramaic was the mother tongue.

THE GREEK ALPHABET

The Greek alphabet may seem a little strange at first because it has different symbols, a different order, and some different sounds. But soon you will know it just as well as the English alphabet. We will mainly use the lower case letters, so begin with them FIRST. The capital forms are given so you can refer to this chart when you find an unknown letter in the Greek text. (And of course, you can learn them if you want to, for it will always be helpful.)

THE INDO-EUROPEAN LANGUAGES

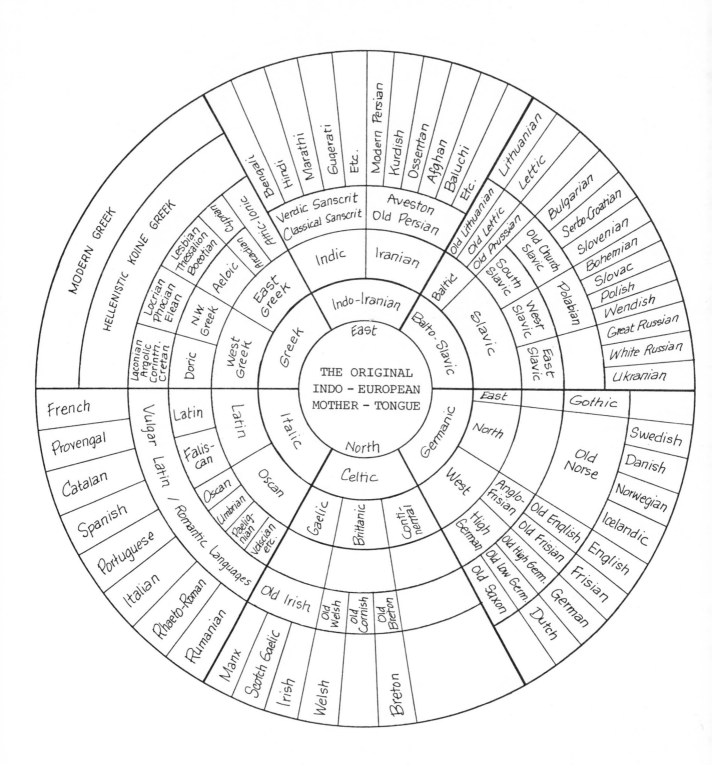

(See also *Lexical Aids for Students of New Testament Greek*, by Bruce M. Metzger, published by author, pp. 74-75.

Hittite belongs somewhere on this chart, along with a half-dozen other ancient languages.

THE SEMITIC LANGUAGES

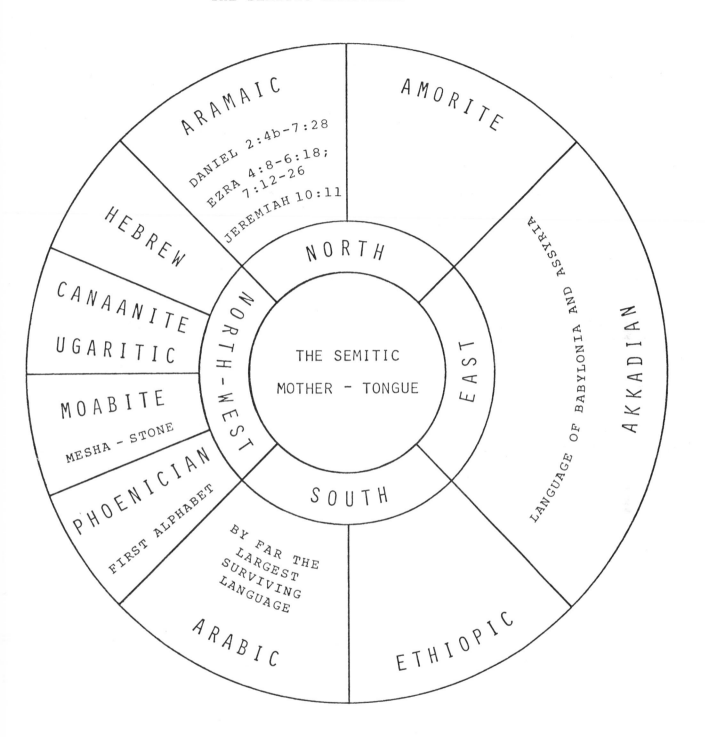

(See also *The Books and the Parchments,* by F. F. Bruce, published by Revell Press, p. 34.)

Hebrew and Aramaic are close cousins, like Norwegian and Swedish. There is no known parent language common to both the Semitic and the Indo-European families.

Let's begin work on the alphabet. Notice the symbol for the first letter is "α" and the name of the letter is "ahl-fah." We have the sound in our English word "father." Practice writing the symbol and saying its name. A good exercise would be to try to think of other English words, beside "father," that have the same SOUND. For instance, "cot, bother, lock, rod." Remember we are looking for the same SOUND, not necessarily the same letter. Now, continue practicing the rest of the alphabet.

Capital	Lower	Name		Pronounced as in:
A	α	Alpha	(ahl-fah)	father
B	β	Beta	(bay-tah)	ball
Γ	γ	Gamma	(gahm-ma)	gone
Δ	δ	Delta	(dell-tah)	dog
E	ε	Epsilon	(ep-sih-lawn)	met
Z	ζ	Zeta	(dzay-tah)	adze
H	η	Eta	(ay-tah)	they
Θ	ϑ	Theta	(thay-tah)	throne
I	ι	Iota	(ee-oh-tah)	fit, machine
K	κ	Kappa	(cop-ah)	king
Λ	λ	Lambda	(lahm-dah)	long
M	μ	Mu	(moo)	men
N	ν	Nu	(new)	new
Ξ	ξ	Xi	(ksee)	likes, asks
O	o	Omicron	(au-mih-crawn)	log
Π	π	Pi	(pea, pie)	pea
P	ρ	Rho	(hrow)	her
Σ	σ,ς	Sigma	(sig-mah)	sign
T	τ	Tau	(rhyme with "how")	ten
Y	υ	Upsilon	(oop-sih-lawn)	new (German "ü")
Φ	φ	Phi	(fee)	phone
X	χ	Chi	(key)	Bach (the composer)
Ψ	ψ	Psi	(psee)	lips
Ω	ω	Omega	(oh-may-gah)	only

Though these Greek letters are far more ancient than the New Testament, their shapes are very modern, less than 100 years. But we learn these because these are the shapes of the letters in modern Greek New Testaments.

See the following illustration of what John 3:16 probably looked like when it was first written.

ΟΥΤωΣΤΑΡΗΓΑΠΗCEW

ΟΘCΤΟΝΚΟCμΟΝωCΤΕΤΟΝ1ΟΝ

ΤΟΝμΟΝΟΤΕΗΕΔωΚΕΝ

Did you notice that many of the sounds are like ones we use in English? But unlike English, the Greek letter is usually pronounced the same way in every word. For instance, every time you see the letter "α" (ahl-fah), you will pronounce it "ah," if it is not with another vowel. This makes Greek much easier. Remember--basically, each Greek letter has only one sound and it is usually pronounced the same way!

There are a couple of pointers that can help you in the future in connection with the letter "γ." When it is doubled in a word (γγ), it is pronounced like the "ng" of "inning." When it joins "κ" or "χ" (γκ, γχ), it is pronounced like "nk" in "conk." When it joins "ξ" (γξ), it is pronounced like "nks" in "oinks."

Vowels

We need to understand just a little bit more of Greek pronunciation, so let's look at the vowels first.

There are seven vowel letters in Greek:

short	ε	ο	ι	α	υ
long	η	ω	ι	α	υ

Notice that η is the long form of ε.
Notice that ω is the long form of ο.
When ι is short, it is pronounced like the "i" in "fit," and when long, it is pronounced like the "i" in "machine." (But you may ignore this inasmuch as the "low roader" has no way of telling when ι is long or short.)
The letters α and υ can be either long or short and are pronounced enough alike that there is no appreciable difference.

Diphthongs

When two vowels join together, making one sound and one syllable, they form what is called a diphthong.

We have an example in English with the word "aisle."
The diphthong is "ai" and it is pronounced like the
word "I."

The following is a list of Greek diphthongs
with their pronunciation and/or an example from an
English word.   Then there are some Greek letters put
together to form English words.   Pronounce them
aloud.   Does it sound like an English word you know?
If not, you are not saying the diphthong correctly.
Go back and check the pronunciation of the diphthong
and try again!

αι - "I"   as in "aisle" --- βαικ, δαικ, θαι, καιτ

αυ - "ow"   as in "kraut" --- καυς, αυλ, δαυτ, ταυλ

ει - "A"   as in "freight" - βειτ, πειδ, τεικ, δειτ

ευ - "you"   as in "feud" ---- κευτ, κευ, μευλ, μευτ

οι - -   as in "oil" ----- τοι, βοι, οιλ, ροιλ

ου - -   as in "group" --- τρουπ, δουκ, τρουθ, βουθ

υι - "we"   as in "suite" --- υικ, κυιν, συιπ, υιδ

You may ignore the rare ηυ and ωυ.   When you see a
"diaeresis," a ¨ over the second vowel of what
appears to be a diphthong, you don't have a diphthong.
See John 1:17 on page 1:9 - Μωϋσέως is pronounced
Moh-oo-seh-ohs.

Subscript

Sometimes the ι unites with the long vowels
α, η, ω.   When this happens, the ι is written underneath and is not pronounced.   It will look like this:
ᾳ, ῃ, ῳ, and is called an "iota subscript."

OTHER MARKS
Punctuation

In Greek there are just four marks of punctuation:

    1.   , = comma (,)
    2.   . = period (.)
    3.   · = semi-colon (;) or colon (:)
    4.   ; = question mark (?)

Notice that the first two are the same as in English,
but the last two are very different.   Whenever you
see ; at the end of a sentence, you should immediately know you have just read a question.

Breathing

Notice the following words: ἀκουω, ἁγιος.
Above the first letter of each word is a special sign
called a "breathing mark" which affects the pronunciation of the word.   The sign that looks like our

English apostrophe (᾿) is called "smooth breathing" and it means that the vowel is pronounced normally. The mark looking like a backward apostrophe (῾) is "rough breathing" and means an h-sound is pronounced before the vowel. For example, ἀ is pronounced "ah," while ἁ is pronounced "hah." What is the difference in sound between ἐν and ἑν? Every Greek word that begins with a vowel <u>must</u> have a breathing mark over it. In the case of a diphthong, the mark falls over the second vowel (αἱμα).

When a word begins with υ or the consonant ρ the rough breathing mark is always used (ὑς, ῥεω).

Because you grew up hearing and speaking English, it is not hard to know where to put the stress or accent on a word. But if you saw a new English word that is quite long, you might not be sure. In many other languages a mark is placed over the syllable in the word that carries the stress. Greek is one of those languages and it uses three kinds of accents. There is the "circumflex" - written either "ᾱ or ᾶ," the acute "ά," and the grave "ὰ."

Accents

If you choose to go on the Greek "high road," you will learn rules for the placement and type of accent. Right now, however, just notice where they are, so you will stress that syllable and pronounce the word correctly. What would be the difference in pronouncing φίλει and φιλεῖ?

Later on you may notice that in certain Greek words there are vowels which have been "contracted" or squeezed together. This will cause a change in spelling. The following chart gives the result when vowels in the left column are joined by another that is listed across the top.

CONTRACTION OF VOWELS

	ε	η	ει	ῃ	ο	ω	ου	οι
ε	ει	η	ει	ῃ	ου	ω	ου	οι
α	α	α	ᾳ	ᾳ	ω	ω	ω	ῳ
ο	ου	ω	οι	οι	ου	ω	ου	οι

The following information may help to show the relationship between the various consonants:

CONSONANTS

1. Consonants spoken without blocking the breath are called "liquids." They are λ, μ, ν, ρ.

2. There is one "sibilant" - σ (ς).

3. The remaining consonants are formed, either in the throat (gutturals), or by placing the tongue against the teeth (dentals), or by closing the lips (labials). Four consonants can then be formed from each of these positions by:

    a. not using the vocal cords,
    b. saying the neutral "ah" with them,
    c. adding "s,"
    d. adding breath.

	Silent	"ah"	Add "s"	Add breath
Throat	κ (k)	γ (g)	ξ (ks)	χ (ch)
Teeth	τ (t)	δ (d)	ζ (ds)	ϑ (th)
Lips	π (p)	β (b)	ψ (ps)	φ (ph)

The "s" category is the sign of a double consonant. The breathed category is the result of the proximity of a rough breathing or another breathed consonant.

ΚΑΤΑ ΙΩΑΝΝΗΝ

1 Ἐν ἀρχῇ ἦν ὁ λόγος, καὶ ὁ λόγος ἦν πρὸς τὸν θεόν, καὶ θεὸς ἦν ὁ λόγος. 2 οὗτος ἦν ἐν ἀρχῇ πρὸς τὸν θεόν. 3 πάντα δι᾽ αὐτοῦ ἐγένετο, καὶ χωρὶς αὐτοῦ ἐγένετο οὐδὲ ἕν ὃ γέγονεν. 4 ἐν αὐτῷ ζωὴ ἦν, καὶ ἡ ζωὴ ἦν τὸ φῶς τῶν ἀνθρώπων· 5 καὶ τὸ φῶς ἐν τῇ σκοτίᾳ φαίνει, καὶ ἡ σκοτία αὐτὸ οὐ κατέλαβεν.

6 Ἐγένετο ἄνθρωπος ἀπεσταλμένος παρὰ θεοῦ, ὄνομα αὐτῷ Ἰωάννης· 7 οὗτος ἦλθεν εἰς μαρτυρίαν, ἵνα μαρτυρήσῃ περὶ τοῦ φωτός, ἵνα πάντες πιστεύσωσιν δι᾽ αὐτοῦ. 8 οὐκ ἦν ἐκεῖνος τὸ φῶς, ἀλλ᾽ ἵνα μαρτυρήσῃ περὶ τοῦ φωτός. 9 Ἦν τὸ φῶς τὸ ἀληθινόν, ὃ φωτίζει πάντα ἄνθρωπον, ἐρχόμενον εἰς τὸν κόσμον. 10 ἐν τῷ κόσμῳ ἦν, καὶ ὁ κόσμος δι᾽ αὐτοῦ ἐγένετο, καὶ ὁ κόσμος αὐτὸν οὐκ ἔγνω. 11 εἰς τὰ ἴδια ἦλθεν, καὶ οἱ ἴδιοι αὐτὸν οὐ παρέλαβον. 12 ὅσοι δὲ ἔλαβον αὐτόν, ἔδωκεν αὐτοῖς ἐξουσίαν τέκνα θεοῦ γενέσθαι, τοῖς πιστεύουσιν εἰς τὸ ὄνομα αὐτοῦ, 13 οἳ οὐκ ἐξ αἱμάτων οὐδὲ ἐκ θελήματος σαρκὸς οὐδὲ ἐκ θελήματος ἀνδρὸς ἀλλ᾽ ἐκ θεοῦ ἐγεννήθησαν.

14 Καὶ ὁ λόγος σὰρξ ἐγένετο καὶ ἐσκήνωσεν ἐν ἡμῖν, καὶ ἐθεασάμεθα τὴν δόξαν αὐτοῦ, δόξαν ὡς μονογενοῦς παρὰ πατρός, πλήρης χάριτος καὶ ἀληθείας. 15 Ἰωάννης μαρτυρεῖ περὶ αὐτοῦ καὶ κέκραγεν λέγων, Οὗτος ἦν ὃν εἶπον, Ὁ ὀπίσω μου ἐρχόμενος ἔμπροσθέν μου γέγονεν, ὅτι πρῶτός μου ἦν. 16 ὅτι ἐκ τοῦ πληρώματος αὐτοῦ ἡμεῖς πάντες ἐλάβομεν, καὶ χάριν ἀντὶ χάριτος· 17 ὅτι ὁ νόμος διὰ Μωϋσέως ἐδόθη, ἡ χάρις καὶ ἡ ἀλήθεια διὰ Ἰησοῦ Χριστοῦ ἐγένετο. 18 θεὸν οὐδεὶς ἑώρακεν πώποτε· μονογενὴς θεὸς ὁ ὢν εἰς τὸν κόλπον τοῦ πατρὸς ἐκεῖνος ἐξηγήσατο.

19 Καὶ αὕτη ἐστὶν ἡ μαρτυρία τοῦ Ἰωάννου, ὅτε ἀπέστειλαν πρὸς αὐτὸν οἱ Ἰουδαῖοι ἐξ Ἱεροσολύμων ἱερεῖς καὶ Λευίτας ἵνα ἐρωτήσωσιν αὐτόν, Σὺ τίς εἶ; **20** καὶ ὡμολόγησεν καὶ οὐκ ἠρνήσατο, καὶ ὡμολόγησεν ὅτι Ἐγὼ οὐκ εἰμὶ ὁ Χριστός. **21** καὶ ἠρώτησαν αὐτόν, Τί οὖν σύ; Ἠλίας εἶ; καὶ λέγει, Οὐκ εἰμί. Ὁ προφήτης εἶ σύ; καὶ ἀπεκρίθη, Οὔ. **22** εἶπαν οὖν αὐτῷ, Τίς εἶ; ἵνα ἀπόκρισιν δῶμεν τοῖς πέμψασιν ἡμᾶς· τί λέγεις περὶ σεαυτοῦ; **23** ἔφη,

　Ἐγὼ **φωνὴ βοῶντος ἐν τῇ ἐρήμῳ,**
　　Εὐθύνατε τὴν ὁδὸν κυρίου,

καθὼς εἶπεν Ἡσαΐας ὁ προφήτης. **24** Καὶ ἀπεσταλμένοι ἦσαν ἐκ τῶν Φαρισαίων. **25** καὶ ἠρώτησαν αὐτὸν καὶ εἶπαν αὐτῷ, Τί οὖν βαπτίζεις εἰ σὺ οὐκ εἶ ὁ Χριστὸς οὐδὲ Ἠλίας οὐδὲ ὁ προφήτης; **26** ἀπεκρίθη αὐτοῖς ὁ Ἰωάννης λέγων, Ἐγὼ βαπτίζω ἐν ὕδατι· μέσος ὑμῶν ἕστηκεν ὃν ὑμεῖς οὐκ οἴδατε, **27** ὁ ὀπίσω μου ἐρχόμενος, οὗ οὐκ εἰμὶ ἐγὼ ἄξιος ἵνα λύσω αὐτοῦ τὸν ἱμάντα τοῦ ὑποδήματος. **28** Ταῦτα ἐν Βηθανίᾳ ἐγένετο πέραν τοῦ Ἰορδάνου, ὅπου ἦν ὁ Ἰωάννης βαπτίζων.

29 Τῇ ἐπαύριον βλέπει τὸν Ἰησοῦν ἐρχόμενον πρὸς αὐτόν, καὶ λέγει, Ἴδε ὁ ἀμνὸς τοῦ θεοῦ ὁ αἴρων τὴν ἁμαρτίαν τοῦ κόσμου. **30** οὗτός ἐστιν ὑπὲρ οὗ ἐγὼ εἶπον, Ὀπίσω μου ἔρχεται ἀνὴρ ὃς ἔμπροσθέν μου γέγονεν, ὅτι πρῶτός μου ἦν. **31** κἀγὼ οὐκ ᾔδειν αὐτόν, ἀλλ᾽ ἵνα φανερωθῇ τῷ Ἰσραὴλ διὰ τοῦτο ἦλθον ἐγὼ ἐν ὕδατι βαπτίζων. **32** Καὶ ἐμαρτύρησεν Ἰωάννης λέγων ὅτι Τεθέαμαι τὸ πνεῦμα καταβαῖνον ὡς περιστερὰν ἐξ οὐρανοῦ, καὶ ἔμεινεν ἐπ᾽ αὐτόν· **33** κἀγὼ οὐκ ᾔδειν αὐτόν, ἀλλ᾽ ὁ πέμψας με βαπτίζειν ἐν ὕδατι ἐκεῖνός μοι εἶπεν, Ἐφ᾽ ὃν ἂν ἴδῃς τὸ πνεῦμα καταβαῖνον καὶ μένον ἐπ᾽ αὐτόν, οὗτός ἐστιν ὁ βαπτίζων ἐν πνεύματι ἁγίῳ. **34** κἀγὼ ἑώρακα, καὶ μεμαρτύρηκα ὅτι οὗτός ἐστιν ὁ υἱὸς τοῦ θεοῦ.

35 Τῇ ἐπαύριον πάλιν εἱστήκει ὁ Ἰωάννης καὶ ἐκ τῶν μαθητῶν αὐτοῦ δύο, 36 καὶ ἐμβλέψας τῷ Ἰησοῦ περιπατοῦντι λέγει, Ἴδε ὁ ἀμνὸς τοῦ θεοῦ. 37 καὶ ἤκουσαν οἱ δύο μαθηταὶ αὐτοῦ λαλοῦντος καὶ ἠκολούθησαν τῷ Ἰησοῦ. 38 στραφεὶς δὲ ὁ Ἰησοῦς καὶ θεασάμενος αὐτοὺς ἀκολουθοῦντας λέγει αὐτοῖς, Τί ζητεῖτε; οἱ δὲ εἶπαν αὐτῷ, Ῥαββί (ὃ λέγεται μεθερμηνευόμενον Διδάσκαλε), ποῦ μένεις; 39 λέγει αὐτοῖς, Ἔρχεσθε καὶ ὄψεσθε. ἦλθαν οὖν καὶ εἶδαν ποῦ μένει, καὶ παρ᾽ αὐτῷ ἔμειναν τὴν ἡμέραν ἐκείνην· ὥρα ἦν ὡς δεκάτη. 40 Ἦν Ἀνδρέας ὁ ἀδελφὸς Σίμωνος Πέτρου εἷς ἐκ τῶν δύο τῶν ἀκουσάντων παρὰ Ἰωάννου καὶ ἀκολουθησάντων αὐτῷ· 41 εὑρίσκει οὗτος πρῶτον τὸν ἀδελφὸν τὸν ἴδιον Σίμωνα καὶ λέγει αὐτῷ, Εὑρήκαμεν τὸν Μεσσίαν (ὅ ἐστιν μεθερμηνευόμενον Χριστός)· 42 ἤγαγεν αὐτὸν πρὸς τὸν Ἰησοῦν. ἐμβλέψας αὐτῷ ὁ Ἰησοῦς εἶπεν, Σὺ εἶ Σίμων ὁ υἱὸς Ἰωάννου · σὺ κληθήσῃ Κηφᾶς (ὃ ἑρμηνεύεται Πέτρος).

43 Τῇ ἐπαύριον ἠθέλησεν ἐξελθεῖν εἰς τὴν Γαλιλαίαν, καὶ εὑρίσκει Φίλιππον. καὶ λέγει αὐτῷ ὁ Ἰησοῦς, Ἀκολούθει μοι. 44 ἦν δὲ ὁ Φίλιππος ἀπὸ Βηθσαϊδά, ἐκ τῆς πόλεως Ἀνδρέου καὶ Πέτρου. 45 εὑρίσκει Φίλιππος τὸν Ναθαναὴλ καὶ λέγει αὐτῷ, Ὃν ἔγραψεν Μωϋσῆς ἐν τῷ νόμῳ καὶ οἱ προφῆται εὑρήκαμεν, Ἰησοῦν υἱὸν τοῦ Ἰωσὴφ τὸν ἀπὸ Ναζαρέτ. 46 καὶ εἶπεν αὐτῷ Ναθαναήλ, Ἐκ Ναζαρὲτ δύναταί τι ἀγαθὸν εἶναι; λέγει αὐτῷ Φίλιππος, Ἔρχου καὶ ἴδε. 47 εἶδεν ὁ Ἰησοῦς τὸν Ναθαναὴλ ἐρχόμενον πρὸς αὐτὸν καὶ λέγει περὶ αὐτοῦ, Ἴδε ἀληθῶς Ἰσραηλίτης ἐν ᾧ δόλος οὐκ ἔστιν.

Like English, the Greek language has nouns, pronouns, adjectives, articles, prepositions, verbs, adverbs and conjunctions. But, Greek also has particles. Most of these parts of speech require little comment.

NOUNS

Nouns are the names of persons, places or things. All nouns have "gender" (masculine, feminine or neuter), "number" (singular or plural) and "case." Because the case idea is new to English speaking people, a special lesson will be devoted to the subject.

Gender

You can say if you like--but only in joking-- that a noun has to be either a man, or a woman, or a thing and that its sex never changes. Actually, gender is only a classification device and class "A" is called masculine because all men "happen" to be placed there and class "B" is called feminine because all of the women "happen" to be placed there. The host of other nouns in these three classes are not there because there is something masculine or feminine or neutered about them.

Adjectives as Nouns

In English, nouns are sometimes made from adjectives as in, "Blessed are the poor." While "poor" usually explains or modifies another word, here it stands alone and becomes a noun equivalent. The Greek language does this more than the English does and it is called the "substantival" use of the adjective.

Infinitives

English manufactures nouns out of verbs by making "gerunds" (adding "-ing") as in, "Swimming is fun." However, the Greek language does this by using "infinitives," ("To swim is fun."). When the Greek infinitive has an article ("the") in front of it, think of it as a noun ("the act of swimming").

PRONOUNS

Pronouns are words used to take the place of nouns, (he, she, it). The Greek language comes equipped with a full roster of pronouns like:

the personal pronoun	"he"	αὐτός
the possessive pronoun	"my"	ἐμός
the reflexive pronoun	"myself"	ἐμαυτοῦ
the reciprocal pronoun	"one another"	ἀλλήλων
the relative pronoun	"who"	ὅς
the interrogative pronoun	"who?"	τίς
the indefinite pronoun	"someone"	τις
the demonstrative pronoun	"this one"	οὗτος

Pronouns have gender, number and case, and must agree with the noun to which they refer in both number and gender. This is called "concord." The case is determined by the way the pronoun is used in its own context and not by the case of its "antecedent" (the noun to which it refers).

ADJECTIVES

Adjectives are words used to modify nouns or pronouns (the good boy, the beautiful house, the tall building). The Greek adjective is very much like the English one. However, it usually follows the noun it modifies (the house white). Adjectives have gender, number and case which always agree with the nouns they modify. For example, in the English phrase, "the hungry boys," the word "hungry" is the same form as in the phrase, "the hungry girl." Not so in Greek! "Hungry" in the first phrase would have the form which shows it is masculine and plural, while in the second example it would be feminine and singular. This is also called "concord." This fact can be very helpful in translation and interpretation.

PARTICIPLES

If the Greeks had a neat way to convert a verb into a noun ("I swim" to "swimming is fun"), they had a neater way to convert a verb into an adjective. They made it into a "participle." So fond did the Greeks become of the procedure and so elaborately did they develop it, that it has become perhaps Greek's most distinguishing feature.

Verb Turned
Adjective

A participle is a verb which has been converted to an adjective by adding an appropriate suffix to the verb stem. It can fill any adjective slot in the sentence. For instance:

You can say, "the good word" (ὁ ἀγαθὸς λόγος). "Good" (ἀγαθός) is the adjective. I may take the Greek verb γράφω (I write) and by adding the appropriate suffix -εις, so it becomes γραφείς (written), make it a participle. Then I can replace "good" with "written" and "the good word" becomes "the written word," (ὁ γραφεὶς λόγος). In this way, a verb can become an adjective.

Not all participles turn out pure adjectives, however. Sometimes they come closer to describing something about the verb than they do about a noun and become adverbs. It's not all that easy to tell.

Take for instance the sentence, "While coming to your house, I saw a bluejay." In this sentence am I being described as the one who is coming to your house? Or is it better to see the temporal idea which is telling you when I saw the bluejay? If you vote "yes" on the first question, the participle is an adjective. If you vote "yes" on the second, it is an adverb. As a rule of thumb, which gets broken so often one must be very cautious, if the participle has an article in front of it, it more often is an adjective and if it doesn't, it probably is an adverb.

Participles can also become an integral part of the verb. The Greek can say "I believe" (πιστεύω) or it can say "I am believing" (εἰμὶ πιστεύων) almost exactly like the English can. However, there is this difference: if the privilege of joining the verb "to be" with a participle were refused us, we would be tongue-tied, but the Greeks would scarcely have missed that construction. This combination of verb and participle is called the "periphrastic construction."

The Greeks managed to introduce all the adjectival properties into their participle (including case, gender and number) without losing the verbal ideas of "voice" and "aspect." Voice and aspect will be explained in Lesson 4. In fact this adjective remains so much a verb that it can even have a subject, a direct object, an indirect object and the whole paraphernalia of a main verb. In Greek, a very elaborate clause with many, many words can actually be nothing more than an adjective and fill a single adjective slot.

Furthermore, because it is an adjective, the participle can still be converted once again, now into a noun (substantival use) by placing the article ("the") in front of it. We saw on page 2:1 how an infinitive works as a noun. Now we learn that a participle with the article can also be a noun. Let me contrast how an infinitive and the substantival use of the participle are used:

article + infinitive = the action itself:

    τὸ ποιεῖν   = "the act of making"

article + participle = the one who is performing the action:

    ὁ ποιῶν   = "the one who is making"

ARTICLES
Only One

English has two articles (definite, "the" and indefinite, "a" or "an"). But there is only one kind of article in Greek and that is the definite kind. There is no word in Greek which answers very well to the English indefinite article, "a" or "an." And the word which comes closest, in no stretch of the imagination can be called an article. It is the Greek indefinite pronoun τις.

The article has gender, number and case, and always agrees with the noun to which it is attached. What is this called? _____ It has more liberties than its English counterpart and can almost approximate a pronoun (ὁ μεν sometimes means "he").

Forms

Because the article is so important and is such an obvious indicator for identifying the syntactic (grammatical) relationships between words, the student is required to memorize it.

	Singular			Plural		
	Masc.	Fem.	Neut.	Masc.	Fem.	Neut.
Nominative	ὁ	ἡ	τὸ	οἱ	αἱ	τὰ
Genitive	τοῦ	τῆς	τοῦ	τῶν	τῶν	τῶν
Dative	τῷ	τῇ	τῷ	τοῖς	ταῖς	τοῖς
Accusative	τὸν	τὴν	τὸ	τοὺς	τὰς	τὰ

Memorize all the singulars before you memorize the plurals. And memorize the Nominative singulars before the Genitive singulars, and thus through the whole "declension."

The purist will insist that the accented article which is not circumflex must be acute. Though he is probably correct technically, it shouldn't be done here because it would only confuse the "low-roader" who never finds these articles accented with other than grave accents in his New Testament.

Complications

The article is the most tricky item in the Greek language. Only the expert is qualified to make exegetical judgments about its use or non-use. Whenever a Bible teacher makes something out of the fact the article appears or is absent, the listener should switch off his hearing aid, because all too often the teacher does not appreciate all the ramifications in the use of the article.

For instance there is the Apollonius' canon, the Anaphoric use, Granville Sharp's principle, Colwell's rule, the Semitic construct state influence, and the pronominal use. After one has mastered these, he must get a firm grasp of the hen-pecking priority between them. You can see how complicated it can get!

Furthermore, English will misslead you badly. You see, English can work with definiteness with three categories: "a," "the," and no article at all. Greek must cover these bases with only two options: the Greek "the," and no article at all (anarthrous).

PREPOSITIONS

Prepositions are words used to show relation-ships between two objects, often spacial or time relationships. The Greek preposition and the prepo-sitional phrases are very much like the English. The common prepositions with emphasis upon their spacial meanings are made into a chart by Bruce M. Metzger (*Lexical Aids for Students of New Testament Greek,* p. 80, published by the author and used by permission, with slight modification).

Geometric (Spacial) Arrangement of the Greek Prepositions

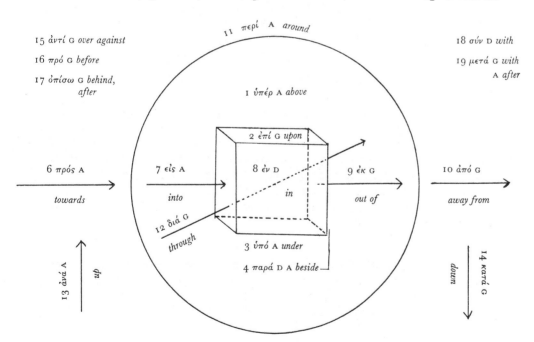

Notes: 1. The symbols, G, D, and A should be read: 'with the genitive case means,' 'with the dative case means,' and 'with the accusative case means.'

2. Only the basic meanings of prepositions with certain cases are given here. For other mean-ings with other cases, a lexicon should be consulted.

3. Preposition 5 (ἀμφί-) has been eliminated from this chart because it never stands by itself, but always is attached to other words.

The prepositions have more meanings than these. The Greek was fond of tacking prepositions to the front of words to add to, or strengthen the meaning. However, one cannot always take the meaning of the preposition plus the meaning of the stem to discover the definition of the word. It is best to use a lexicon.

For instance: βαίνω means "I go," and the word στάσις means "standing," and ἐκ we learn from the above chart means "out of." If I put ἐκ and βαίνω together (ἐκβαίνω) I get "I go out," but if I put ἐκ and στάσις together (ἔκστασις) I do not get "outstanding" but rather what its English transliteration means, "ecstasy."

VERBS

Verbs are words used to express action, being, or state of being (run, is, am rejoicing). Verbs in Greek have the same function as they do in English. So different from English, however, is the verb inflection system, that a special lesson must be set aside to describe it (Lesson 4).

ADVERBS

Adverbs are words used to modify verbs, adjectives, or other adverbs. (She sings beautifully. He is a very great man. She smiled rather sadly.)

The Greek adverb is much the same as the English adverb. When the student sees a word ending in -ως, he can be fairly certain that it is an adverb. However, just as all adverbs do not end in -ly in English, so the above help will not always apply in Greek.

CONJUNCTIONS

Conjunctions are words used to connect other words or groups of words (and, but, as well as, etc.). The Greek conjunction is much the same as in English and needs no further comment here.

PARTICLES

"Particles" is the title of the "catch-all bin" for the little words that won't fit into any other. It is populated by many "feeling words." Experts can't agree on them; some put the "negatives" here (μή and οὐ, meaning "no" or "not"); others, all the conjunctions.

Particles may be ignored by those taking the "low road."

The basic unit in any language is the sentence. Essentially, a sentence relates a happening. Take, for example, this happening: "validated." It is a verb. That's why I chose a word starting with a "V." The sentence, at least in Greek, more or less builds up around the verb. Let's diagram a verb:

```
_____|verb_____        _____|validated_____
        |                              |
```

THE SUBJECT SLOT

Usually somebody (or something) makes the happening happen. We call what does this the "subject." In this example, we make him the "notary." I bet you are wondering what the "N" stands for.

```
subject |verb_____        notary |validated_____
        |                              |
```

THE DIRECT OBJECT SLOT

And more often than not, this happening happens to somebody (or something). We call the victim (even when he is lucky, like finding tickets to the Super Bowl) the "direct object." And because the logical flow goes from the cause through the action to the object, we draw an arrow over the verb which points in this direction. In our example, we make the receiver of the action of the verb an "affidavit." I bet you are wondering what the "A" stands for.

```
          ———→                          ———→
subject |verb |direct object   notary |validated |affidavit
        |                              |
```

THE INDIRECT OBJECT SLOT

And very often, this happening is for somebody (or something) else's benefit who doesn't actually receive the blow of the action. Sometimes it isn't a good benefit. We call this the "indirect object." In the sentence we are building, we make a "deputy" the indirect object. I bet you wonder what the "D" stands for.

```
          ———→                          ———→
subject |verb |d. object/i. object   notary |validated |affidavit/deputy
        |                              |
```

If you have learned how to diagram an English sentence, it will help you a lot now. However, not in every instance. Take here, for example. The English indirect object is awkward. It is a prepositional phrase and is diagramed like this:

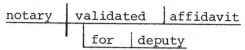

or something like that. But in Greek it is <u>not</u> a prepositional phrase and the "to" or "for" or what have you is <u>not</u> to be considered as "understood."   It is not "understood." You just use a plain, ordinary noun. A more appropriate location for an "object," be it direct or indirect, is on the same line with the subject and the verb.

The places on our diagram which we have named "subject," "direct object," and "indirect object" are "noun slots," better to be called "substantival slots," and are only to be filled in with nouns or their substitute, pronouns. Often infinitives and participles can be converted into nouns. These, also, can be found in substantival slots.

substantival slot	verb slot	substantival slot	substantival slot

THE ADJECTIVE SLOT

Your diagram also has a place to insert adjectives and adverbs so as to show the connection between the nouns and their adjectives and the verb and its adverbs. Take the sentence: "The new notary validated the appropriate affidavit for the dejected deputy."

notary	validated	affidavit	/ deputy
new		appropriate	dejected
the		the	the

I bet you wonder why I made alliterations between the nouns and their adjectives. I did it to illustrate concord. What is the definition of concord?

_____

_____

I have only located three substantival slots on my diagram. Here is another. Often a noun can serve as an adjective. "He saw a city slicker," makes the noun an adjective.

he	saw	slicker
		city
		a

The Greeks were sort of shy on adjectives so they did a lot of this. Most of the time you can't tell the difference between ὁ ἅγιος ἄνθρωπος (literally: "the holy man") and ὁ ἄνθρωπος ἁγιασμοῦ (literally: "the man of holiness") in meaning, although there is a difference in concord which will be discussed shortly.

So if I were to use nouns for adjectives, I would then write: "The government notary validated the graft affidavit for the grand jury deputy." And I would diagram the sentence, putting these nouns turned adjectives in their adjective slots like this:

notary	validated	affidavit	deputy
government		graft	grand jury
the		the	the

THE CASE NAMES

I bet you wonder why all of these new nouns placed in the adjective slots start with the letter "G." Let me explain. The Greeks indicated in which substantival slot the noun should go by adding the appropriate suffix to the noun stem.

The subject slot they called "Nominative,"
so the "N."

The adjective slot they called "Genitive,"
so the "G."

The indirect object slot they called "Dative,"
so the "D."

The direct object slot they called "Accusative,"
so the "A."

You've got to memorize these fancy names and remember which slot each is a name for.

Nominative	verb	Accusative	Dative
Genitive		Genitive	Genitive

I wonder if you noticed a problem? Look again and see if you can't find a problem with the Genitive. If you can't see it, don't get too dejected. For the problem is far worse than it appears when you put it in English. Here is the problem: If you spell the noun exactly the same, no matter what adjective slot you put it into, then how can you tell which you are describing; the subject, direct object, or indirect object?

Here is the answer: You cannot be absolutely positive. The rule holds good in almost all situations that the Genitive noun usually follows the word it is describing.

You memorized the 24 forms of the article, already. You understood well enough about "singular" and "plural." And it wasn't too hard to get the idea that all nouns have "gender" and that the "the" that goes with the noun must have the same gender and number.

But what was this Nominative, Genitive, Dative and Accusative thing all about? It is the same way. The "the" a noun has must also be the same "case" as the noun.

So let's diagram our sentence, locating every "the." We will give each noun a "the." To make it easier, let's assume all the nouns are masculine and singular.

"The notary of the government validated the affidavit of the graft for the deputy of the grand jury."

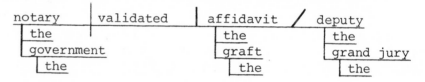

I replace the English "the" with the appropriate Greek article:

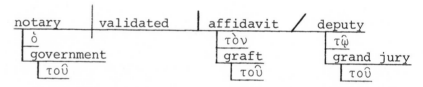

See how perfectly the articles match up when I replace our example sentence with the case names of the various noun slots:

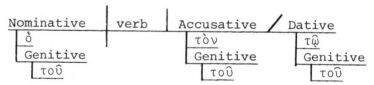

Just for practice, let's make our nouns all plural: "The notaries of the governments validated the affidavits of the grafts for the deputies of the grand juries."

OBJECT OF THE PREPOSITION SLOT

The sentence has one more--and a very important one at that--noun slot. It is the "object of the preposition." The preposition, plus its noun, plus the modifiers of that noun compose a word cluster called a "prepositional phrase." For example, take the sentence: "She wanted to be noticed by the very handsome young man." "By the very handsome young man" is a prepositional phrase:

"by" is the preposition

"man" is the object of the preposition

"the" is the article which goes with "man"

"very handsome young" further modify the object.

The Greek has to put every noun it uses into some case or other. This noun slot, the object of the preposition, can be written either in the Genitive, Dative or Accusative cases. Certain prepositions, however, have developed, for good reasons, affinities for certain cases, for instance:

the object of ἐκ (out of) is always in the Genitive case

the object of ἐν (in) is always in the Dative case

the object of εἰς (into) is always in the Accusative case.

Some prepositions are not all that particular. For instance: ἐπί (upon) can have an object in any of the three cases, but it would mean different things. This is why the little letters D, G, and A on your preposition chart are so important that they must be memorized.

So let's see if we can add a prepositional phrase or two to the sentence we have been working with: "The notary of the government validated with an obvious personal satisfaction the affidavit by the subpoenaed witness of graft concerning bribery for the deputy of the grand jury in the waiting room."

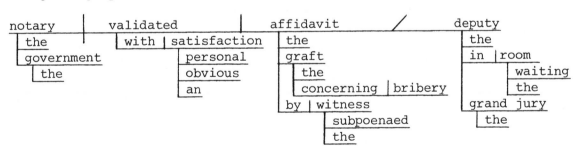

Replace the English prepositions with the Greek translation and underline the object of each and place in parentheses after each a G or D or A indicating what case would be required of a Greek noun which would replace the English object:

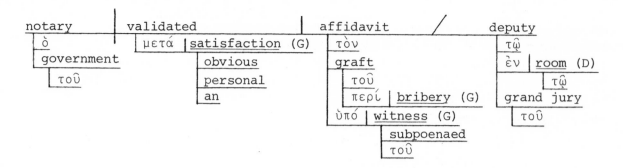

THE VOCATIVE CASE

There is a fifth case that really has no sentence slot to live in. Maybe it isn't a true case. But it does seem to have a discrete ending sometimes. It did not show up on the article chart because this case has no article.

It is the way you spell someone (or something) when you are talking directly to him (it):

πάτερ, ἄφες αὐτοῖς (Father, forgive them.)

Here, "Father" is written in the Vocative case.

New Testament Vocatives are rare and those with discrete endings differing from the Nominative endings are extremely rare.

THE EIGHT CASE SYSTEM

A few Greek *Grammars* teach an eight case system as taught by A. T. Robertson. The two systems are compared as follows:

THE FIVE CASE SYSTEM	THE EIGHT CASE SYSTEM
1. Nominative	1. Nominative
2. Genitive	
a. Possession	2. Genitive (Possession)
b. Separation	3. Ablative (Separation)
3. Dative	
a. Locative	4. Locative
b. Instrumental	5. Instrumental
c. Indirect Object	6. Dative (Indirect Object)
4. Accusative (Direct Object)	7. Accusative (Direct Object)
5. Vocative	8. Vocative

Both the genitival and ablatival functions have the same genitive endings. And all three functions; the locative, the instrumental, and the dative, have the same dative endings. Hence there are only five distinct sets of endings, even though the eight case system offers a name for eight principal functions.

These cases not only identify substantives with their substantival slot, they sometimes can be more explicit with respect to time and motion. For instance, the word "day" could be used in the accusative, genitive or dative case, depending on the precise meaning you wish to convey.

He ate that day, accusative case: He ate throughout
                                   that day.
He ate that day, dative case: He ate when it was
                                   daytime.
He ate that day, genitive case: He ate a daytime
                                   type meal.

When you have motion with the accusative case, you usually have motion toward. Motion with the genitive is usually away, and with the dative there is no motion.

The table on page 3:8 gives a summary of the cases, their function and the more common endings associated with them, and their relation to time and motion. Study it well and know where to find it. You will be referring to it often.

Questions to ask nouns, pronouns and adjectives (including participles and infinitives):

You should ask a noun two questions:
1. What is its *case*? Options: Nominative or Genitive or
     Dative or Accusative.
2. What is its *number*? Options: Singular or Plural.

You should ask an adjective or pronoun three questions:
1. What is its *case*? Options: Nominative or Genitive or
     Dative or Accusative.
2. What is its *number*? Options: Singular or Plural.
3. What is its *gender*? Options: Masculine or Feminine
     or Neuter.

Because verbs turned adjectives retain two of their verbal functions, you should ask a participle and an infinitive* five questions:
1. What is its *case*? Options: Nominative or Genitive or
     Dative or Accusative.
2. What is its *number*?* Options: Singular or Plural.
3. What is its *gender*?* Options: Masculine or Feminine
     or Neuter.
4. What is its *voice*? Options: Active or Middle or
     Passive. (These will be explained in Lesson 4.)
5. What is its *aspect*? Options: Punctiliar or Linear or
     Combined. (These will be explained in Lesson 4.)

*Infinitives are always singular in number; neuter in gender.

THE GREEK CASE SYSTEM

All Nouns, Pronouns, Adjectives, Participles, Articles and Infinitives* have Gender, Number, and Case

CASE	ENDINGS (sg.)(pl.)	USE IN SENTENCE	FINE TUNING WITH PREPOSITIONS	QUANTITY	TIME	MOTION	ARTICLE (sg.)(pl.)
NOMINATIVE	ος οι η αι ον ες α α ης η ες εις ους εις	Subject Complement of "to be"	No Prepositions				ὁ οἱ ἡ αἱ τό τά
GENITIVE	ου ων τος εως ης ας ους ο	Possession ("of" phrases) Absolute	ἀντί instead of περί concerning ἀπό away from πρό before διά through πρός for ἐκ out of ὑπέρ behalf of ἐπί on (contact) ὑπό by (agent) κατά down μετά with	Part of	Qualitative time (kind of time)	Motion away	τοῦ τῶν τῆς
DATIVE	ι εσι ᾳ σι ῃ ις ῳ ους ει αις εουσι	Indirect Object Object	ἐν in, with (means) ἐπί on (position) παρά beside πρός at σύν with		Time at which	No motion	τῷ τοῖς τῇ ταῖς

ACCUSATIVE	ον ους
	ην ας
	αν α
	ο εις
	α
	ους
	ον
		Direct Object
		Subject of Infinitive
			ἀνά up μετά after
			διά because of παρά alongside
			εἰς into (result) περί around
			ἐπί on (motion) πρός toward
			κατά down, ὑπέρ over
			  along, ὑπό under
			  according to
				All of	Time throughout which	Motion toward	τόν τούς
							τήν τάς
							τό τά

VOCATIVE	ε οι υ αι α ες αι	Direct Address	No Prepositions				

*(Infinitives are neuter, singular nouns without case endings. When it has an article, one can determine its case. Otherwise, case is determined by its use in the sentence.)

Last time we learned that a noun (and adjective and pronoun) has to be divided into two elements, the stem and the ending. It is the same with a verb, except you also can add something on the front.

But the verb is much more complicated. For instead of finding eight (for nouns) or twenty-four (for adjectives and pronouns) endings, the verb has almost 500!

So once more you take the stem (or root) and separate it from the ending. Then you examine the ending to find all the information it has for you. The same word will take on an awful lot of different appearances.

Call these additions to the stem, "inflections." They sort out such things as *who* is doing the action, or *how many* are, whether the subject is doing it or it is being done *to* him, or how the speaker sees the *kind* of action or views the *fulfillment* of it or *when* it happens.

That is, these inflections ask and answer the following questions:

1. Who is doing the action?
2. How many are doing the action?
3. Is the subject doing it or is it being done to him?
4. How does the speaker look at the kind of action?
5. How does the speaker look at the fulfillment of it?
6. And sometimes we add a sixth: When does it happen?

These six areas have six names. We'll call them, in order: (1) person, (2) number, (3) voice, (4) aspect, (5) mood, and sometimes (6) time. Number 6 is asked only when number 5 is answered in a certain way. You simply <u>must</u> get a hold of this. Everytime you see a verb, you must ask its inflection these five and sometimes six questions.

**WHAT IS ITS
PERSON?**

When you talk, it's about what you, yourself do, or the person you are talking to does, or what somebody (or something) else does.

1st person: "I hear the voice."
ἀκούω τὴν φωνήν: ἀκου = "hear," ω = "I"

2nd person: "You hear the voice."
ἀκούεις τὴν φωνήν: ἀκου = "hear," εις = "You"

3rd person: "He hears the voice."
ἀκούει τὴν φωνήν: ἀκου = "hear," ει = "He"

IMPORTANT! Look where the subject is! It is in the inflection. The Greeks did not add the pronoun to give the verb a subject. When they did - which was rare - it was not to give the verb a subject, but rather to give *emphasis* to the subject. So we must not write one in. Neither may we say it was "understood," like when we command people, "Go away." It is not "understood" to be there, it *is* there.

IMPORTANT! Of course, you have to write in the subject when it is something or somebody special.

"He hears."   ἀκούει
but "God hears."   Θεὸς ἀκούει

To the first question, "What is its person?", there are three possible answers: 1st person, 2nd person, or 3rd person.

**WHAT IS ITS
NUMBER?**

When you are talking, you also imply whether somebody else is helping you, or whether you are talking to more than one person, or whether more than one person is doing something. Now you repeat the three persons. Only this time you make all three plural.

1st person plural: "We hear the voice."
ἀκούομεν τὴν φωνήν: ομεν = "We"

2nd person plural: "Y'all hear the voice."
ἀκούετε τὴν φωνήν: ετε = "Y'all"

3rd person plural: "They hear the voice."
ἀκούουσι τὴν φωνήν: ουσι = "They"

Add these two threes together; you get six. The verb will be falling into these groups of six.

To the second question, "What is its number?", there are two possible answers: singular or plural.

**WHAT IS ITS
VOICE?**

These inflectional endings also tell you

whether you are doing the action or if it is being
done to you. Take the sentence, "I will make a
house," (ποιήσω οἶκον). You will understand it
better if I diagram it:

I	will make	house
		a

	ποιήσω	οἶκον

Notice the direction the action is going, from the
left to the right; from "I" to "house." The verb
tells you what I will do to the house. So I place
an arrow over the verb pointing in the right
direction of the action:

I	will make →	house
		a

	ποιήσω →	οἶκον

It is possible, however, to turn the arrow
around so it points in the opposite direction. Then
something will happen *to* me.

I	← will be made
	by | God

	← ποιηθήσομαι
	ὑπό | θεοῦ

Now it is something that will happen to me
because I am the subject. If I had said, "You will
be made by God," then you would have been the
subject. Anybody who has enough sense to come in
out of the rain can tell the big difference between
"I kicked the ball" and "I got kicked by a mule."
Yet in both sentences the subject "I" and the verb
"kick" are the same words.

When the arrow is pointing to the right, we
will call it the "active" voice. And when it is
pointing to the left, we will call it the "passive"
voice. It works the same way with English or
with Greek.

However, the Greek had a third way of writing
the arrow. It made the arrow do a "U-turn" ⟵⟝ .
Something like, "I will make myself." This third
way of writing the arrow we will call the "middle"
voice, and put the "middle" voice in the middle:

ACTIVE VOICE	MIDDLE VOICE	PASSIVE VOICE
⟶	⟵⟝	⟵
"I will make"	"I will make myself"	"I will be made"
ποιήσω	ποιήσομαι	ποιηθήσομαι

I have translated and diagramed the middle
voice as if it were reflexive in meaning. But that
is only the way it started. By the time the New
Testament was being written down, this reflexive

meaning was almost totally gone. The sense of the middle voice is really sort of like putting the subject into italics:

ACTIVE VOICE	MIDDLE VOICE	PASSIVE VOICE
"I will make"	"*I* will make"	"I will be made"

Or it might mean that the subject is more implicated in the result of the action than he would be if the simple active voice were used.

Or look at it differently: The middle voice is used when the subject of the verb, logically, should also occupy the indirect object slot.

"I open the gate *for myself*."

Or even (rarely by New Testament times) when the subject of the verb, logically, should also occupy the direct object slot.

"I promote *myself*."

(But this reflexive meaning is almost always taken over by the active voice in the verb plus a reflexive pronoun in the direct object slot:

not ὑψουμαι; but ὕψω ἐμαυτόν.)

Deponents

IMPORTANT! There are a lot of verbs, too many, which do not have active voice endings. The meaning is active, alright, but the ending is middle voice, and sometimes passive voice. These are called "Deponent" verbs.

πιστεύω (active voice ending -ω) is a "regular" verb. (some end in -μι).

ἔρχομαι (middle voice ending -μαι) is a "deponent" verb.

The only way you can tell a deponent verb is from the Greek lexicon. Regular verbs will end in -ω or -μι. Deponent verbs will end in -ομαι.

To the third question, "What is its voice?", there are three possible answers: active, middle, or passive.

WHAT IS ITS ASPECT?

Two ways

Sorry, there's nothing in English that will help you. Aspect is new. The Greek speaker regarded an action in two fundamentally different ways. He either wanted you to notice how long the action was taking or he didn't want you to pay any attention to its duration. Most of the time the duration wasn't all that important; so usually the "timeless" aspect suffix was attached to the stem of the verb.

If you can think of a moving picture as duration, then a snapshot would be timeless. Or, to
change the figure, if you think of the timeless one,
the snapshot, as a point (.), then you could also
think of the one with duration, the moving picture,
as a line (———). In fact, we give the two aspects
names which indicate dot and line.

      snapshot   · "punctiliar" "I believed"   (ἐπίστευσα)

   moving picture ———   "linear" "I was believing" (ἐπίστευον)

In the New Testament, it was quite the normal
way to say, "He rolled up his sleeping bag (· punctiliar) and was walking around (——— linear)."

But when Paul used a punctiliar ending, we must
not jump to the conclusion that the action was
instantaneous. It could have taken years. What he
would be saying is, "How long it took is not important to what I am trying to say; so just ignore it."
It just happened: a lightning flash, or the 40 plus
years it took to build Herod's temple. In the case
of Herod's temple, the duration, to use the words of
a Greek expert, "was reduced to a point by perspective."

Some events seem to be very sudden and brief.
Naturally, unless there were some special reason,
the speaker would use a punctiliar ending to describe
it. Similarly, with actions which take a long time,
you normally get a linear ending. In fact, "I am"
(εἰμί) never has a punctiliar ending.

In those cases there would be no particular
point in noticing the aspect. Only when you catch
a mismatch, would you conclude that the writer is
trying to say something by it. Like how Luke
expresses it in Acts 28:30, "He (Paul) remained
(ἐνέμεινε, a linear type stem with a punctiliar
aspect) for two whole years in his own rented apart-
ment." Apparently nothing significant happened in
that interim.

I am sure you must have heard the word "Aorist" before.
And the way it was used probably filled your mind with
curiosity about the wonders of its exotic content.

Actually, it's about as pedestrian a category as you
can find. It's the old word for what I call "punctiliar."
I waited to the last minute to tell you this. I have
my reasons.

And it doesn't mean, "once and for all," no matter who
tells you it does. It is the workhorse of the aspects,
used more frequently than the others. Its special
meaning is that it does not have a special meaning.
It states an action simply done; no trimmings.

Combined

When I first started talking about aspect, I said that the Greeks "regarded an action in two fundamentally different ways." But they sort of combined the two so as to wind up with one more, making the total three. This "combined" aspect looks at an action as an event with ensuing results. Take, for example, how you might go about talking about eating a green apple:

    ·   punctiliar: "I ate the green apple." (simple event)

   —— linear: "I was eating the green apple."
                          (when I got caught, maybe)

  ·—— combined: "I ate the green apple and boy, do I
                          need an Alka-Seltzer!"

When it comes to the combined aspect, you can't talk simply about suffixes, because you have to change the spelling at the start of the word also.

·	——	·——
snap-shot	moving picture	combination of both
punctiliar	linear	combined
"It was written"	"It was being written"	"It is written"
ἐγράφη	ἐγράφετο	γέγραπται

Suppose you are talking about God's law being written. In the first instance, the punctiliar, you are simply saying that it happened; God's law got written down. If you add the linear spellings, you are saying that God's law was being written down, and you notice the duration or what was happening when this was going on. But if you use the combined spelling, you see the event having been done and the continuing application of that law to life, "It *is* right now, viable and in force." The New Testament liked this aspect when quoting Scripture. See, for instance, Luke 24:46.

Notice how I divide the combined form between the root and the combined inflection: γέγραπται breaks down into γε-γραφ-ται.

    Root: γραφ   "write"

    Suffix: ται   "he, she or it"

    Prefix: γε   combined aspect (In most cases you
                              sort of "stutter" the first syllable.)

To the fourth question, "What is its aspect?", there are three possibilities: punctiliar, linear, or combined.

WHAT IS ITS
MOOD?

In contrast to the aspect which indicates the

speaker's attitude toward the kind of action, the mood indicates the speaker's attitude toward the kind of reality behind his statement. Maybe it could happen, or maybe someone wished that it would happen or commanded it to happen. Or possibly, it really did happen.

Greek has four moods:

1. Indicative: "It *is* true."

2. Subjunctive: "It *could be* true."

3. Imperative: "I *command* to make it true."

4. Optative: "I *wish* it would come true."

The Indicative mood is the simplest and most common. You simply make a statement about something or somebody. All the examples I have given you in this chapter in Greek are written in the indicative mood. And the English examples are the English equivalent.   **Indicative**

"You *do believe* in Christ." πιστεύεις εἰς Χριστόν.

The Subjunctive mood expresses possibility or probability. It is almost like the indicative in the future time with a "maybe" or "possibly" or even "probably" attached to it. However, its use this way purely is very rare. So you would be wiser to see how it works in its most frequent specialized uses.   **Subjunctive**

1. As a condition with some doubt:
   "If you *would believe* in Christ, you will be saved."
   ἐὰν πιστεύῃς εἰς Χριστόν, σωθήσῃ.

2. As expressing purpose:
   "I preached in order that you *might believe*."
   ἐκήρυξα, ἵνα πιστεύῃς.

3. As a command in the 1st person (hortatory):
   "*Let's believe* in Christ."
   πιστεύωμεν εἰς Χριστόν.

4. As a deliberative question expecting a command for an answer:
   "*Should* you *believe* in Christ? Believe in Him!"
   πιστεύῃς εἰς Χριστόν; πίστευε εἰς αὐτόν.

The Imperative mood is like the English. But ours is only in the second person. You can't tell somebody to do something who is not there. The closest we can come to it would be something like this: "I won't do it and you refuse to do it, so John *must do* it." This linguistic sleight-of-hand was just as simple as the second person command for the Greeks. And by using the "hortatory subjunctive,"   **Imperative** (number three in the above paragraph) you can even do it for the first person (though it seems it must be plural), like saying, "We've just got to do it."

So when you see the paradigms of the Greek imperative mood, they will be in patterns of four, not the normal six of the other Greek moods.

For example, the paradigm for active voice, linear aspect, indicative mood, present time is:

	Singular	Plural
1 prs.	πιστεύω "I believe"	πιστεύομεν "We believe"
2 prs.	πιστεύεις "You believe"	πιστεύετε "Y'all believe"
3 prs.	πιστεύει "He believes"	πιστεύουσι "They believe"

But for the active voice, linear aspect, imperative mood, the paradigm is:

	Singular	Plural
2 prs.	πίστευε "Believe!"	πιστεύετε "Y'all believe!"
3 prs.	πιστευέτω "He should believe"	πιστευέτωσαν "They should believe"

Optative

The Optative mood was in its last throes when Paul took up Greek. You can only find it 68 times in the whole New Testament. More often than not it expresses a wish. "Low roaders" should forget about this mood.

Aspect and Mood

I have the feeling that the punctiliar aspect is more significant for exegesis in the potential moods (subjunctive, imperative and optative) than in the indicative mood.

The combined aspect is very rare in the potential moods, and "did not really belong to the people" (Robertson p. 908). In the New Testament, the combined aspect doesn't even appear in the subjunctive or optative and at the most three times (if you include two very doubtful occurrences) in the imperative.

In fact, when the element of time (past, present or future) is missing, the true distinction between the punctiliar and the linear aspects is clearer to see. So look for pristine examples which contrast the punctiliar and linear aspects in the potential moods.

Punctiliar: ἵνα πορεύσωμαι = "so that I might go"

Linear: ἵνα πορεύωμαι = "so that I might be on my wa

The general idea is very clear in the imperative mood when the linear and punctiliar aspects are being contrasted; something to be done once, compared to something to be repeated.

Punctiliar: δὸς ἡμῖν σήμερον = "give us today" (Mt. 6:11)

Linear: δίδου ἡμῖν τὸ καθ' ἡμέραν = "keep giving to us day after day" (Lk. 11:3)

An added implication is sometimes seen in the imperative:

Punctiliar: "Start!" (The person being addressed is not doing it.)
    Matthew 5:24: διαλλάγηθι = "Get reconciled!"

Linear: "Keep on!" (The person addressed is already doing it.)
    Matthew 5:24: πρόσφερε = "Continue your offering!"

This added implication becomes quite significant in prohibitions:

Punctiliar: "Don't start!" (The person addressed is not doing it.)
    Matthew 1:20 μὴ φοβηθῇς = "When the time comes, don't be afraid to, that is, don't hesitate!"

Linear: "Quit!" (The person addressed is already doing it.)
    Luke 1:30: μὴ φοβοῦ = "Stop being afraid!"

To the fifth question, "What is its mood?", there are four possible answers: indicative, subjunctive, imperative, or optative.

WHAT IS ITS TIME?

Only if the mood is right do you ask the sixth question. The mood must, I repeat, *must* be indicative for there to be any time!

For some strange reason or other, this seems to be one of the most difficult things for a fledgling Greek student to get a grip on. Always stop with question five unless your answer to question five is that the verb is in the indicative mood.

When the indicative mood is used, either past, present or future time must be expressed. Draw a line from left to right across the page, with some arrows pointing to the right. Make this the "time line" with time going from left to right.

Next draw a vertical line through the middle of the time line. Make this the point where you are now.

NOW

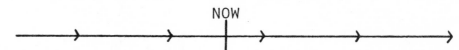

Everything to the left of the "Now" line has already happened, and everything on the right of it hasn't happened yet. So you write "Past" on the left side and "Future" on the right side, and "Present" where you first wrote "Now."

Notice how I didn't call this "tense" because "tense" has become polluted with aspect ideas. And it is absolutely necessary that we keep time and aspect separate. Remember what aspect is? Remember its signs?

snap-shot	"punctiliar"	•
moving picture	"linear"	———
combination of both	"combined"	• ——

Combining Aspect and Time

You can have aspect in each of the three times. Let's draw them in:

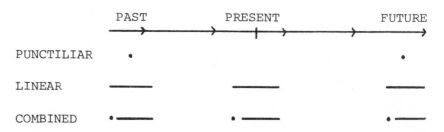

Notice that one aspect is missing in the present time. And be sure to remember that this combination of time and aspect happens only in the indicative mood because that is the only place where you will find time.

Past Time Indicator

When you put a Greek ἐ in front of an indicative verb, you throw it into the past time.

"I was believing"	"I am believing"
ἐπίστευον	πιστεύω
ε πιστευ ον	πιστευ ω
past "believe" "I"	"believe" "I"

IMPORTANT! When you attach both a preposition plus
an ε for past time onto the front end of a verb, you
attach the ε on first, and then you add the preposition.

    "I was receiving"   "I am receiving"

      παρελάμβανον   παραλαμβάνω

παρα ε λαμβαν ον   παρα λαμβαν ω
prep. past "take" "I"   prep. "take" "I"

(The second α of the preposition drops out because
the Greeks resisted the idea of one vowel following
another and the ε was necessary to get the past
time in.)

IMPORTANT! When the verb starts with a vowel, instead
of adding another vowel, that vowel becomes long:

          ε to η or ει
          α to η
          ο to ω

  "I was having"   "I have"

    εἶχον   ἔχω

εἰ εχ ω   ἐχ   ω
past "have" "I"   "have" "I"

When you put a Greek σ next to the stem and   Future Time
before the ending which indicates person and number, Indicator
you throw the indicative into the future.

  "I will believe"   "I am believing"

    πιστεύσω   πιστεύω

πιστευ   σ   ω   πιστευ   ω
"believe" future "I"   "believe"   "I"

There are many other indicators at the beginning Thematic Vowel
and end of the stem which you will notice and will
soon get on to. But before I list the more common of
them, there is a sticky little item I must explain.
"Sticky" is a good word for it. It seems that in
most cases, some glue was needed to fix an inflectional ending to a stem. The Greek used either an
ο or an ε, or in the case of the subjunctive mood,
the long forms of the two, ω and η. This is called
the "Thematic Vowel." I must confess I have been
hiding it from you. Half the time it has been con-
cealed by contraction into other vowels. It surfaces
in such words as πιστεύομεν ("we believe"): πιστευ
(stem: "believe), ο (the thematic vowel: the glue
that fixes the stem to the inflection), μεν (the
inflection: "we," first person plural). And the ε
surfaces in the form πιστεύετε ("y'all believe"):
πιστευ (stem: "believe"), ε (the thematic vowel),

τε (the inflection: "y'all," second person plural).

> The rules for the surfacing and submerging of the thematic vowel are not for the "low roaders." You will be wanting to try to split the inflection off from the stem by yourself. And if this mysterious bit of glue winds up stuck to one or the other, your surgery will not be downgraded.

FREQUENT INFLECTION INDICATORS

Here is a list of the more common inflectional affixes you will find. Before you seize on this as the solution to all your problems, I must warn you that altogether too often you will run across these letters and syllables and they won't, in that particular place, be part of the inflectional system. These are only to be considered as clues.

Prefixes (additions or changes in front of the stem):
ε-   = past time (augment)
reduplication = combined aspect (you stutter the
        first consonant as in: πεπίστευκα)

πε   πιστευ   κ   α
reduplication stem: "believe" combined "I"

Suffixes directly behind the stem ("sub-final"):
-σ-   = punctiliar (future if verb has no augment)
-κ-   = combined aspect
-ω/η-   = subjunctive mood (lengthened thematic vowel)
-ι-   = optative mood
-θη/θε- = passive voice

Suffixes at the very end of the word ("final"):
-ω   = "I" (active voice)
-μαι   = "I" (deponent or middle or passive voice)
-μην   = "I" (deponent, middle or passive voice; past time)
-ς   = "you" (active voice)
-ε/ει   = "he, she or it" (active voice; sometimes ε is εν)
-ται   = "he, she or it" (deponent, middle or passive voice)
-το   = "he, she or it" (deponent, middle or passive; past)
-μεν   = "we" (active voice)
-μεθα   = "we" (deponent, middle or passive voice)
-τε   = "y'all" (active voice)
-σθε   = "y'all" (deponent, middle or passive voice)
-σι   = "they" (active voice; sometimes it is σιν)
-νται   = "they" (deponent, middle or passive voice)
-ντο   = "they" (deponent, middle or passive; past time)

CONVERTING INFLECTION TERMS

I have introduced some new terms which will not be used in many of the reference works you will be using. These new terms replace a system which confused time with aspect. You have to learn how to use these reference works and understand what these old terms mean. So you must learn to extract the time and the aspect from them.

In order to help you do this, I have made an
overlay of these eight possibilities we talked about
on page 4:9 with the titles which these older reference works attached to these eight. I indicate at the
top headings, the proper time to be extracted; and at
the left hand side, the proper aspect to be extracted.

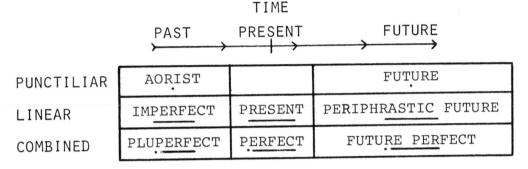

The need for this chart could be illustrated in this
example. Most reference books would consider
πίστευε to be 2 person, singular, present, imperative.
But we have already seen that time is only found in
the indicative mood. So we would need to take the
reference to present "tense" and use the above chart
to extrapolate it to linear aspect, no time.

SUMMARY

To summarize this lesson: You should ask
every verb five, maybe six questions:

1. What is its *person*? Options: First Person, or
    Second Person, or Third Person.

2. What is its *number*? Options: Singular or Plural.

3. What is its *voice*? Options: Active Voice, or
    Middle Voice, or Passive Voice.

4. What is its *aspect*? Options: Punctiliar Aspect,
    or Linear Aspect, or Combined Aspect.

5. What is its *mood*? Options: Indicative Mood, or
    Subjunctive Mood, or Imperative Mood or
    Optative Mood.

6. AND ONLY IF YOUR ANSWER TO QUESTION FIVE IS
    "INDICATIVE MOOD" CAN YOU ASK THE QUESTION,
    What is its *time*? Options: Past Time, or
    Present Time, or Future Time.

By the way, when we ask all these forms these
questions and then proceed to answer them we are
doing what grammarians call "parsing." You *must*
remember this word!

Lexical studies (we call them "word studies") investigate the meanings of words in and of themselves; that is, the stems. "Syntactical studies" show how words relate to each other through grammatical principles and by means of prefixes and suffixes.

UNITS OF SYNTAX

Words have affinities towards other words and thereby form clusters (modifiers) which will modify other words. These clusters can then form phrases, clauses, or sentences. Let's explain by giving some examples.

Word Cluster

In the English cluster "the very handsome young man," there is the single word "man" with modifier-words (an article, adverb, and two adjectives) which give more information about him. The modifiers "belong" to the word they modify. The nucleus of the cluster could be the direct object of a sentence like, "The freshman girl saw the very handsome young *man*." Words can even cluster around the verb as, "She *wanted* very badly to meet him." "Very badly" belongs to the verb "wanted." The Greek constructs modifiers in exactly the same way.

As a Prepositional Phrase

The cluster might be connected to the rest of the sentence by a preposition as, "She wanted to be noticed *by* the handsome young man." "By" connects and implies a relationship between the sentence and "the handsome young man." The Greek constructs it the same way.

As a Clause

Sometimes the cluster includes some action (or state), but is insufficient to stand alone. In the sentence, "She wondered *if he was going steady with anyone*," the italicized clause has some action to it (perhaps too much), but is not complete in itself. There are a variety of clauses in the Greek. Some of the principal ones are:

Relative: "She wondered *who he was*."

Conditional: ". . . and *if he had noticed her*."

Purpose:	"She signed up for 'Greek' *in order to sit near him*."
Result:	"But he signed up for 'Hebrew' *so that her plan was foiled*."
Participial:	"Saturday morning she was embarrassed because he saw her *wearing her curlers*."
Indirect quote:	"She said to herself *that that would finish it for her*."
Infinitive:	"Imagine her surprise when he stopped her and asked *to escort her to the Freshman Mixer*."
Temporal:	"This began something which she hoped would last *until death do them part*."

As a Sentence

The Greek sentence is more complex than the English, involving a considerable amount of elaboration, especially with participial clauses. The Classical Greek was even more elaborate than Biblical Greek. Greek is essentially "hypotactic," whereas the Semitic languages are "paratactic." An hypotactic sentence has one main clause and is embellished by subordinate clauses. The verb is usually the nucleus to the sentence.

Already having noticed the handsome young man, and wondering who he was and if he had noticed her, and having had her plans to sign up for "Greek" in order to sit near him foiled by his signing up for "Hebrew," and although she thought her chances were finished with him because he embarrassed her by catching her in her curlers on Saturday morning, she was surprised when he stopped her to ask if he could escort her to the Freshman Mixer, the start of something which she hoped would last until death do them part.

The Greeks could take this 100 word sentence in stride (an impossible situation in English) without batting an eye. As an exercise in English grammar, the student should try to find the main verb. What is it? _____ (The answer is on the next page.)

A paratactic sentence joins independent clauses with "and."

She had already noticed the handsome young man and wondered if he had noticed her and planned to sign up for "Greek" because she wanted to sit next to him, but her plans were foiled because he signed up for "Hebrew" and Saturday morning she thought it was finished for her because he caught her wearing curlers, but he stopped her and asked if he could escort her to the Freshman Mixer and she hoped this was the start of something which would last until death would them part.

The Semitic languages would do it this way.
The New Testament, though written in Greek, was
written by men of a Semitic culture and language.
In addition, the Greek Old Testament, having been
translated directly from the Hebrew, was their guide
in theological truth, supplying a theological vocabulary and adding the flavor of a paratactic Greek to
their writings.

So the sentence in Biblical Greek is more
paratactic than a sentence in Classical Greek, but
more hypotactic than a sentence in the Semitic
language.

WORD ORDER

It is amazing how much the meaning of an
English sentence changes when the order of the words
is changed. The Greeks would say we talk in a
straightjacket. They played fast and loose with the
location of words in the sentence. They even put a
main verb between a noun and its modifiers.

In spite of their seeming lack of order, they   Attributive and
were very particular about the position of the   Predicate Position
article and any of the other modifiers of a word.
This is very tricky and very important.

"The good man" (ὁ ἀγαθὸς ἄνθρωπος) means "the good man" -
      the "Attributive" position.

"Good the man" (ἀγαθὸς ὁ ἄνθρωπος) means "the man is
      good" - the "Predicate" position.

The article always comes before the word it is making
definite, but not necessarily immediately before.
Sometimes modifiers belonging to the word come between.
The adjective usually follows the word to which it
belongs.

A very few unaccented particles are so self-
effacing that they refuse to start a sentence or clause
and so always seem to be out of place by a few notches
(μεν, δε, τε). These are called "Post Positives."

The most important part of the sentence is put   Emphasis
first. The secondary emphatic position is at the
last. What is not so important is buried in the
middle of the sentence. The Greek is not nearly as
limited as the English. Usually the order is verb,
subject and direct object; or subject, verb and
direct object.

Remember, as far as word order is concerned,
and compared to English, the Greek language is really
a swinging language.

(Answer to the question on page 5:2: "was surprised.")

CONCORD

When it came to concord, the Greeks were very firm. Pronouns must agree with their antecedents in gender and number. Adjectives must agree with the nouns to which they belong in gender, number and case. Subjects and their verbs agree in number. Sometimes a relative pronoun can be convinced by "attraction" to change its gender. Neuter plural subjects usually employ a singular verb. Often the third person personal pronoun serves to emphasize the subject of verbs when their subjects are first or second person. It is this strict adherence to concord which enables the Greek reader, even in the midst of a 100-word sentence to know his whereabouts.

The Bible student should make an effort to understand every breach of concord which he finds in the New Testament (even in the Apocalypse). There must have been a reason for it, since the writers were so careful about concord. An exegetical point probably turns on that very breach!

IDIOMS

No language lives up to its own grammatical rules. Language is too human and dynamic, and communication is too important to be stymied by logic. So language evolves ways of saying things which defy its own categories. In order to accommodate "tidy souls," all these peculiar expressions are pigeon-holed into the category called "idioms."

For the person who does not really know and feel the language, the idiom is an indetectable boobytrap. Feeling for the language is necessary because there is no gulf fixed between idioms on the one hand, and constructions which adhere to the letter of the law on the other. One blends into the other, and no one can pinpoint when one leaves off and the other begins.

Some idioms, of course, can be isolated and described, but they are at the end of the spectrum.

For instance, there is the reduplication of the preposition which the Greeks loved to profligate. That is, they would have a prepositional phrase which belongs with the verb and then would attach the same preposition to the verb itself. In English it would be like the tautological, "She entered *into* the house."

At other times they had a neuter plural subject with a singular verb; a clear defiance of the number concord rule. Or they would leave out the main verb, especially "to be" (εἰμί), apparently thinking that anyone with even a questionable I.Q.

could replace it with a verb from his own imagination.

A whole carload of idioms is imported from the Semitic languages, some arriving from the Aramaic mother tongue and others from the Septuagint.

> For instance, although the construction is indigenous to the Greek also, the Semitic tongues loved the "cognate accusative," "I kicked him a kick." The paratactic constructions already mentioned and poetic parallelisms are further examples. For instance, in the familiar verse, "He maketh me to lie down in green pastures; He leadeth me beside the still waters," the writer is trying to say the same thing twice by using different words and figures. One's exegetical thrust, therefore, should not be in the direction of discovering what each has in contrast, but in what both are saying in common.

> Another example might be Matthew 5:45, "for He makes His sun to rise on the evil and on the good, and sends rain on the just and on the unjust." If the Lord were using a Semitic poetic parallelism, then an exegesis of contrasts would work against the Author.

One Hebrew idom has crept into English and made itself so much at home that few are aware of its existence. Almost anyone can quote the Ten Commandments, but who has noticed that all but one are in the future tense?

> Another very common Hebrew idiom in the New Testament is the familiar "and it came to pass."

> The Jews did everything they could to avoid pronouncing the word "Jehovah" or "Yahweh," the proper name of God. In its place they substituted "name, glory, heaven" and other words. "Heaven" probably does not mean "heaven" in Luke 15:18. If the prodigal son was talking like a Jew, he more probably meant, "I have sinned against God." And that is the way the word should be interpreted, if not translated.

> No one has any business judging if there is any difference between the "kingdom of God" and the "kingdom of heaven" until he has settled in his mind if these phrases are in the same category.

STYLE

The formal rhetorical literary style was the result of man-made standards superimposed upon plain Greek. The "in" generation of that day went to college to practice talking and writing that way.

There is nothing rhetorical in the Greek New

Testament.   It is plain Greek.   The only time Paul
saw the inside of a Greek school was when he leased
a hall from Tyrannus in Ephesus (Acts 19:9).

When reading the letters of the New Testament,
one should keep in mind that they were written like
letters ought to be written, following a chain of
consciousness more than a formal outline.   Digres-
sions balloon subordinate clauses all out of pro-
portion.   The author, together with his own
situation at the time of writing, makes his presence
felt on every page.   When a letter is forced into
the mold of a formal dissertation, the sap is
squeezed out of it.

"I wonder what that word is in Greek?" No doubt you have asked yourself this question many times. To find the answer, there are four possible routes, some of which are much simpler than others.

Let's suppose you are working on the idea "ye tasted that the Lord is gracious," and you want to know the Greek word for "tasted" in I Peter 2:3.

ROUTE 1

1. Look up I Peter 2:3 in the *Interlinear Greek - English New Testament*. (See the sample page which follows on page 6:2.) Underneath each Greek word is an English translation of that word. (Remember that the *Interlinear* only translates word for word, following the Greek word order. Therefore it will rarely read the same as the normal English version.)

The English of verse 3 as found in the *Interlinear* reads, "if ye tasted that good the Lord (is)." Look at the Greek directly above "ye tasted" and you will see the word ἐγεύσασθε. Remember Lesson 4 said that you can spell a Greek verb nearly 500 different ways? This is one of those 500 ways, so now you come to the next step.

2. Look up the word ἐγεύσασθε in a special book called *The Analytical Greek Lexicon*. (See the sample page which follows on page 6:3.) This book lists in alphabetical order all the 500 or less forms of all the words which appear in a Greek New Testament. Looking up the word, you find that to the right of it, after some abbreviations, is the word γεύομαι. This is called the "lexical form" and is the word you need to write down. In the following lessons you will learn the importance of this "lexical form," but for now it is sufficient to just find out what it is.

The Analytical Greek Lexicon is an important tool in that it gives you the lexical form of the Greek word. It also gives a limited meaning of the lexical form and will list other nouns, verbs and adjectives which come from the same stem.

I. PETER 2

born babes, long for the pure spiritual milk, that by it you may grow up to salvation; ³for you have tasted the kindness of the Lord.

4 Come to him, to that living stone, rejected by men but in God's sight chosen and precious; ⁵and like living stones be yourselves built into a spiritual house, to be a holy priesthood, to offer spiritual sacrifices acceptable to God through Jesus Christ. ⁶For it stands in scripture:

"Behold, I am laying in Zion a stone, a cornerstone chosen and precious, and he who believes in him will not be put to shame."

⁷To you therefore who believe, he is precious, but for those who do not believe,

"The very stone which the builders rejected has become the head of the corner,"

⁸and

"A stone that will make men stumble, a rock that will make them fall";

for they stumble because they disobey the word, as they were destined to do.

9 But you are a chosen race, a royal priesthood, a holy nation, God's own people, that you may declare the wonderful

βρέφη τὸ λογικὸν ἄδολον γάλα ἐπιποθήσατε,
babes ²the ³spiritual ⁴pure ¹milk ¹desire ye,

ἵνα ἐν αὐτῷ αὐξηθῆτε εἰς σωτηρίαν,
in or- by it ye may grow to salvation,
der that

3 εἰ ἐγεύσασθε ὅτι χρηστὸς ὁ κύριος.
if ye tasted that ⁵good ¹the ¹Lord [is].

4 πρὸς ὃν προσερχόμενοι, λίθον ζῶντα,
to whom approaching, ¹stone ¹a living,

ὑπὸ ἀνθρώπων μὲν ἀποδεδοκιμασμένον παρὰ
by men on one having been rejected ²by
hand

δὲ θεῷ ἐκλεκτὸν ἔντιμον, 5 καὶ
¹on the ⁴God ²chosen[,] precious, ¹also
other

αὐτοὶ ὡς λίθοι ζῶντες οἰκοδομεῖσθε οἶκος
¹[your]- ²as ³stones ⁴living are being built ²house
selves

πνευματικὸς εἰς ἱεράτευμα ἅγιον, ἀνενέγκαι
¹a spiritual for ²priesthood, ¹a holy, to offer

πνευματικὰς θυσίας εὐπροσδέκτους θεῷ διὰ
spiritual sacrifices acceptable to through
God

Ἰησοῦ Χριστοῦ· 6 διότι περιέχει ἐν γραφῇ·
Jesus Christ; because it is in scripture:
contained

ἰδοὺ τίθημι ἐν Σιὼν λίθον ἐκλεκτὸν
Behold I lay in Sion ⁴stone ¹a chosen

ἀκρογωνιαῖον ἔντιμον, καὶ ὁ πιστεύων
²corner foundation ³precious, and the [one] believing

ἐπ᾽ αὐτῷ οὐ μὴ καταισχυνθῇ. 7 ὑμῖν
on it(him) by no means will be shamed. To you
=Yours

οὖν ἡ τιμὴ τοῖς πιστεύουσιν· ἀπιστοῦσιν
there- ²[is] ³honour ¹the [ones] ²believingᵉ; ³to unbelieving
fore ¹the [ones]
therefore who believe is the honour;

δὲ λίθος ὃν ἀπεδοκίμασαν οἱ οἰκοδομοῦντες,
¹but a stone which ²rejected ¹the [ones] ²building,

οὗτος ἐγενήθη εἰς κεφαλὴν γωνίας 8 καὶ
this came to be for head of [the] corner and

λίθος προσκόμματος καὶ πέτρα σκανδάλου·
a stone of stumbling and a rock of offence;

οἱ προσκόπτουσιν τῷ λόγῳ ἀπειθοῦντες,
who stumble at the word disobeying,

9 εἰς ὃ καὶ ἐτέθησαν· ὑμεῖς δὲ γένος
ι to which indeed they were but ye [are] ²race
appointed;

ἐκλεκτόν, βασίλειον ἱεράτευμα, ἔθνος ἅγιον,
¹a chosen, a royal priesthood, nation a holy,

λαὸς εἰς περιποίησιν, ὅπως τὰς ἀρετὰς
a people for possession, so as ²the ²virtues

ἐγείρει, 3 pers. sing. pres. ind. act. . . ἐγείρω
ἐγείρειν, pres. infin. act. . . . . id.
ἐγείρεσθε, 2 pers. pl. pres. imper. mid. . id.
ἐγείρεται, 3 pers. sing. pres. ind. mid. . id.
ἐγείρετε, 2 pers. pl. pres. imper. act. . id.
ἐγείρηται, 3 pers. sing. pres. subj. mid. . id.
ἐγείρομαι, 1 pers. sing. pres. ind. mid. . id.
ἐγείρονται, 3 pers. pl. pres. ind. mid. . id.
ἐγείροντι, dat. sing. masc. part. pres. act. . id.
ἐγείρου, 2 pers. sing. pres. imper. mid. . id.

ἐγείρω], (§ 37. rem. 1) fut. ἐγερῶ, perf. ἐγήγερκα, aor. 1, ἤγειρα, perf. pass. ἐγήγερμαι, aor. 1, pass. ἠγέρθην, *to excite, arouse, awaken*, Mat. 8.25, et al.; mid. *to awake*, Mat. 2. 13, 20, 21, et al.; met. mid. *to rouse one's self* to a better course of conduct, Ro. 13. 11; Ep. 5. 14; *to raise from* the dead, Jno. 12. 1, et al.; and mid. *to rise* from the dead, Mat. 27. 52; Jno. 5. 21, et al.; met. *to raise* as it were from the dead, 2 Co. 4. 14; *to raise up, cause to rise up* from a recumbent posture, Ac. 3. 7; and mid. *to rise up*, Mat. 17. 7, et al.; *to restore to health*, Ja. 5. 15; met. et seq. ἐπί, *to excite* to war; mid. *to rise up against*, Mat. 24. 7, et al.; *to raise up again, rebuild*, Jno. 2. 19, 20; *to raise up from a lower place, to draw up or out of* a ditch, Mat. 12. 11; from Heb. *to raise up, to cause to arise or exist*, Ac. 13. 22, 23; mid. *to arise, exist, appear*, Mat. 3. 9; 11. 11, et al.

ἔγερσις, εως, ἡ, (§ 5. tab. E. c) pr. *the act of waking* or *rising up; resurrection, resuscitation*, Mat. 27. 53.

ἐγέμισαν, 3 pers. pl. aor. 1, ind. act. . γεμίζω
ἐγέμισε, 3 pers. sing. aor 1, ind. act. . id.
ἐγεμίσθη, 3 pers. sing. aor. ind. pass. . id.
ἐγένεσθε, 2 pers. pl. aor. 2, ind. mid. . γίνομαι
ἐγένετο, 3 pers. sing. aor. 2, ind. (§ 37. rem. 1) id.
ἐγενήθη, 3 pers. sing. aor. 1, ind. pass. . id.
ἐγενήθημεν, 1 pers. pl. aor. 1, ind. pass. . id.
ἐγενήθησαν, 3 pers. pl. aor. 1, ind. pass. . id.
ἐγενήθητε, 2 pers. pl. aor. 1, ind. pass. . id.
ἐγεννήθη, 3 pers. sing. aor. 1, ind. pass. . γεννάω
ἐγεννήθημεν, 1 pers. pl. aor. 1, ind. pass. . id.
ἐγεννήθης, 2 pers. sing. aor. 1, ind. pass. . id.

ἐγεννήθησαν, 3 pers. pl. aor. 1, ind. pass. . γεννάω
ἐγέννησα, 1 pers. sing. aor. 1, ind. act. . id.
ἐγέννησαν, 3 pers. pl. aor. 1, ind. act. . id
ἐγέννησε, 3 pers. sing. aor. 1, ind. act. . id.
ἐγενόμην, 1 pers. sing. aor. 2, ind. mid. . γίνομαι
ἐγένοντο, 3 pers. pl. aor. 2, ind. mid. . id.
ἐγένου, 2 pers. sing. aor. 2, ind. mid. . . id.
ἐγερεῖ, 3 pers. sing. fut. ind. act. (§ 37. rem. 1) ἐγείρω
ἐγερεῖς, 2 pers. sing. fut. ind. act. . . id.
ἐγερθείς, nom. sing. masc. part. aor. 1, pass. . id.
ἐγερθέντι, dat. sing. masc. part. aor. 1, pass. id.
ἐγερθῇ, 3 pers. sing. aor. 1, subj. pass. . id.
ἐγερθῆναι, aor. 1, infin. pass. . . . id.
ἐγερθήσεται, 3 pers. sing. fut. 1, ind. pass. . id.
ἐγερθήσονται, 3 pers. pl. fut. 1, ind. pass. . id.
ἐγέρθητε, 2 pers. pl. aor. 1, imper. pass. . id.
ἐγέρθητι, 2 pers. sing. aor. 1, imper. pass. . id.
ἔγερσιν,ᵃ acc. sing. . . . ἔγερσις
ἔγερσις], εως, ἡ, (§ 5. tab. E. c) . ἐγείρω
ἐγερῶ, 1 pers. sing. fut. ind. act. . . id.
ἐγεύσασθε, 2 pers. pl. aor. 1, ind. . γεύομαι
ἐγεύσατο, 3 pers. sing. aor. 1, ind. (§ 15. tab. O) id.
ἐγηγερμένον, acc. sing. masc. part. perf. pass. ἐγείρω
ἐγήγερται, 3 pers. sing. perf. ind. pass. . id.
ἔγημα, 1 pers. sing. aor. 1, ind. (§ 37. rem. 2) γαμέω
ἐγίνετο, 3 pers. sing. imperf. . . γίνομαι
ἐγίνωσκε, 3 pers. sing. imperf. act. . γινώσκω
ἐγίνωσκον, 3 pers. pl. imperf. act. . . id.
ἐγκάθετος], ου, ὁ, ἡ, (§ 7. rem. 2) (ἐν & καθίημι) *suborned*.

ἐγκαθέτους,ᵇ acc. pl. masc. . . . ἐγκάθετος
ἐγκαίνια,ᶜ ίων, τά, (§ 6. rem. 5) (ἐν & καινός) *initiation, consecration*; in N.T. *the feast of dedication*, an annual festival of eight days in the month Kisleu.

ἐγκαινίζω], fut. ίσω, (§ 26. rem. 1) aor. 1, ἐνεκαί-νισα, perf. pass. ἐγκεκαίνισμαι, *to handsel, initiate, consecrate, dedicate, renovate; to institute*, He. 9. 18; 10. 20. LXX.

ἐγκακεῖν, pres. infin.—Al. Ln. Tdf. }
ἐκκακεῖν, Rec. Gr. Sch. (Lu. 18. 1) } ἐγκακέω

ἐγκᾰκέω, ῶ], fut. ήσω, v.r. probably the same in signification as ἐκκακέω, *to despond, be faint-hearted, be remiss*.

ἐγκακήσητε, 2 pers. pl. aor. 1, subj.—B. Ln. Tdf. }
ἐκκακήσητε, Rec. Gr. Sch. (2 Thes. 3. 13) } ἐγκακέω

ἐγκακοῦμεν, 1 pers. pl. pres. ind.—A. D. Ln. Tdf. }
ἐκκακοῦμεν, Rec. Gr. Sch. (2 Co. 4. 1) } id.

ᵃ Mat. 27. 53.   ᵇ Lu. 20. 20.   ᶜ Jno. 10. 22.

So, Route 1 has two steps for finding the Greek word: the *Interlinear Greek - English New Testament* and *The Analytical Greek Lexicon*.

ROUTE 2

1. Take *The Englishman's Greek Concordance of the New Testament* and look in the back (between pages 783 and 943) for the word "taste." (See the sample page which follows on page 6:5.) Under this word will be a list of all the Greek words that are translated "taste" in the King James Version. In this case, there is only one Greek word, γεύομαι. Did you notice that it is listed in its lexical form? So you have the word you need in just one easy step.

Route 2 may seem shorter, but this example is easy since there is only one Greek word for "taste." However if you had looked up the word "take" from I Peter 2:20, the problem would have been more complicated, since the King James Version employs the English word "take" to translate 21 different Greek words. What would you do in that situation? There is an answer, but let's take a different route instead.

ROUTE 3

1. Look up the word "tasted" in the *Exhaustive Concordance of the Bible* by James Strong. (See the sample page which follows on page 6:6.) It must be the exact form that is found in the King James Version, i.e. "tast<u>ed</u>;" not "taste." You will find a list of eight references and so must look until you come to I Peter 2:3. In a column to the right of this verse there are ditto marks which carry down from the italicized number *1089*.

It is very important to notice whether or not the number is in italics. At the back of Strong's *Concordance* are two different dictionaries: one for the Hebrew and Aramaic words of the Old Testament, and the other for the Greek words of the New Testament. The numbers which are not in italics refer to the Hebrew and Aramaic section, while the italicized numbers refer to the Greek dictionary.

2. Look up the italicized number *1089* in the back of the *Concordance* in the section entitled "A Concise Dictionary of the Words in the Greek Testament." (See the sample page which follows on page 6:7.) Number *1089* will be found on page 20. Notice that you are given the lexical form, γεύομαι, along with a brief definition.

Again, you find that there are two steps involved: the main section in Strong's *Concordance* and the dictionary in the back of the same book.

SUR   (932)   TEL

surety, εγγυος 176
surety (of a), αληθως 28
surfeiting, κραιπαλη 431
surmising, ὑπονοια......... 779
surname is, (whose), επικαλεομαι 284
surname (Mar. {επιτιθημι . 288
3:16, 17), {ονομα 532
surname was (whose), καλεω 401
surnamed (be), επικαλεομαι 284
sustenance, χορτασμα 802
swaddling clothes (wrap in), σπαργανοω 695
swallow, } καταπινω 414
swallow up,}
swear, ομνυμι 530
sweat, ιδρως 382
sweep, σαροω............... 681
sweet, γλυκυς 124
sweet, see savour, smell, spices.
sweetsmelling, ευωδια 328
swelling (great), ὑπερογκος . 775
swellings φυσιωσις 792
swerve, αστοχεω........... 89
swift, οξυς 534
    ταχινος 724
    ταχυς .... —
swim, κολυμβαω 428
swim out, εκκολυμβαω..... 228
swine, χοιρος............. 801
swollen (be), πιμπραμαι.... 621
sword, μαχαιρα 473
    ρομφαια............. 678
sycamine tree, συκαμινος .. 704
sycomore tree, συκομωραια . 705
synagogue, συναγωγη 709
synagogue (chief ruler of), αρχισυναγωγος 85
synagogue (put out of the), αποσυναγωγος........... 78
synagogue (ruler of the), αρχισυναγωγος 85
synagogues (out of the), αποσυναγωγος............ 78

tabernacle, σκηνη 687
    σκηνος .... —
    σκηνωμα .... —
tabernacles (Joh.7:2), σκηνοπηγια .... —
table, κλινη............. 425
    πλαξ................. 627
    τραπεζα 748
table, see write.
table (with), see sit.
tackling, σκευη 686
tail, ουρα 571
take, αιρω 17
    αναλαμβανω 43
    απαιρομαι 59
    απολαμβανω 73
    ἁρπαζω.............. 82
    δεχομαι 137
    δρασσομαι 164
    επιλαμβανομαι....... 284
    επιφερω............. 289

take, καταλαμβανω 412
    κατεχω 417
    κρατεω 431
    λαμβανω 445
    μεταλαμβανω 488
    παραλαμβανω 591
    πιαζω................ 621
    ποιεω 636
    προσδεχομαι 662
    προσλαμβανω 666
    συλλαμβανω 705
    συναιρω 709
take, see accusation, captive, care, counsel, ease, hand, heed, hold, journey, knowledge, oversight, part, pleasure, rest, thought, throat, tithe, wrong.
take away, αιρω 17
    αναιρεω 42
    απαγω 59
    απαιρομαι ...... —
    αφαιρεω 96
    εξαιρω 265
    λαμβανω........ 445
    παραφερω 593
    περιαιρεω 615
take before, προλαμβανω . 656
take by, επιλαμβανομαι ... 284
    κρατεω 431
take by force, ἁρπαζω 82
take down, καθαιρεω 394
take for, εχω 329
take heed, βλεπω 108
    σκοπεω 688
take heed to, προσεχω...... 664
    επεχω 275
take in, αναλαμβανω 43
    συναγω 708
take into, see number.
take leave, αποτασσομαι.... 78
take leave, ασπαζομαι 88
take none, see effect.
take off from, εκδυω 224
take on, επιλαμβανομαι ... 284
take out, εκβαλλω 222
take patiently, ὑπομενω ... 779
take (ship), εμβαινω 235
    επιβαινω 281
take unto, παραλαμβανω ... 591
(αναλαμβανω43)προσλαμβανω 666
take up, αναγω 41
    αναιρεω............ 42
    αναλαμβανω 43
    βασταζω 105
    εγειρω 176
    επαιρω 272
    λαμβανω 445
    περιαιρεω......... 615
take up, see carriages.
take up in, see arms.
take upon, επιχειρεω....... 289
take (vengeance), διδωμι .. 151
take with, παραλαμβανω .. 591
    συμπαραλαμβανω 706
take with, see palsy.
taken away, ανακαλυπτω .. 42

taken (be), ἁλωσις......... 32
taken (be), απορφανιζομαι 75
taken (be), γινομαι 117
taken with (be), συνεχω.... 712
talent, ταλαντον........... 719
talent (weight of a), ταλαντιαιος .... —
Talitha, ταλιθα............. —
talk, λογος 462
talk, λαλεω 443
    ὁμιλεω 529
talk, see idle.
talk with, συλλαλεω 705
    συνομιλεω....... 713
talker (vain), ματαιολογος.. 473
talking (foolish), μωρολογια 512
tame, δαμαζω 132
tanner, βυρσευς 111
tares, ζιζανια 338
tarry, βραδυνω 110
    διατριβω............. 149
    επιμενω 285
    καθιζω............. 396
    μελλω 478
    ποιεω 636
    προσδοκαω 662
    προσμενω 666
    χρονιζω 803
tarry behind, ὑπομενω...... 779
tarry for, εκδεχομαι 223
    μενω............. 481
taste, γευομαι 115
tattler, φλυαρος 788
taught, διδακτος 150
taught, see God.
taught (as hath been), διδαχη 151
Taverns (The Three), Τρεις Ταβερναι 865
taxed (be), απογραφω 68
taxing, απογραφη .... —
teach, διδασκω 150
    καταγγελλω........... 410
    κατηχεω............... 418
    μαθητευω 466
    παιδευω 582
teach see sober.
teach other doc-} ἑτεροδιδ-
trine, } ασκαλεω.. 317
teach otherwise,}
teacher, διδασκαλος 150
teacher (false), ψευδοδιδασκαλος 806
teacher of the law, νομοδιδασκαλος 517
teachers of good things, καλοδιδασκαλος 402
teacheth (which...), διδακτος 150
teaching, διδασκαλια .... —
tear, ῥηγνυμι................ 677
    σπαρασσω 695
    συσπαρασσω 714
tears, δακρυ 131
tedious unto (be), εγκοπτω 178
teeth, see cast.
tell, αναγγελλω 40
    απαγγελλω............ 58

Ac 9:43 he t' many days in Joppa with one*3306
15:33 after they had t' there a space. *4160
18:18 Paul after this t' there yet a good 4357
20: 5 These going before t'...at Troas. *3306
15 at Samos, and t' at Trogyllium; * "
21: 4 disciples, we t' there seven days: 1961
10 And as we t' there many days, "
25: 6 he had t' among them more than 1304
27:33 the fourteenth day that ye have t'*4328
28:12 at Syracuse, we t' there three days. 1961

tarriest
Ac 22:16 And now why t' thou? arise, and be3195

tarrieth
1Sa 30:24 his part be that t' by the stuff; 3427
Mic 5: 7 upon the grass, that t' not for man. 6960

tarry See also TARRIED; TARRIEST; TARRIETH; TARRYING.
Ge 19: 2 t' all night, and wash your feet, 3885
27:44 And t' with him a few days, until 3427
30:27 I have found favour in thine eyes, t':
45: 9 Egypt: come down unto me, t' not:5975
Ex 12:39 out of Egypt, and could not t', 4102
24:14 T' ye here for us, until we come 3427
Le 14: 8 t' abroad out of his tent seven days.*"
Nu 22:19 t' ye also here this night, that I may"
J'g 5:28 why t' the wheels of his chariots? 309
6:18 I will t' until thou come again. 3427
19: 6 and t' all night, and let thine 3885
9 evening, I pray you t' all night: "
10 But the man would not t' that night,"
Ru 1:13 t' for them till they were grown? 7663
3:13 T' this night, and it shall be in the3885
1Sa 1:23 t' until thou have weaned him; 3427
10: 8 seven days shalt thou t', till I come3176
14: 9 T' until we come to you; then we 1826
2Sa 10: 5 T' at Jericho until your beards be 3427
11:12 T' here to day also, and to morrow "
15:28 t' in the plain of the wilderness, 4102
18:14 Joab, I may not t' thus with thee. 3176
19: 7 there will not t' one with thee this 3885
2Ki 2: 2 unto Elisha, T' here, I pray thee; 3427
4 him, Elisha, t' here, I pray thee; "
6 unto him, T', I pray thee, here; "
7: 9 if we t' till the morning light, some2442
9: 3 open the door, and flee, and t' not. "
14:10 glory of this, and t' at home: for *3427
1Ch 19: 5 T' at Jericho until your beards be "
Ps 101: 7 he that telleth lies shall not t' in *3559
Pr 23:30 They that t' long at the wine; they 309
Isa 46:13 off, and my salvation shall not t': "
Jer 14: 8 that turneth aside to t' for a night?3885
Hab 2: 3 not lie: though it t', wait for it; 4102
3 it will surely come, it will not t'. * 309
M't 26:38 t' ye here, and watch with me. *3306
M'r 14:34 unto death: t' ye here, and watch.* "
Lu 24:29 And he went in to t' with them. * "
49 but t' ye in the city of Jerusalem, 2523
Joh 4:40 him that he would t' with them: *3306
21:22, 23 If I will that he t' till I come, "
Ac 10:48 prayed they him to t' certain days. 1961
18:20 they desired him to t' longer time*3306
28:14 desired to t' with them seven days:1961
1Co 11:33 together to eat, t' one for another.*1551
16: 7 I trust to t' a while with you, if the1961
8 will t' at Ephesus until Pentecost. "
1Ti 3:15 But if I t' long, that thou mayest 1019
Heb 10:37 come will come, and will not t'. 5549

tarrying
Ps 40:17 deliverer; make no t', O my God. 309
70: 5 my deliverer; O Lord, make no t'. "

Tarshish (*tar'-shish*) See also THARSHISH.
Ge 10: 4 sons of Javan; Elishah, and T', 8659
1Ch 1: 7 the sons of Javan; Elishah and T', "
2Ch 9:21 For the king's ships went to T' "
21 came the ships of T' bringing gold,"
20:36 him to make ships to go to T': "
37 they were not able to go to T'. "
Es 1:14 Admatha, T', Meres, Marsena, "
Ps 48: 7 Thou breakest the ships of T' "
72:10 The kings of T' and of the isles "
Isa 2:16 And upon all the ships of T', and "
23: 1 Howl, ye ships of T'; for it is laid "
6 Pass ye over to T'; howl, ye "
10 land as a river, O daughter of T': "
14 Howl, ye ships of T': for your "
60: 9 for me, and the ships of T' first, "
66:19 them unto the nations, to T', Pul, "
Jer 10: 9 into plates is brought from T', "
Eze 27:12 T' was thy merchant by reason of "
25 The ships of T' did sing of thee "
38:13 Dedan, and the merchants of T', "
Jon 1: 3 But Jonah rose up to flee unto T' "
3 and he found a ship going to T': "
3 unto it, to go with them unto T' "
4: 2 Therefore I fled before unto T': "

Tarsus (*tar'-sus*)
Ac 9:11 Judas for one called Saul, of T': 5018
30 Cæsarea, and sent him forth to T'. 5019
11:25 Then departed Barnabas to T', "
21:39 I am a man which am a Jew of T', 5018
22: 3 man which am a Jew, born in T', 5019

taskmasters
Ex 1:11 they did set over them t' 8269,4522
3: 7 their cry by reason of their t'; 5065
5: 6 And Pharaoh commanded...the t' "
10 And the t' of the people went out, "
13 And the t' hasted them, saying, "
14 Pharaoh's t' had set over them, "

tasks
Ex 5:13 Fulfil your works, your daily t', 1697

taste See also TASTED; TASTETH.
Ex 16:31 t' of it was like wafers made with 2940
Nu 11: 8 the t' of it was as the t' of fresh oil. "
1Sa 14:43 I did but t' a little honey with the 2938
2Sa 3:35 to me, and more also, if I t' bread, "
19:35 t' what I eat or what I drink? "
Job 6: 6 there any t' in the white of an egg?2940
30 my t' discern perverse things? 2441
12:11 and the mouth t' his meat? *2938
Ps 34: 8 O t' and see that the Lord is good: "
119:103 sweet are thy words unto my t'! 2441
Pr 24:13 honeycomb, which is sweet to thy t':"
Ca 2: 3 and his fruit was sweet to my t'. "
Jer 48:11 therefore his t' remained in him, 2940
Jon 3: 7 beast, herd nor flock, t' any thing: 2938
M't 16:28 here, which shall not t' of death, 1089
M'r 9: 1 here, which shall not t' of death, "
Lu 9:27 here, which shall not t' of death, "
14:24 were bidden shall t' of my supper. "
Joh 8:52 saying, he shall never t' of death. "
Col 2:21 (Touch not; t' not; handle not; "
Heb 2: 9 should t' death for every man. "

tasted
1Sa 14:24 So none of the people t' any food. 2938
29 because I t' a little of this honey. "
Da 5: 2 Belshazzar, whiles he t' the wine, 2942
M't 27:34 had t' thereof, he would not drink. 1089
Joh 2: 9 t' the water that was made wine, "
Heb 6: 4 and have t' of the heavenly gift, and "
5 And have t' the good word of God, "
1Pe 2: 3 ye have t' that the Lord is gracious."

tasteth
Job 34: 3 words, as the mouth t' meat. 2938

Tatnai (*tat'-nahee*)
Ezr 5: 3, 6 T', governor on this side the *8674
6: 6 T', governor beyond the river, * "
13 T', governor on this side the river,*"

tattlers
1Ti 5:13 idle, but t' also and busybodies, 5397

taught
De 4: 5 Behold, I have t' you statutes and 3925
31:22 day, and t' it the children of Israel. "
J'g 8:16 them he t' the men of Succoth. 3045
2Ki 17:28 t' them how they should fear the 3384
2Ch 6:27 thou hast t' them the good way, * "
17: 9 they t' in Judah, and had the book3925
9 cities of Judah, and t' the people. "
23:13 and such as t' to sing praise. *3045
30:22 t' the good knowledge of the Lord:*7919
35: 3 unto the Levites that t' all Israel, 4000
Ne 8: 9 and the Levites that t' the people, 995
Ps 71:17 thou hast t' me from my youth: 3925
119:102 judgments: for thou hast t' me. 3384
171 when thou hast t' me thy statutes.*3925
Pr 4: 4 He t' me also, and said unto me, 3384
11 I have t' thee in the way of wisdom;"
31: 1 prophecy that his mother t' him. 3256
Ec 12: 9 he still t' the people knowledge; 3925
Isa 29:13 fear toward me is t' by the precept*"
40:13 being his counsellor hath t' him? 3045
14 t' him in the path of judgment, 3925
14 and t' him knowledge, and shewed "
54:13 children shall be t' of the Lord; 3928
Jer 2:33 hast thou also t' the wicked ones 3925
9: 5 have t' their tongue to speak lies, "
14 Baalim, which their fathers t' them:"
12:16 they t' my people to swear by Baal;"
13:21 thou hast t' them to be captains, † "
28:16 hast t' rebellion against the Lord.*1696
29:32 hath t' rebellion against the Lord.* "
32:33 though I t' them, rising up early 3925
Eze 23:48 be t' not to do after your lewdness. 3256
Ho 10:11 Ephraim is as an heifer that is t', 3925
11: 3 I t' Ephraim also to go, taking 8637
Zec 13: 5 t' me to keep cattle from my youth.*
M't 5: 2 he opened his mouth, and t' them, 1321
7:29 he t' them as one having 2258, "
13:54 he t' them in their synagogue, "
28:15 the money, and did as they were t': "
M'r 1:21 entered into the synagogue, and t'. "
22 for he t' them as one that had 2258, "
2:13 resorted unto him, and he t' them. "
4: 2 he t' them many things by parables,"
6:30 they had done, and what they had t'. "
9:31 For he t' his disciples, and said unto"
10: 1 as he was wont, he t' them again. "
11:17 he t', saying unto them, Is it not "
12:35 and said, while he t' in the temple, "
Lu 4:15 And he t' in their synagogues, being"
31 t' them on the sabbath days. *2258, "
5: 3 and t' the people out of the ship. "
6: 6 entered into the synagogue and t': "
11: 1 pray, as John also t' his disciples. "
13:26 and thou hast t' in our streets. * "
Ac 5:21 temple early in the morning, and t'. 1321
11:26 the church, and t' much people. "
14:21 to that city, and had t' many, *3100
15: 1 down from Judæa t' the brethren, 1321
18:25 t' diligently the things of the Lord, "
20:20 you, and have t' you publickly, * "
22: 3 t' according to the perfect manner*3811
Ga 1:12 it of man, neither was I t' it, 1321
6: 6 Let him that is t' in the word 2727
Eph 4:21 heard him, and...been t' by him, 1321
Col 2: 7 in the faith, as ye have been t', "
1Th 4: 9 are t' of God to love one another. 2312
2Th 2:15 traditions which ye have been t', 1321
Tit 1: 9 faithful word as he hath been t', *1322
1Joh 2:27 no lie, and even as it hath t' you, 1321
Re 2:14 t' Balac to cast a stumblingblock "

taunt See also TAUNTING.
Jer 24: 9 and a proverb, a t' and a curse, 8148
Eze 5:15 So it shall be a reproach and a t', 1422

taunting
Hab 2: 6 and a t' proverb against him, and 4426

taverns
Ac 28:15 far as Appii forum,...The three t': 4999

taxation
2Ki 23:35 of every one according to his t', to 6187

taxed
2Ki 23:35 he t' the land to give the money 6186
Lu 2: 1 that all the world should be t'. * 582
3 all went to be t', every one into his* "
5 be t' with Mary his espoused wife, * "

taxes
Da 11:20 a raiser of t' in the glory of the *5065

taxing
Lu 2: 2 And this t' was first made when * 583
Ac 5:37 Judas of Galilee in the days of the t',*"

teach See also TAUGHT; TEACHER; TEACHEST; TEACHETH; TEACHING.
Ex 4:12 and t' thee what thou shalt say. 3384
15 and will t' you what ye shall do. "
18:20 thou shalt t' them ordinances and 2094
24:12 written; that thou mayest t' them. 3384
35:34 hath put in his heart that he may t'."
Le 10:11 may t' the children of Israel all the "
14:57 t' when it is unclean, and when it is"
De 4: 1 the judgments, which I t' you, for 3925
9 but t' them thy sons, and thy sons'*3045
10 and that they may t' their children. 3925
14 me at that time to t' you statutes "
5:31 judgments, which thou shalt t' them,"
6: 1 your God commanded to t' you, "
7 shalt t' them diligently unto thy 8150
11:19 And ye shall t' them your children, 3925
17:11 of the law which they shall t' thee, 3384
20:18 they t' you not to do after all their3925
24: 8 the priests the Levites shall t' you: 3384
31:19 you, and t' it the children of Israel: 3925
33:10 They shall t' Jacob thy judgments, 3384
J'g 3: 2 Israel might know, to t' them war, 3925
13: 8 and t' us what we shall do unto the3384
1Sa 12:23 I will t' you the good and the right*"
2Sa 1:18 bade them t' the children of Judah3925
1Ki 8:36 that thou t' them the good way *3384
2Ki 17:27 t' them the manner of the God of "
2Ch 17: 7 to t' in the cities of Judah. 3925
Ezr 7:10 and to t' in Israel statutes and "
25 and t' ye them that know them not. 3046
Job 6:24 T' me, and I will hold my tongue: 3384
8:10 Shall not they t' thee, and tell thee, "
12: 7 the beasts, and they shall t' thee: "
8 to the earth, and it shall t' thee: "
21:22 Shall any t' God knowledge? seeing3925
27:11 I will t' you by the hand of God: 3384
32: 7 multitude of years...t' wisdom. 3045
33:33 peace, and I shall t' thee wisdom. 502
34:32 That which I see not t' thou me: 3384
37:19 T' us what we shall say unto him; 3045
Ps 25: 4 thy ways, O Lord; t' me thy paths. 3925
5 Lead me in thy truth, and t' me: "
8 will he t' sinners in the way. *3384
9 and the meek will he t' his way. 3925
12 him shall he t' in the way that he*3384
27:11 T' me thy way, O Lord, and lead "
32: 8 I will instruct thee and t' thee in the"
34:11 I will t' you the fear of the Lord. 3925
45: 4 thy right hand shall t' thee terrible3384
51:13 will I t' transgressors thy ways; 3925
60: *title* Michtam of David, to t'; when "
86:11 T' me thy way, O Lord; I will 3384
90:12 t' us to number our days, that we 3045
105:22 pleasure; and t' his senators wisdom. "
119:12 thou, O Lord: t' me thy statutes. 3925
26 heardest me: t' me thy statutes. "
33 T' me, O Lord, the way of thy 3384
64 of thy mercy: t' me thy statutes. 3925
66 T' me...judgment and knowledge; "
68 and doest good; t' me thy statutes. "
108 O Lord, and t' me thy judgments. "
124 thy mercy, and t' me thy statutes. "
135 thy servant; and t' me thy statutes."
132:12 my testimony that I shall t' them, "
143:10 T' me to do thy will; for thou art "
Pr 9: 9 t' a just man, and he will increase 3045

Taken from the *Exhaustive Concordance of the Bible* by James Strong, published by Abingdon Press, and is used by permission.

1043. Γαβριήλ **Gabriēl**, *gab-ree-ale';* of Heb. or. [1403]; *Gabriel,* an archangel:—Gabriel.

1044. γάγγραινα **gaggraina**, *gang'-grahee-nah;* from γραίνω **grainō** (to *gnaw*); an *ulcer* (" gangrene"):—canker.

1045. Γάδ **Gad**, *gad;* of Heb. or. [1410]; *Gad,* a tribe of Isr.:—Gad.

1046. Γαδαρηνός **Gadarēnŏs**, *gad-ar-ay-nos';* from Γαδαρά (a town E. of the Jordan); a *Gadarene* or inhab. of Gadara:—Gadarene.

1047. γάζα **gaza**, *gad'-zah;* of for. or.; a *treasure:*—treasure.

1048. Γάζα **Gaza**, *gad'-zah;* of Heb. or. [5804]; *Gazah* (i.e. 'Azzah), a place in Pal.:—Gaza.

1049. γαζοφυλάκιον **gazŏphulakiŏn**, *gad-zof-oo-lak'-ee-on;* from *1047* and *5438;* a *treasure-house,* i.e. a court in the temple for the collection-boxes:—treasury.

1050. Γάϊος **Gaiŏs**, *gah'-ee-os;* of Lat. or.; *Gaius* (i.e. *Caius*), a Chr.:—Gaius.

1051. γάλα **gala**, *gal'-ah;* of uncert. affin.; *milk* (fig.):—milk.

1052. Γαλάτης **Galatēs**, *gal-at'-ace;* from *1053;* a *Galatian* or inhab. of Galatia:—Galatian.

1053. Γαλατία **Galatia**, *gal-at-ee'-ah;* of for. or.; *Galatia,* a region of Asia:—Galatia.

1054. Γαλατικός **Galatikŏs**, *gal-at-ee-kos';* from *1053;* *Galatic* or relating to Galatia:—of Galatia.

1055. γαλήνη **galēnē**, *gal-ay'-nay;* of uncert. der.; *tranquillity:*—calm.

1056. Γαλιλαία **Galilaia**, *gal-il-ah'-yah;* of Heb. or. [1551]; *Galilæa* (i.e. the heathen *circle*), a region of Pal.:—Galilee.

1057. Γαλιλαῖος **Galilaiŏs**, *gal-ee-loh'-yos;* from *1056;* *Galilæan* or belonging to Galilæa:—Galilæan, of Galilee.

1058. Γαλλίων **Galliōn**, *gal-lee'-own;* of Lat. or.; *Gallion* (i.e. *Gallio*), a Roman officer:—Gallio.

1059. Γαμαλιήλ **Gamaliēl**, *gam-al-ee-ale';* of Heb. or. [1583]; *Gamaliel* (i.e. *Gamliel*), an Isr.:—Gamaliel.

1060. γαμέω **gamĕō**, *gam-eh'-o;* from *1062;* to *wed* (of either sex):—marry (a wife).

1061. γαμίσκω **gamiskō**, *gam-is'-ko;* from *1062;* to *espouse* (a daughter to a husband):—give in marriage.

1062. γάμος **gamŏs**, *gam'-os;* of uncert. affin.; *nuptials:*—marriage, wedding.

1063. γάρ **gar**, *gar;* a prim. particle; prop. assigning a *reason* (used in argument, explanation or intensification; often with other particles):—and, as, because (that), but, even, for, indeed, no doubt, seeing, then, therefore, verily, what, why, yet.

1064. γαστήρ **gastĕr**, *gas-tare';* of uncert. der.; the *stomach;* by anal. the *matrix;* fig. a *gourmand:*—belly, + with child, womb.

1065. γέ **gĕ**, *gheh;* a prim. particle of *emphasis* or *qualification* (often used with other particles prefixed):—and besides, doubtless, at least, yet.

1066. Γεδεών **Gĕdĕōn**, *ghed-eh-own';* of Heb. or. [1439]; *Gedeon* (i.e. *Gid[e]on*), an Isr.:—Gedeon.

1067. γέεννα **gĕĕnna**, *gheh'-en-nah;* of Heb. or. [1516 and 2011]; *valley of* (the son of) *Hinnom; gehenna* (or *Ge-Hinnom*), a valley of Jerus., used (fig.) as a name for the place (or state) of everlasting punishment:—hell.

1068. Γεθσημανή **Gĕthsēmanē**, *gheth-say-man-ay';* of Chald. or. [comp. 1660 and 8081]; *oil-press; Gethsemane,* a garden near Jerus.:—Gethsemane.

1069. γείτων **gĕitōn**, *ghi'-tone;* from *1093;* a

1073. γέμω **gĕmō**, *ghem'-o;* a prim. verb; to *swell out,* i.e. *be full:*—be full.

1074. γενεά **gĕnĕa**, *ghen-eh-ah';* from (a presumed der. of) *1085;* a *generation;* by impl. an *age* (the period or the persons):—age, generation, nation, time.

1075. γενεαλογέω **gĕnĕalŏgĕō**, *ghen-eh-al-og-eh'-o;* from *1074* and *3056;* to *reckon by generations,* i.e. *trace in genealogy:*—count by descent.

1076. γενεαλογία **gĕnĕalŏgia**, *ghen-eh-al-og-ee'-ah;* from the same as *1075:* *tracing by generations,* i.e. "*genealogy*":—genealogy.

1077. γενέσια **gĕnĕsia**, *ghen-es'-ee-ah;* neut. plur. of a der. of *1078;* *birthday* ceremonies:—birthday.

1078. γένεσις **genesis**, *ghen'-es-is;* from the same as *1074;* *nativity;* fig. *nature:*—generation, nature (-ral).

1079. γενετή **gĕnĕtē**, *ghen-et-ay';* fem. of a presumed der. of the base of *1074;* *birth:*—birth.

1080. γεννάω **gĕnnaō**, *ghen-nah'-o;* from a var. of *1085;* to *procreate* (prop. of the father, but by extens. of the mother); fig. to *regenerate:*—bear, beget, be born, bring forth, conceive, be delivered of, gender, make, spring.

1081. γέννημα **gĕnnēma**, *ghen'-nay-mah;* from *1080; offspring;* by anal. *produce* (lit. or fig.):—fruit, generation.

1082. Γεννησαρέτ **Gĕnnēsarĕt**, *ghen-nay-sar-et';* of Heb. or. [comp. 3672]; *Gennesaret* (i.e. *Kinnereth*), a lake and plain in Pal.:—Gennesaret.

1083. γέννησις **gĕnnēsis**, *ghen'-nay-sis;* from *1080; nativity:*—birth.

1084. γεννητός **gĕnnētŏs**, *ghen-nay-tos';* from *1080; born:*—they that are born.

1085. γένος **gĕnŏs**, *ghen'-os;* from *1096;* "*kin*" (abstr. or concr., lit. or fig., indiv. or coll.):—born, country (-man), diversity, generation, kind (-red), nation, offspring, stock.

1086. Γεργεσηνός **Gĕrgĕsēnŏs**, *gher-ghes-ay-nos';* of Heb. or. [1622]; a *Gergesene* (i.e. *Girgashite*) or one of the aborigines of Pal.:—Gergesene.

1087. γερουσία **gĕrŏusia**, *gher-oo-see'-ah;* from *1088;* the *eldership,* i.e. (collect.) the Jewish *Sanhedrim:*—senate.

1088. γέρων **gĕrōn**, *gher'-own;* of uncert. affin. [comp. *1094*]; *aged:*—old.

1089. γεύομαι **gĕuŏmai**, *ghyoo'-om-ahee;* a prim. verb; to *taste;* by impl. to *eat;* fig. to *experience* (good or ill):—eat, taste.

1090. γεωργέω **gĕōrgĕō**, *gheh-ore-gheh'-o;* from *1092;* to *till* (the soil):—dress.

1091. γεώργιον **gĕōrgiŏn**, *gheh-ore'-ghee-on;* neut. of a (presumed) der. of *1092; cultivable,* i.e. a *farm:*—husbandry.

1092. γεωργός **gĕōrgŏs**, *gheh-ore-gos';* from *1093* and the base of *2041;* a *land-worker,* i.e. *farmer:*—husbandman.

1093. γῆ **gĕ**, *ghay;* contr. from a prim. word; *soil;* by extens. a *region,* or the solid part or the whole of the *terrene* globe (includ. the occupants in each application):—country, earth (-ly), ground, land, world.

1094. γῆρας **gēras**, *ghay'-ras;* akin to *1088; senility:*—old age.

1095. γηράσκω **gēraskō**, *ghay-ras'-ko;* from *1094;* to *be senescent:*—be (wax) old.

1096. γίνομαι **ginŏmai**, *ghin'-om-ahee;* a prol. and mid. form of a prim. verb; to *cause to be* (" *generate*), i.e. (reflex.) to *become* (*come into being*), used with great latitude (lit., fig., intens., etc.):—arise, be assembled, be (-come, -fall, -have self), be brought (to pass), (be) come (to pass), continue, be divided, draw, be ended, fall, be finished, follow, be found, be ful-

be aware (of), feel, (have) know (-ledge), perceive, be resolved, can speak, be sure, understand.

1098. γλεῦκος **glĕukŏs**, *glyoo'-kos;* akin to *1099; sweet* wine, i.e. (prop.) *must* (fresh juice), but used of the more saccharine (and therefore highly inebriating) fermented *wine:*—new wine.

1099. γλυκύς **glukus**, *gloo-koos';* of uncert. affin.; *sweet* (i.e. not bitter nor salt):—sweet, fresh.

1100. γλῶσσα **glōssa**, *gloce-sah';* of uncert. affin.; the *tongue;* by impl. a *language* (spec. one naturally unacquired):—tongue.

1101. γλωσσόκομον **glōssŏkŏmŏn**, *gloce-sok'-om-on;* from *1100* and the base of *2889;* prop. a *case* (to keep mouthpieces of wind-instruments in), i.e. (by extens.) a *casket* or (spec.) *purse:*—bag.

1102. γναφεύς **gnaphĕus**, *gnaf-yuce';* by var. for a der. from κνάπτω **knaptō** (to *tease* cloth); a *cloth-dresser:*—fuller.

1103. γνήσιος **gnēsiŏs**, *gnay'-see-os;* from the same as *1077; legitimate* (of birth), i.e. *genuine:*—own, sincerity, true.

1104. γνησίως **gnēsiōs**, *gnay-see'-oce;* adv. from *1103; genuinely,* i.e. *really:*—naturally.

1105. γνόφος **gnŏphŏs**, *gnof'-os;* akin to *3509; gloom* (as of a storm):—blackness.

1106. γνώμη **gnōmē**, *gno'-may;* from *1097; cognition,* i.e. (subj.) *opinion,* or (obj.) *resolve* (counsel, consent, etc.):—advice, + agree, judgment, mind, purpose, will.

1107. γνωρίζω **gnōrizō**, *gno-rid'-zo;* from a der. of *1097;* to *make known;* subj. to *know:*—certify, declare, make known, give to understand, do to wit, wot.

1108. γνῶσις **gnōsis**, *gno'-sis;* from *1097; knowing* (the act), i.e. (by impl.) *knowledge:*—knowledge, science.

1109. γνώστης **gnōstēs**, *gnoce'-tace;* from *1097;* a *knower:*—expert.

1110. γνωστός **gnōstŏs**, *gnoce-tos';* from *1097;* well *known:*—acquaintance, (which may be) known, notable.

1111. γογγύζω **gŏgguzō**, *gong-good'-zo;* of uncert. der.; to *grumble:*—murmur.

1112. γογγυσμός **gŏggusmŏs**, *gong-goos-mos';* from *1111;* a *grumbling:*—grudging, murmuring.

1113. γογγυστής **gŏggustēs**, *gong-goos-tace';* from *1111;* a *grumbler:*—murmurer.

1114. γόης **gŏēs**, *gŏ'-ace;* from γοάω **gŏaō** (to *wail*); prop. a *wizard* (as *muttering* spells), i.e. (by impl.) an *impostor:*—seducer.

1115. Γολγοθᾶ **Gŏlgŏtha**, *gol-goth-ah';* of Chald. or. [comp. 1538]; *the skull; Golgotha,* a knoll near Jerus.:—Golgotha.

1116. Γόμοῤῥα **Gŏmŏrrha**, *gom'-or-hrhah';* of Heb. or. [6017]; *Gomorrha* (i.e. '*Amorah*), a place near the Dead Sea:—Gomorrha.

1117. γόμος **gŏmŏs**, *gom'-os;* from *1073;* a *load* (as *filling*), i.e. (spec.) a *cargo,* or (by extens.) *wares:*—burden, merchandise.

1118. γονεύς **gŏnĕus**, *gon-yooce';* from the base of *1096;* a *parent:*—parent.

1119. γόνυ **gŏnu**, *gon-oo';* of uncert. affin.; the "*knee*":—knee (× -l).

1120. γονυπετέω **gŏnupĕtĕō**, *gon-oo-pet-eh'-o;* from a comp. of *1119* and the alt. of *4098;* to *fall on the knee:*—bow the knee, kneel down.

1121. γράμμα **gramma**, *gram'-mah;* from *1125;* a *writing,* i.e. a *letter, note, epistle, book,* etc.; plur. *learning:*—bill, learning, letter, scripture, writing, written.

ROUTE 4

1. Take the *Analytical Concordance to the Bible* by Robert Young and look up the word "taste." (See the sample page which follows on page 6:9.) You are confronted with a list of five numbers, but only #5 has a Greek word with New Testament references. I Peter 2:3 is one of those twelve verses listed. Notice that the Greek word listed after #5 is the lexical form, γεύομαι, rather than the actual form of the Greek word of I Peter 2:3.

This route is the easiest and most preferable since it only involves one step to find the lexical form.

However, there is one disadvantage in routes 2, 3, and 4 in that they require the use of the King James Version. If you are using another version that has a word other than "taste," you will have to find out what the King James' word is before you can use the *Concordance*. This will add another step to each of the last three routes.

Acts 9. 11 enquire..for..Saul, of T.: for, behold, he pr.
9. 30 brought him..and sent him forth to T.
11. 25 Then departed Barnabas to T., for to seek
21. 39 Paul said, I am a man..a Jew of T...in C.
22. 3 I am verily a man..a Jew, born in T...in

TAR'-TAK, תַּרְתָּק *hero of darkness.*
A god worshipped by the Avites whom Shalmaneser removed to Samaria.
2 Ki. 17. 31 the Avites made Nibhaz and T., and the

TAR'-TAN, תַּרְתָּן.
An official of Sargon and of Sennacherib, kings of Assyria, sent to Hezekiah. B.C. 710.
2 Ki. 18. 17 the king of Assyria sent T., and Rabsaris
Isa. 20. 1 In the year that T. came unto Ashdod, wh.

TASK, taskmaster —

1. *A word, matter,* דָּבָר *dabar.*
Exod. 5. 13 Fulfil your works, (your) daily tasks, as
5. 19 shall not minish (ought)..of your daily ta.

2. *A statute, statutory work,* חֹק *choq.*
Exod. 5. 14 Wherefore have ye not fulfilled your task

3. *To exact,* נָגַשׂ *nagas.*
Exod. 3. 7 heard their cry by reason of their taskm.
5. 6 commanded the same day the taskmaste.
5. 10 the taskmasters of the people went out
5. 13 the taskmasters hasted (them), saying, F.
5. 14 which Pharaoh's taskmasters had set over

4. *Head or chief of the burden or levy,* שַׂר מַס *sar mas.*
Exod. 1. 11 they did set over them taskmasters to affl.

TASTE (to) —

1. *Palate, taste,* חֵךְ *chek.*
Job 6. 30 cannot my taste discern perverse things?
Psa. 119. 103 How sweet are thy words unto my taste!
Prov 24. 13 the honeycomb, (which is) sweet to thy ta.
Song 2. 3 I sat down..his fruit (was) sweet to my ta.

2. *Taste, reason,* טַעַם *taam.*
Exod 16. 31 the taste of it (was) like wafers (made) wi.
Num 11. 8 the taste of it was as the taste of fresh oil
Job 6. 6 or is there (any) taste in the white of an
Jer. 48. 11 his taste remained in him, and his scent

3. *To taste, perceive,* טָעַם *taam.*
1 Sa. 14. 24 So none of the people tasted (any) food
14. 29 enlightened, because I tasted a little of
14. 43 I did but taste a little honey with the end
2 Sa. 3. 35 if I taste bread, or ought else, till the sun
19. 35 can thy servant taste what I eat or what
Job 12. 11 Doth not..the mouth taste his meat?
34. 3 the ear trieth words, as the mouth tasteth
Psa. 34. 8 O taste and see that the LORD (is) good
Jon. 3. 7 Let neither man nor beast..taste any th.

4. *Taste,* טְעֵם *teem.*
Dan. 5. 2 Belshazzar, whiles he tasted the wine, c.

5. *To taste, experience,* γεύομαι *geuomai.*
Matt 16. 28 There be some..which shall not taste of
27. 34 when he had tasted (thereof), he would
Mark 9. 1 there be some..which shall not taste of
Luke 9. 27 there be some..which shall not taste of
14. 24 none..which were bidden shall taste of
John. 2. 9 When the ruler of the feast had tasted
8. 52 a man keep my saying, he shall never ta.
Col. 2. 21 Touch not; taste not; handle not
Heb. 2. 9 he by the grace of God should taste death
6. 4 have tasted of the heavenly gift, and were
6. 5 have tasted the good word of God, and
1 Pe. 2. 3 If so be ye have tasted that the Lord (is)

TAT'-NAI, תַּתְּנַי.
A governor of the king of Persia on the W. of the Jordan, in Samaria, who opposed the Jews, and wrote to Darius to stop the temple. B.C. 520.
Ezra 5. 3 At the same time came to them T., gov.
5. 6 The copy of the letter that T...sent unto
6. 6 Now..T...and your companions..be ye
6. 13 Then T...Shethar-boznai, and their com.

TATTLER —
A prater, tattler, φλύαρος *phluaros.*
1 Ti. 5. 13 not only idle, but tattlers also and busy.

TAUGHT, (to be) —

1. *To be chastised, instructed,* יָסַר *yasar,* 2.
Eze. 23. 48 that all women may be taught not to do

2. *To be taught,* לָמַד *lamad,* 4.
Isa. 29. 13 their fear toward me is taught by the pr.
Hos. 10. 11 Ephraim (is as) an heifer (that is) taught

3. *Taught, learned,* לִמּוּד *limmud.*
Isa. 54. 13 all thy children (shall be) taught of the

4. *Causing to understand,* מְבוֹנִים *mebonim.*
2 Ch. 35. 3 said unto the Levites that taught all Is.

5. *Taught,* διδακτός *didaktos.*
John 6. 45 It is written..they shall be all taught of

TAUGHT, as hath been —
Teaching, doctrine, κατὰ διδαχήν *kata didachēn.*
Titus 1. 9 Holding fast..as he hath been taught, that

TAUGHT of God —
God taught, θεοδίδακτος *theodidaktos.*
1 Th. 4. 9 ye yourselves are taught of God to love

3. *Sharp saying, byeword,* שְׁנִינָה *sheninah.*
Jer. 24. 9 (to be) a reproach and a proverb, a taunt

TAX, be taxed, taxation —

1. *To set in array, value,* עָרַךְ *arak,* 5.
2 Ki. 23. 35 he taxed the land to give the money acc.

2. *Array, valuation,* עֵרֶךְ *erek.*
2 Ki. 23. 35 exacted..of every one according to his ta.

3. *A writing off, register,* ἀπογραφή *apographē.*
Luke 2. 2 this taxing was first made when Cyrenius
Acts 5. 37 rose up Judas..in the days of the taxing

4. *To write off, register,* ἀπογράφω *apographō.*
Luke 2. 1 a decree..that all the world should be ta.
2. 3 all went to be taxed, every one into his
2. 5 To be taxed with Mary his espoused wife

TEACH, to —

1. *To teach,* אָלַף *alaph,* 3.
Job 33. 33 hold thy peace, and I shall teach thee wi.
35. 11 Who teacheth us more than the beasts of

2. *To cause to understand,* בִּין *bin,* 5.
2 Ch. 35. 3 said unto the Levites that taught all Isr.
Neh. 8. 9 the Levites that taught the people, said

3. *To speak,* דָּבַר *dabar,* 3.
Jer. 28. 16 thou hast taught rebellion against the L.
29. 32 he hath taught rebellion against the LORD

4. *To warn, cause to shine,* זָהַר *zahar,* 5.
Exod 18. 20 thou shalt teach them ordinances and la.

5. *To cause to know,* יָדַע *yada,* 5.
Deut. 4. 9 but teach them thy sons, and thy sons' so.
Judg. 8. 16 and with them he taught the men of Suc.
2 Ch. 23. 13 the singers..and such as taught to sing
Job 32. 7 and multitude of years should teach wis.
37. 19 Teach us what we shall say unto him; (for)
Psa. 90. 12 So teach (us) to number our days, that we
Prov. 9. 9 teach a just (man), and he will increase
Isa. 40. 13 or, (being) his counsellor, hath taught him?

6. *To cause to know,* יְדַע *yeda,* 5.
Ezra 7. 25 and teach ye them that know (them) not

7. *To chastise, instruct, teach,* יָסַר *yasar,* 3.
Prov 31. 1 the prophecy that his mother taught him

8. *To cast, show, direct, teach,* יָרָה *yarah,* 5.
Exod. 4. 12 I will be with thy mouth, and teach thee
4. 15 and will teach you what ye shall do
24. 12 commandments..that thou mayest teach
35. 34 he hath put in his heart that he may teach
Lev. 10. 11 that ye may teach the children of Israel
14. 57 To teach when (it is) unclean, and when
Deut 17. 11 sentence of the law which they shall teach
24. 8 all that the priests the Levites shall teach
33. 10 They shall teach Jacob thy judgments, and
Judg 13. 8 teach us what we shall do unto the child
1 Sa. 12. 23 I will teach you the good and the right
1 Ki. 8. 36 that thou teach them the good way wher.
2 Ki. 17. 27 let him teach them the manner of the God
17. 28 taught them how they should fear the L.
2 Ch. 6. 27 when thou hast taught them the good way
Job 6. 24 Teach me, and I will hold my tongue
8. 10 Shall not they teach thee, (and) tell thee
12. 7 ask now the beasts, and they shall teach
12. 8 speak to the earth, and it shall teach thee
27. 11 I will teach you by the hand of God: (that)
34. 32 (That which) I see not, teach thou me
36. 22 God exalteth by his power: who teacheth
Psa. 25. 8 therefore will he teach sinners in the way
25. 12 him shall he teach in the way (that) he sh.
27. 11 Teach me thy way, O LORD, and lead me
32. 8 I will instruct thee and teach thee in the
45. 4 thy right hand shall teach thee terrible
86. 11 Teach me thy way, O LORD; I will walk
119. 33 Teach me, O LORD, the way of thy statut.
119. 102 I have not departed..for thou hast tau.
Prov. 4. 4 He taught me also, and said unto me, Let
4. 11 I have taught thee in the way of wisdom
6. 13 he speaketh with his feet, he teacheth wi.
Isa. 2. 3 he will teach us of his ways, and we will
9. 15 the prophet that teacheth lies, he (is) the
28. 9 Whom shall he teach knowledge? and w.
28. 26 God doth instruct..(and) doth teach him
Eze. 44. 23 they shall teach my people (the difference)
Mic. 3. 11 the priests thereof teach for hire, and the
4. 2 he will teach us of his ways, and we will
Hab. 2. 19 to the dumb stone, Arise, it shall teach!

9. *To teach,* לָמַד *lamad,* 3.
Deut. 4. 1 and unto the judgments, which I teach
4. 5 I have taught you statutes and judgments
4. 10 and (that) they may teach their children
4. 14 commanded me at that time to teach you
5. 31 the judgments, which thou shalt teach
6. 1 the LORD your God commanded to teach
11. 19 ye shall teach them your children, speak.
20. 18 That they teach you not to do after all th.
31. 19 write ye this song for you, and teach it
31. 22 Moses therefore..taught it the children of
Judg. 3. 2 the children of Israel might know to tea.
2 Sa. 1. 18 he bade them teach the children of Judah
22. 35 He teacheth my hands to war; so that a
2 Ch. 17. 7 he sent to his princes..to teach in the ci.
17. 9 they taught in Judah, and (had) the book

Psa. 25. 9 and the meek will he teach his way
34. 11 hearken unto me; I will teach you the
51. 13 (Then) will I teach transgressors thy ways
60. *title.* To the chief Musician..to teach: when
71. 17 thou hast taught me from my youth: and
94. 10 he that teacheth man knowledge, (shall
94. 12 thou..LORD..teachest him out of thy law
119. 12, 26, 64, 68, 124, 135 teach me thy statutes
119. 66 Teach me good judgment and knowledge
119. 108 I beseech thee..teach me thy judgments
119. 171 when thou hast taught me thy statutes
132. 12 and my testimony that I shall teach them
143. 10 Teach me to do thy will; for thou (art) my
144. 1 which teacheth my hands to war, (and)
Eccl. 12. 9 the preacher was wise, he still taught the
Isa. 40. 14 taught him in the path of judgment, and
48. 17 the LORD thy God which teacheth thee to
Jer. 2. 33 therefore hast thou also taught the wic.
9. 5 they have taught their tongue to speak
9. 14 after Baalim, which their fathers taught
9. 20 teach your daughters wailing, and every
12. 16 as they taught my people to swear by B.
13. 21 thou hast taught them (to be) captains
31. 34 they shall teach no more every man his
32. 33 I taught them, rising up early and teach.
Dan. 1. 4 whom they might teach the learning and

10. *To cause to act wisely,* שָׂכַל *sakal,* 5.
2 Ch. 30. 22 the Levites that taught the good know.
Prov 16. 23 The heart of the wise teacheth his mouth

11. *Taught,* διδακτός *didaktos.*
1 Co. 2. 13 not in the words which man's wisdom te.
2. 13 but which the Holy Ghost teacheth; com.

12. *To teach,* διδάσκω *didaskō.*
Matt. 4. 23 teaching in their synagogues, and preach.
5. 2 he opened his mouth, and taught them
5. 19 Whosoever..shall teach men so, he shall
5. 19 whosoever shall do and teach (them), the
7. 29 he taught them as (one) having authority
9. 35 teaching in their synagogues, and preach.
11. 1 he departed thence, to teach and to preach
13. 54 he taught them in their synagogue, inso.
15. 9 teaching (for) doctrines the commandme.
21. 23 the elders..came unto him as he was te.
22. 16 thou art true, and teachest the way of
26. 55 I sat daily with you [teaching] in the te.
28. 15 took the money, and did as they were ta.
28. 20 Teaching them to observe all things wh.
Mark 1. 21 he entered into the synagogue, and tau.
1. 22 for he taught them as one that had auth.
2. 13 resorted unto him, and he taught them
4. 1 he began again to teach by the sea side
4. 2 he taught them many things by parables
6. 2 he began to teach in the synagogue: an
6. 6 he went round about the villages, teach.
6. 30 what they had done, and what they had t.
6. 34 and he began to teach them many things
7. 7 teaching (for) doctrines the commandm.
8. 31 he began to teach them, that the Son of
9. 31 he taught his disciples, and said unto th.
10. 1 and, as he was wont, he taught them ag.
11. 17 he taught, saying unto them, Is it not wr.
12. 14 for thou..teachest the way of God in tru.
12. 35 Jesus answered and said, while he taught
14. 49 I was daily with you..teaching, and ye
Luke 4. 15 he taught in their synagogues, being glo.
4. 31 and taught them on the sabbath days
5. 3 he sat down, and taught the people out
5. 17 on a certain day, as he was teaching, that
6. 6 he entered into the synagogue and taught
11. 1 teach us to pray, as John also taught his
12. 12 the Holy Ghost shall teach you in the same
13. 10 he was teaching in one of the synagogues
13. 22 teaching and journeying toward Jerusal.
13. 26 We have eaten..and thou hast taught in
19. 47 And he taught daily in the temple
20. 1 he taught the people in the temple, and
20. 21 thou sayest and teachest rightly, neither
20. 21 we know that thou..teachest the way of
21. 37 in the day time he was teaching in the te.
23. 5 He stirreth up the people, teaching thro.
John 6. 59 These things said he..as he taught in Ca.
7. 14 Jesus went up into the temple, and tau.
7. 28 Then cried Jesus in the temple, as he ta.
7. 35 will he go..among the Gentiles, and tea.
8. 2 [people came unto him; and he..taught]
8. 20 These words spake Jesus..as he taught in
8. 28 as my Father hath taught me, I speak th.
9. 34 born in sins, and dost thou teach us?
14. 26 he shall teach you all things, and bring
18. 20 I ever taught in the synagogue, and in the
Acts 1. 1 all that Jesus began both to do and teach
4. 2 Being grieved that they taught the peop.
4. 18 commanded them not to..teach in the na.
5. 21 they entered into the temple..and taught
5. 25 standing in the temple, and teaching the
5. 28 command you, that ye should not teach
5. 42 they ceased not to teach and preach Jesus
11. 26 they assembled..and taught much people
15. 1 certain men which came..taught the br.
15. 35 teaching and preaching the word of the
18. 11 he continued..teaching the word of God
18. 25 taught diligently the things of the Lord
20. 20 have taught you publicly, and from hou.
21. 21 thou teachest all the Jews which are among

LESSON 7

IDENTIFYING THE FORM

PARSING THE WORD

As you have seen in the previous lessons, Greek words may have many forms. A single noun has 10, a single adjective 24, and a single verb almost 500. These changes occur at the end of the nouns, adjectives and pronouns and at the beginning and end of the verbs. Other parts of speech have only one form.

The different meanings in these forms are as important as the meaning of the stem itself. They not only embellish the meaning of the stem, itself, but they also may establish the sentence slot where the word belongs. In other words, the glue which holds a word cluster together is located in the inflections.

Identifying these forms is called "parsing."

The most useful tool to identify these forms is called *The Analytical Greek Lexicon*. You have already used this book when you used Route 1 in the previous lesson.

In Lesson 6 you discovered that the Greek word translated "tasted" in I Peter 2:3 was ἐγεύσασθε. From *The Analytical Greek Lexicon* you learned that the lexical form for ἐγεύσασθε was γεύομαι. When you used this *Analytical Greek Lexicon*, you skipped over a lot of abbreviations to get to the Greek word on the right hand side of the column.

Now you have to go back to examine and identify these abbreviations.

ἐγεύσασθε, 2 pers. pl. aor. 1, ind.   .   . γεύομαι

At the beginning of the *Lexicon* is a list of abbreviations with their meanings. I have copied this page (7:2). This list is not complete; so I have tried to add those which have been omitted. Let's make a list of these abbreviations found after the Greek word ἐγεύσασθε in *The Analytical Greek Lexicon* as above. Then by consulting the abbreviation page (p. 7:3), write out completely what these abbreviations mean:

ABBREVIATION TABLE FOUND AT THE BEGINNING OF
THE ANALYTICAL GREEK LEXICON

absol.	absolutely, without case or adjunct.
acc.	accusative case
adj.	adjective
adv.	adverb.
Æol.	Æolic dialect.
al.	*alibi*, in other texts.
al. freq.	*alibi frequenter*, in many other texts.
aor.	aorist.
apoc.	apocope, cutting off the last syllable.
Aram.	Aramæan dialect.
Att.	Attic dialect.
bis	twice.
compar.	comparative.
conj.	conjunction.
contr.	contraction, contracted.
dat.	dative case.
dimin.	diminutive.
enclit.	enclitic, throwing the accent on the preceding syllable.
&, et,	and.
&c., etc.	*et cætera*.
e. g.	*exempli gratia*, for example.
f., fem.	feminine.
f., fut.	future tense.
fr.	from.
gen.	genitive case.
genr.	generally, in a general sense, not affected by adjuncts.
Heb.	Hebrew, or the Hebrew idiom.
i. e.	*id est*, that is.
id., idem.	the same.
imp., imper., imperat. }	imperative mood.

imperf.	imperfect tense.
impers.	impersonal.
impl.	implication.
ind.	indicative mood.
indec.	indeclinable.
inf., infin.	infinitive mood.
interj.	interjection.
interrog.	interrogation.
intrans.	intransitive.
Ion.	Ionic dialect.
i. q.	*idemque*, the same as.
L. G.	later Greek.
lit.	literally.
LXX.	Septuagint.
m., masc	masculine.
met.	metaphorically.
metath.	metathesis, the transposition of letters.
meton.	by metonymy.
mid.	middle voice
n., neut.	neuter.
N. T.	New Testament.
obsol.	obsolete.
O. T.	Old Testament.
om.	*omittit*, or *omittunt*.
opt., optat.	optative mood.
part.	participle.
partic.	particle.
pass.	passive voice.
perf.	perfect tense.
p., pers.	person.
pl., plur	plural.
pluperf.	pluperfect tense.
pr.	properly, proper.
prep.	preposition.
pron.	pronoun.
q. d.	*quasi dicas*, as if, as it were.
q. v.	*quod vide*, which see.
sc.	*scilicet*, that is to say.

seq.	*sequente*, as seq. gen., *sequente genitivo*, with a genitive following.
s., sing.	singular. The figures placed before sing. or pl. denote the person.
spc.	specially, i. e. in a special and local meaning.
subj.	subjunctive mood.
subs.	substantive.
superl.	superlative.
sync.	syncope, contraction.
synec.	synecdoche.
ter	thrice.
trans.	transitively.
trop.	tropically, i. e. turned aside from its strict literal meaning.
v.	*vel*, or.
v r.	a various reading to the common text.
viz.	*videlicet*, that is, namely.
voc.	vocative case.

ὁ attached to a word shows it to be masculine; ἡ, to be feminine; ὁ, ἡ, to be common, i. e. masculine or feminine; and τό, to be neuter.

§, tab., rem., refer to sections, tables, and remarks in the Tables of Paradigms.

AUTHORITIES REFERRED TO.

A. B. C. D.	Codices.
Rec.	*Textus Receptus*, the Received Text.
Gb.	Griesbach.
Sch.	Scholz.
Ln.	Lachmann.
Tdf.	Tischendorf.
Elz.	Elzevir.
Ste.	Stephens

FURTHER ABBREVIATIONS EMPLOYED WITHOUT EXPLANATION BY
THE ANALYTICAL GREEK LEXICON

act.   =   active voice (often omitted, but assumed if "pass." or "mid." does not appear)

aor. 1
aor. 2   =   the "1" and "2" (first aorist and second aorist) may be ignored as they only indicate an inflectional system. The meaning of the form is the same in either case.

pres.   =   present

1 pers. =   first person (singular = "I";   plural = "we")

2 pers. =   second person (singular = "you";   plural = "y'all")

3 pers. =   third person (singular = "he, she, or it";   plural = "they")

Taken from *The Analytical Greek Lexicon* by George Wigram, published by Zondervan Publishing House, and is used by permission.

(continued from page 7:1)

2 pers. = second person (either "you" or "y'all,"
            depending upon the next entry)

pl.   = plural (therefore the meaning is "y'all")

aor. 1   = aorist (In Lesson 4 you learned that "aorist
            indicative" should be understood as "past time,
            punctiliar aspect." You will learn from the
            next entry it is indicative. Remember: Don't
            bother about the "1" that appears after "aor.".)

ind.   = indicative mood (Always remember that *only*
            indicative mood has both time and aspect. So,
            if the verb form is "aorist," but the mood is
            other than indicative; namely, subjunctive,
            imperative or optative, the verb will not have
            past time, but only punctiliar aspect.)

                If there is no mention of mood; no "subj."
                or "opt." or "ind." or "imper." or "part."
                or "infin.", the form may safely be consid-
                ered to be in the indicative mood.

                The apparent contradictions for the future
                infinitive and the future participle are
                so rare that they need not concern the
                beginning Greek student.

         = active voice (If there is no other word like
            "pass." for passive, or "mid." for middle here,
            you may assume that the verb form indicates
            an active voice.)

Now we are ready to parse the Greek word for
"tasted" in I Peter 2:3: ἐγεύσασθε.

    Because the form is in the indicative mood, we must first
    extract the time and aspect from the word "aorist." Turn
    back to page 4:13. Find the word "aorist" in the boxes.
    Read up for time. What is it? _____ Read left
    for aspect. What is it? _____

Now write the 5 or 6 questions you are supposed
to ask verb forms, and then answer each question:

QUESTIONS   ANSWERS

1._____   _____

2._____   _____

3._____   _____

4._____   _____

5._____   _____

Do you ask question 6?_____ What is your reason?

_____

6._____   _____

The verb in I Peter 2:3 translated by "tasted"
is ἐγεύσασθε; the second person, plural, deponent,
punctiliar aspect, indicative mood, past time form
of γεύομαι.

Can you understand why I said "deponent" rather than
"active voice"? Go back and read the paragraph called
IMPORTANT at the middle of page 4:4. Now do you understand? A deponent verb is a verb which has a middle
voice or a passive voice form, but still has an active
voice meaning. You tell a deponent verb by how the
lexical form is spelled. If the lexical form of a
verb ends in -ω or -μι, you know it is not a deponent
verb. If it ends in -μαι, you know it is.

In Lesson 8 we will try to interpret this
information. But for now it is sufficient to be
able simply to parse the word.

DISCOVERING ITS
COGNATES

Do you remember that you also noticed the
lexical form of this verb? What was it?_____
This lexical form becomes important because it is
the word you must look up in a good lexicon to
find its definition. It is also important because
its "cognate" words will be listed with this form
in *The Analytical Greek Lexicon*.

When you know a person, you should get
acquainted with the whole family. Words belong to
families and have brothers and sisters. These related
words are called "cognates." The same stem may take
the form of a verb, a noun, an adjective, an adverb,
or it may even be used to form more than one of each.

So, it is important, when you want to do a
thorough job, to take a look at these brothers and
sisters. To find the family that a lexical form
belongs in, if it has a family, requires two more
steps with *The Analytical Greek Lexicon*. Let's go
through the whole process by the numbers and in so
doing, get acquainted with the marvelous δικ family.

Let's say you are reading along in Revelation,
chapter 19. When you come across the fact in verse
eight that the fine linen is the "righteousnesses"
of the saints, you wonder what Greek word translates
"righteousnesses."

1. The *Interlinear Greek - English New Testament* at Revelation 19:8 has the words "righteous
deeds" under the Greek word δικαιώματα.

2. Parse δικαιώματα.   (The next page, 7:6, has a reproduction of the appropriate page from *The Analytical Greek Lexicon*.)

nom.	=	nominative case
& acc.	=	and accusative case
pl.	=	plural number
δικαίωμα	=	lexical form

3. Look up this lexical form (on the same page following; 7:6).

ατος	=	the genitive ending (always given with nouns)
τό	=	this is a noun in the neuter gender (appropriate article always given with nouns)
(§ 4. tab. D. c.)	=	(ignore this for now)
δίκη	=	Because δικαίωμα is already a lexical form, δίκη cannot be another one. It is the "Clan Leader" of the fabulous δικ family.

4. Look up the "Clan Leader": δίκη. Notice I do not call it the "patriarch," because the word could be a younger brother or sister. It was an arbitrary selection made by the grammarian or the lexicographer. Notice that following ης, the Greek article ἡ appears. This tells you that δίκη is a noun which is feminine in gender.

Notice the indentation on the seventh line down, forming a second paragraph. The indented word, δίκαιος, is a "relative" or cognate of the "Clan Leader." This word has three endings following it, but not an article. That means that δίκαιος is an adjective.

Look for the next cognate. It will be in the next paragraph. What is it? _____ What is the abbreviation which follows it?_____ Look at the abbreviation page (7:2). What does it mean?_____ What part of speech is this Greek word?_____

What is the next cognate?_____ Look at what follows it. What part of speech is it? _____ How do you know?_____

_____

In the next column is still another cognate. After the three lines of various Greek forms, notice the English definition, "to make or render right. . . to act with justice . . . ." Whenever you find the English definition beginning with the word "to" followed by an English verb, you know the Greek word is also a verb.

Counting the "Clan Leader," how many cognates

δικαιωθήτω, 3 pers. sing. aor. 1, imper. pass.   δικαιόω
δικαιωθῶμεν, 1 pers. pl. aor. 1, subj. pass.   id.
δικαίωμα, ατος, τό, (§ 4. tab. D. c)   δίκη
δικαιώμασι, dat. pl.   δικαίωμα
δικαιώματα, nom. and acc. pl.   id.
δικαιώματος, gen. sing.   id.
δικαιῶν, nom. sing. masc. part. pres. act.   δικαιόω
δικαίων, gen. pl.   δίκαιος
δικαίως, adv.   δίκη
δικαιῶσαι, aor. 1, infin. act.—B. C. D. Ln. Tdf.
δικαιοῦν, Rec. Gr. Sch. (Lu. 10. 29)   δικαιόω
δικαιώσει, 3 pers. sing. fut. ind. act.   id.
δικαίωσιν, acc. sing.   δικαίωσις
δικαίωσις], εως, ἡ, (§ 5. tab. E. c)   δίκη
δικαστήν, acc. sing.   δικαστής
δικαστής], οῦ, ὁ, (§ 2. tab. B. c)   δίκη

δίκη, ης, ἡ, (§ 2. tab. B. a) right, justice; in N.T. judicial punishment, vengeance, 2 Thes. 1. 9; Jude 7; sentence of punishment, judgment, Ac. 25. 15; personified, the goddess of justice or vengeance, Nemesis, Pœna, Ac. 28. 4.

δίκαιος, αία, αιον, (§ 7. rem. 1) used of things, just, equitable, fair, Mat. 20. 4; Lu. 12. 57; Jno. 5. 30; Col. 4. 1, et al.; of persons, just, righteous, absolutely, Jno. 17. 25; Ro. 3. 10, 26; 2 Ti. 4. 8; 1 Pe. 3. 18; 1 Jno. 1. 9; 2. 1, 29; Re. 16. 5; righteous by account and acceptance, Ro. 2. 13; 5. 19, et al.; in ordinary usage, just, upright, innocent, pious, Mat. 5. 45; 9. 13, et al. freq.; ὁ δίκαιος, the Just One, one of the distinctive titles of the Messiah, Ac. 3. 14; 7. 52; 22. 14.

δικαίως, adv. justly, with strict justice, 1 Pe. 2. 23; deservedly, Lu. 23. 41; as it is right, fit or proper, 1 Co. 15. 34; uprightly, honestly, piously, religiously, 1 Thes. 2. 10; Tit. 2. 12.

δικαιοσύνη, ης, ἡ, (§ 2. tab. B. a) fair and equitable dealing, justice, Ac. 17. 31; He. 11. 33; Ro. 9. 28; rectitude, virtue, Lu. 1. 75; Ep. 5. 9; in N.T. generosity, alms, 2 Co. 9. 10, v.r.; Mat. 6. 1; piety, godliness, Ro. 6. 13, et al.; investiture with the attribute of righteousness, acceptance as righteous, justification, Ro.

4. 11; 10. 4, et al. freq.; a provision or means for justification, Ro. 1. 17; 2 Co. 3. 9, et al.; an instance of justification, 2 Co. 5. 21. (ῠ).

δικαιόω, ῶ, fut. ώσομαι & ώσω, aor. 1, ἐδικαίωσα, perf. pass. δεδικαίωμαι, aor. 1, pass. ἐδικαιώθην, (§ 20. tab. T; § 21 tab. U) pr. to make or render right or just; mid. to act with justice, Re. 22. 11; to avouch to be good and true, to vindicate, Mat. 11. 19; Lu. 7. 29, et al.; to set forth as good and just, Lu. 10. 29; 16. 15; in N.T. to hold as guiltless, to accept as righteous, to justify, Ro. 3. 26, 30; 4. 5; 8. 30, 33, et al.; pass. to be held acquitted, to be cleared, Ac. 13. 39; Ro. 3. 24; 6. 7; to be approved, to stand approved, to stand accepted, Ro. 2. 13; 3. 20, 28, et al.

δικαίωμα, ατος, τό, (§ 4. tab. D. c) pr. a rightful act, act of justice, equity; a sentence, of condemnation, Re. 15. 4; in N.T., of acquittal, justification, Ro. 5. 16; a decree, law, ordinance, Lu. 1. 6; Ro. 1. 32; 2. 26; 8. 4; He. 9. 1, 10; a meritorious act, an instance of perfect righteousness, Ro. 5. 18; state of righteousness, Re. 19. 8.

δικαίωσις, εως, ἡ, (§ 5. tab. E. c) pr. a making right or just; a declaration of right or justice; a judicial sentence; in N.T., acquittal, acceptance, justification, Ro. 4. 25; 5. 18.

δικαστής, οῦ, ὁ, (§ 2. tab. B. c) δικάζω, to judge) a judge, Lu. 12. 14; Ac. 7. 27, 35.

δίκην, acc. sing.   δίκη
δίκτυα, acc. pl.   δίκτυον

δίκτυον, ου, τό, (§ 3. tab. C. c) a net, fishing-net, Mat. 4. 20, 21, et al.

δίλογος], ου, ὁ, ἡ, (§ 7. rem. 2) (δίς & λόγος) pr. saying the same thing twice; in N.T. double-tongued, speaking one thing and meaning another, deceitful in words. N.T.

δίλογους,[a] acc. pl. masc.   δίλογος
διό, (i.e. δι' ὅ) on which account, wherefore, therefore, Mat. 27. 8; 1 Co. 12. 3, et al.
διοδεύσαντες, nom. pl. masc. part. aor. 1   διοδεύω

[a] 1 Ti. 3. 8.

are there?_____

   The following is the easiest way to distinguish
what part of speech the Greek word is:

   1. If the English definition begins with "to" followed
      by an English verb, it is a verb.

   2. If there is an article (ὁ, ἡ, or τό) following the
      word, it is a noun.

   3. If there are two or three endings, but no article,
      it is an adjective.

   4. If it is followed by "pro.", it is a pronoun.

   5. If it is followed by "adv.", it is an adverb.

   So, when you study a word, you should also find
out if there are any brothers and sisters, how they
are alike, and how they differ.

   Words may also have "cousins." These more
remote relatives have introduced strange blood by
alliances with prepositions. Often the prepositions
come in with such strong blood that the meaning of
the combination doesn't have much in common with the
stem meaning.

   For example: ἀνά means "up" and γινώσκω means "I know";
   yet the two words have joined together in ἀναγινώσκω,
   which means "I read." You can hardly call "know" and
   "read" kissin' kin!

   A branch of the family might move to a far
country and stay so long and take on such airs as to
become "feudin' kin," like our own "zeal" and "jeal-
ousy." You wouldn't suspect them of having the same
stem (ζῆλος).

   So, when studying kinfolk among words, beware!
The family likeness may have gotten lost. It is no
use climbing the family tree, trying to retrieve it.
Genealogy among words is called "etymology," and is
a "no-no." Only experts understand and apply it
properly, and you aren't an expert! Of course, if
a word appears only once or twice, you might *have*
to do it. And proper names, when first given,
usually have etymological significance.

REMINDERS

   1. Remember that *The Analytical Greek Lexicon*
does not distinguish between time and aspect. You
must refer to your chart on page 4:13 in order to
know how to interpret both, when you are dealing
with verbs in the *indicative mood*.

2. *The Analytical Greek Lexicon* will always use the same form of the word when giving the lexical form:

    a. For the noun, it is the nominative singular form.

    b. For the pronoun, it is the nominative, masculine, singular form.

    c. For the adjective, it is the nominative, masculine, singular form.

    d. For the verb, it is the first person, singular, active voice, linear aspect, indicative mood, present time form.

LESSON 8

INTERPRETING THE FORM

Now that you have learned to identify the form of an inflected Greek word, how do you go about interpreting that form? One semester of intensive study will not qualify you to draw profound conclusions from your knowledge of how the inflectional spellings of Greek words work. To do this would require, not only a thorough knowledge of Greek grammar, but also such a familiarity with the language that you can scan it with ease and be able to feel its idioms.

DON'T BE
INDEPENDENT

Before you despair over this ugly truth, be informed that the same must be said for him who has embarked on the "high road." Only those who have ventured a considerable distance along this road are competent to venture into independent exegesis.

I remember my traumatic disappointment in college when my Greek teacher informed us that not until one has studied Greek for ten years may one launch into independent exegesis.

But he was very young--in his twenties--and can be excused for his mistake. He missed the lower limit by another ten years.

When I say this, I am completely conscious of the fact that in so doing I have relegated 95% of all Biblical exegesis to the trash heap where it belongs.

I don't mean to suggest that through this long apprenticeship you are no more than a fledgling flapping his wings. Rather, as you continue to listen to and submit to your linguistic "betters," you continue to gain competency.

Greek is not all that easy to come by.

HIGHLY SELECTED
EXAMPLES

However, it would be well to spend some time experimenting a little in this area, since occasionally there is a particular part of the word form that is simple and uncomplicated enough for you, even as a beginner, to understand. Also, it is a necessary preparation for study of the better commentaries, whose authors, first rate exegetes as they are, draw on a word's particular form to bring out precise meanings.

It is very difficult to discover "parade ground examples" which would be of interest to the student and which at the same time would contain no hidden booby-traps or pitfalls. The examples I have selected for your exercise required a time-consuming search on my part.

If you gather from this exercise that Greek exegesis is a "piece of cake," you are committing a horrendous blunder!

An Example

We have been studying "taste" in I Peter 2:3. We have already learned that "taste" is a translation of ἐγεύσασθε, and is second person, plural number, punctiliar aspect, deponent, indicative mood, and (because the mood is indicative, it must also have time) in the past time. Let's do some interpretation of the inflections which attach to the root, γευ, the ἐ which attaches at the beginning of the stem and the σασθε, which attaches to the end of it.

1. *It is in the second person.* The apostle is talking directly about whom he is addressing, not about somebody else, nor about himself.

2. *It is the plural number.* The apostle is talking to a group of people. The fact is not limited to a single person, but extends to the church as a whole.

3. *It is in the punctiliar aspect.* This action of the stem, the tasting, or the eating as the case may be, is looked upon like a photograph. The duration, for the purposes of the author, of the action is not to be considered. It simply happened. "Y'all tasted or ate."

4. *It is deponent.* Though the form is a middle form, the action is to be considered active. "You acted yourselves; took the initiative. It wasn't done to you."

5. *It is in the indicative mood.* We are talking about an actual event; not something that might or should take place.

6. *It is in the past time.* Because number five identifies the mood as indicative, we must notice the time. "The action y'all participated in already happened in the past."

MUCH IS
TRANSLATABLE

If you are trying to show off your knowledge of Greek, you might make your Bible lesson outline: "The Personal, Plural, Punctiliar, Possession, Positive Past of Tasting the Lord."

However, after all is said and done, how much of all this is not already seen in the English, "Ye have tasted"? Only when you are trying to impress another with your profound knowledge, do you parade your Greek to make these points!

Most of what you will learn from interpreting the Greek word's inflectional form will not supply new information to you because it is obvious in the English translation. Nevertheless, there are instances where the word form can make a difference in interpretation which is not readily seen in the translation. A review of Lesson 3 on the case system might be good at this point. Discovering the aspect of a negative command can bring added light to an otherwise obscure statement. Lesson 4 on the Greek verb makes a distinction between these commands which you might wish to review. These are only two examples of the types of conclusions that even you, as a beginner, can come to through the study of inflections. The following exercise will help you to get started in developing this kind of skill.

QUESTION SUMMARY

In Greek, only nouns (including infinitives), pronouns, adjectives (including participles) and verbs are inflected.

ASK A NOUN TWO QUESTIONS:

1. What is your *case*? (Options: nominative, genitive, dative, accusative, vocative)
2. What is your *number*? (Options: singular or plural)

ASK A PRONOUN AND AN ADJECTIVE THREE QUESTIONS:

1. What is your *case*? (Options: nominative, genitive, dative, accusative, vocative)
2. What is your *number*? (Options: singular or plural)
3. What is your *gender*? (Options: masculine, feminine, neuter)

ASK A PARTICIPLE AND AN INFINITIVE* FIVE QUESTIONS:

1. What is your *case*?* (Options: nominative, genitive, dative or accusative)
2. What is your *number*?* (Options: singular or plural)
3. What is your *gender*?* (Options: masculine, feminine, neuter)
4. What is your *voice*? (Options: active, middle, passive)
5. What is your *aspect*? (Options: punctiliar, linear, combined)

*An infinitive is always singular in number and neuter

in gender. The case is determined by the case of
its article, or by the context if it has no article.

ASK A VERB FIVE OR SIX QUESTIONS:

1. What is your *person*? (Options: first, second,
   third)
2. What is your *number*? (Options: singular or
   plural)
3. What is your *aspect*? (Options: punctiliar,
   linear, combined)
4. What is your *voice*? (Options: active,
   middle, passive, deponent)
5. What is your *mood*? (Options: indicative,
   subjunctive, imperative, optative)
6. Only if your answer to number 5 is "indicative"
   do you ask: What is your *time*? (Options:
   past, present, future)

LESSON 9

HOW TO DO A WORD STUDY

To the fledgling Bible student, "word studies" seem to be almost the epitome of exegesis. Not true at all! In fact, this kind of study is really just about the easiest part of exegesis. Word studies, really, are lexical studies; an investigation into what a word stem, rather than its particular inflectional forms, means.

You take our word, ἐγεύσασθε, that we have been studying in I Peter 2:3. You break it down into its stem and inflectional endings: ε / γευ / σα / σθε.

ε = past time, indicative mood (the augment)
γευ = the stem
σα = punctiliar aspect
σθε = 2nd person plural (middle form because the verb is deponent)

We have already studied how to interpret these inflectional endings (Lessons 7 and 8). Lexical study is an inquiry into what the *stem* means.

Lexicography (word studies) plus syntax (inflectional studies) equal grammatical exegesis.

Actually, it isn't all that simple; for syntax must always involve the whole sentence, and the sentence within its context. So, lexical studies involve the meanings which a stem is capable of bearing if the context is compatible to it. On the other hand, syntax involves all the filaments which bind these stems to other stems in a countless number of differing patterns. Always consider that these inflectional endings are as pregnant with meanings as are the stems themselves.

And, grammatical exegesis is only the half of it; the easier half, actually. To this must be added the more difficult: external exegesis - the study of a literary unit in the light of its historical, cultural and geographical context.

Have you done much thinking about where the writers of dictionaries get their information?

When a lexicographer wants to write a definition of a word, he first engages in extensive samplings of the way that word is used in different periods of time, in different geographical areas, and among different kinds of people.

From this extensive sampling, he isolates various ways the word is used and writes a separate definition for each way.

ETYMOLOGY IS A "NO-NO"

What he does not do is analyze each part of a word for meaning and then conclude that the sum of the meanings of these parts is the definition of a word. Remember, you were told that as far as "low roaders" were concerned, etymology is a "no-no." Rarely, the original flavor of a word perseveres in the thinking of a person who is using the word. Only the experts can tell.

You would go far afield if you tried to understand what the English word "pioneer" means from its etymology, for it shares a common etymology with "pawn." The etymology of "atonement" is very simple: at-one-ment. What a wonderful idea! The Christian faith makes much of the idea of the believer being at one with God. But, that is not at all what we think of when we use the word "atonement." We rather think of what is paid for sins so that they may be forgiven.

SORTING OUT THE SAMPLES

All the samples you can dig up do not have the same degree of relevance when you are trying to be precise about a word in some particular statement. Call that statement your "Target Text"; your T.T.

You sort out these samples by considering their proximity to your "Target Text"; your T.T.

You are right to assume that the most significant examples come from the author of your T.T. And among those examples, the more important ones come from the same literary piece, or from the same period of time. And, any that appear in the context of your T.T. have the highest priority of all.

Call this special meaning which an author attaches to a word "*Usus Loquendi*."

Because the samplings of the word we are setting out to define will be less and less significant, we illustrate their growing remoteness by drawing concentric circles that become more and more distant from your T.T.

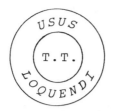

We next examine the examples found in the rest of the New Testament. How do the other writers of the New Testament use this word?

Because the writers of the New Testament were Greek-speaking Jews who spoke Aramaic as their native language, and because their Greek Bible, the Septuagint (LXX), was a translation of the Hebrew Old Testament, and contained a ready-made theological vocabulary, the Old Testament, both LXX and Hebrew, becomes the next important circle. You must ask yourself the question, "How is the word which I am studying used there?"

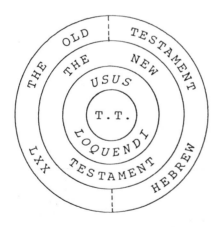

This will be the "outer limits" for the "low roader." And in this course, he will gain very little experience in the tricky, but necessary procedure in converting a LXX Greek word back into the Hebrew word which the Greek word translates. One has to use an exhaustive Old Testament Greek concordance. Hatch and Redpath's *A Concordance to the Septuagint* is all Greek, but has keyed in the Hebrew words which the Greek word translates. Every student should take down a volume from the library shelf and look it over.

The Jewish Bible, written in Hebrew, is the Christian's Old Testament. Jews and Christians both claim the same Jehovah as their God. The Christian writers of the New Testament were converts from Judaism. When they became Christians, they had no idea of abandoning their Jewish faith. They brought with them a theological vocabulary with Greek terms from their Hebrew Bible *via* the LXX. And with little or no change, they used these terms in the New Testament they were writing.

New Testament scholars, therefore, must retrace these steps. Often a New Testament Greek word is nothing more than a different symbol for the same Old Testament Hebrew word. Δόξα is no more or less than the Old Testament כָּבוֹד. So, to do a proper lexical study of the New Testament δόξα requires a proper lexical study of the Old Testament כָּבוֹד. And to fail to study the Old Testament קָהָל, is to fail to understand the important New Testament word, ἐκκλησία.

After the samples of our word which appear in the Septuagint are examined, one turns to the "Fathers" We call them the "Patristics."

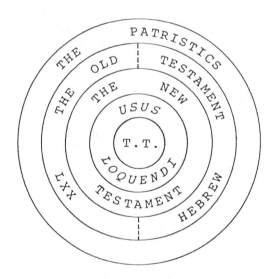

These are the earliest Christian writings we have outside the New Testament itself. The earliest actually overlapped a bit the times of the writing of the New Testament. Clement of Rome wrote an epistle to the church at Corinth in about 94 A.D., and the *Didache* and the *Epistle of Barnabas* were not much later.

For our use, we are interested primarily in the Fathers who wrote in Greek. These men, because their native tongue was the same as the Greek New Testament, and because they were familiar with the New Testament Greek, give us understanding we cannot get in any other way about what these words mean.

We call the earliest of these writers, "The Apostolic Fathers." They extend to the latter half of the second century. You can buy a paperback edition of these edited and translated by Lightfoot, and published by Baker Book House.

You can't get a comprehensive set of all the Patristics in English. The best you can do is the 38 volume combination of *The Ante-Nicene Fathers* and *The Nicene and Post-Nicene Fathers* published by Eerdmans.

There is no concordance for the Patristics, not even of the Apostolic Fathers. The nearest you can get to one on the Apostolic Fathers is Edgar J. Goodspeed's *Index Patristicus* published by Alec R. Allenson, Inc.

However, there is an excellent Greek lexicon of the Patristics done by G. W. H. Lampe; *A Patristic Greek Lexicon,* published by Oxford, and costing over one hundred dollars.

From the Patristics, we move out to embrace the Jewish Greek writers. Among them will be men like Philo and Josephus, the letter of Aristeas, and the Greek Pseudepigraphal writers, like Enoch, etc. They have the same Semitic orientation as those in the smaller circles.

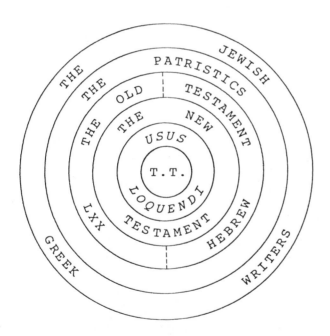

The next circle embraces the non-Semitic Hellenistic writings. On the one hand, there are the pedestrian matters of daily life coming to us through the recovery from the papyrus dumps of Egypt, memoranda, letters, receipts, etc. Then there are the literary works of such men as Epectitus, Polybius and Plutarch.

These, now without the Semitic cast, express
the Koine Greek, that dialect which thrived from about
333 B.C. to about 333 A.D, replacing Classical Greek,
only to be replaced by Byzantine Greek.

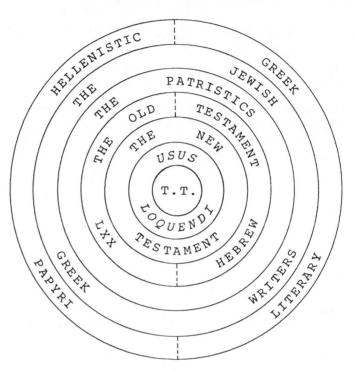

And now, at long last, we consider what samples
the Classical and Byzantine Greek may have to offer.
For all practical purposes, this is as far as the
Greek lexicographer need go in Greek proper.

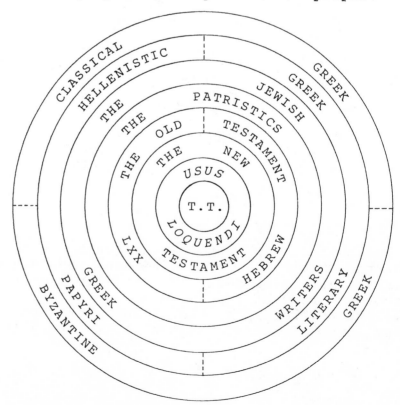

Until this century, the Classical Greek had altogether
too much influence upon what meaning we place upon a
New Testament Greek word. You can see how remote
Classical Greek really is.

The influence of Classical Greek was usurped by the
Papyri, which for the first half of the twentieth century
exerted an inordinate amount of influence upon our
understanding of New Testament word meanings.

To the degree you have a lot of samples in the
smaller rings, you don't need the ones in the larger
rings. But, some words are so very rare you need all
the samples you can find anywhere.

WHEN IT'S GOD'S
WORD

Some of you will have a problem reconciling the fact that the same word will not have exactly the same meaning when used by different New Testament authors. You may be reasoning: If we are looking at the Word of God, then *usus loquendi* should extend without a ripple from Genesis through Revelation. But to reason this way is to ignore some important facts.

The Bible is a human-Divine cooperative effort. These humans, numbering more than thirty, did not have equal vocabularies with identical ways that they would use each word.

One might envisage different ways this cooperative effort worked between God, on the one hand, and the 30+ men, on the other. I, personally, take a very strong position about God's superintendence, so that the outcome was exactly as He wanted it to be, and reflected, perfectly, His integrity. Whichever way you take it, you still have to go with the fact that the Divine Author employed the vocabulary of the human writers, attaching the meanings to the words which the human writers did.

In each case of the 30+, some distinctions are there. And those distinctions, a serious Bible student seeks to discover.

For instance, I have an idea that Paul and James didn't use the common word for faith (πίστις) in exactly the same way. Paul saw it as strong enough to produce appropriate reactions on the part of the person believing. On the other hand, James, seeing more exclusively a naked faith, felt that he must qualify his statements about faith, insisting it be accompanied by those appropriate responses.

So Paul points his wide-angle lens at faith and photographs the works that accompany faith. And James points his telescopic lens in the same direction and photographs only the faith itself.

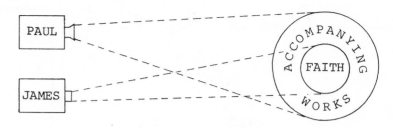

The Bible is not one iota less the Word of man because it is also at the same time the Word of God. To go any other way requires a non-human, Divine lexicography and a non-human, Divine syntax in a human language, and a non-human, Divine hermeneutic to interpret it, and an outrageous denial of any characteristic style on the part of the various human Biblical writers. Nobody is prepared to go this far.

BIBLICAL COINAGE

When we talk about the Spirit of God employing the vocabulary and meanings the human writers already had, we do not rule out that old words might take on new Christian meanings when used in the New Testament or that there might even be some brand new words made up for the occasion.

For instance, the older Classical literature doesn't prepare one at all for the way the Bible uses ἀγάπη (love). The New Testament attaches considerable content to ἐκκλησία (church), not found in either the Classical literature or even the Septuagint. In the Greek Bible, δόξα (glory) is practically unrecognizable compared with the same word in Classical literature. We can see distinct differences also in the meanings of μαθητής (disciple), and δικαιοσύνη (righteousness), to name a few more.

This is not God breaking His own rules. Rather, it is just another example of a universal, but natural process where man makes-do with the language he has to describe ideas that are new to him.

We might even have a brand new word made up for the occasion. Many think Paul did this in II Timothy 3:16 with the word θεόπνευστος, "given by the inspiration of God," or "God-breathed," or something like that.

MORE THAN ONE MEANING

You will discover that most words have more than one meaning, just like in English. Take the harmless little English word, "up." The following was clipped out of the *Reader's Digest*, of August, 1970; p. 134, and is used by permission.

We've got a two-letter word we use constantly that may have more meanings than any other. The word is *up*.

It is easy to understand *up* meaning toward the sky or

toward the top of a list. But when we waken, why do we
wake *up*? At a meeting, why does a topic come *up,* why do
participants speak *up,* and why are officers *up* for elec-
tion? And why is it *up* to the secretary to write *up* a
report?

Often the little word isn't needed, but we use it anyway.
We brighten *up* a room, light *up* a cigar, polish *up* the
silver, lock *up* the house, and fix *up* the old car. At
other times, it has special meanings. People stir *up*
trouble, line *up* for tickets, work *up* an appetite, think
up excuses, get tied *up* in traffic. To be dressed is
one thing, but to be dressed *up* is special. It may be
confusing, but a drain must be opened *up* because it is
stopped *up.* We open *up* a store in the morning and
close it *up* at night. We seem to be mixed *up* about *up.*

To be *up* on the proper use of *up* look *up* the word in
your dictionary. In one desk-size dictionary *up* takes
up half a page, and listed definitions add *up* to about
40. If you are *up* to it, you might try building *up* a
list of the many ways in which *up* is used. It will
take *up* a lot of your time but, if you don't give *up,*
you may wind *up* with a thousand.   -Frank S. Endicott

Although this sample is about as bad as it can
get, all languages have the same problem. Greek is
no exception. So, when the dictionary writer is going
through his samples, he finds the word used in different ways and sorts them out by putting all the examples
of a certain way in one pile.

We are going to practice a little, doing what
the lexicographer does. So, we must *look* for different
meanings of the same word.

For instance, to pick on a very obvious one, if you
examine all the uses for ἐκκλησία (church), you would
be picking up an idea about a special, ongoing group of
people belonging to Christ, like a body, a family and a
building. But when you come to the way it is used in
Acts 19:32, 39, and 41, it doesn't fit "church" at all.
You would find these three appearances fit much better
the old Classical use. So you start a new pile. And,
Acts 7:38 doesn't belong in either one. You would find
that it would go in the LXX pile.

We will say more about this in the next lesson
when we describe how to use a lexicon.

COGNATE STUDY

Before the dictionary writer is done, he must
consult the word's brothers and sisters and the more
remote cousins. Be sure you go back and reread 7:5-9
about these cognates before you continue.

It all depends on the abundance of the examples.
If they are already coming out of your ears, there is
little profit in cognate study. But when it is a
rare word, sometimes you *have* to do this.

For example, if you want to understand what "for the
καταρτισμός of the saints" means, you cannot look up
the other appearances of καταρτισμός, because this
is its only appearance. The verb form, which in this
instance has the same idea, appears thirteen times.

And, you will be studying the meaning of ἀποστασία,
which does not appear very often. So you must consult
the cognate, ἀφίστημι, which does *not* have the identical
meaning.

CAUTION: The cognate can go its own way, so
that it is not at all synonymous with its relatives.
For example, the cognates δοκέω (I think so), δόξα
(glory), and δογματίζω (I issue a decree) have meanings very different from one another.

SYNONYM AND ANTONYM

One must always be on the lookout for synonyms
and antonyms of the word one is studying. There is
a New Testament book of Greek synonyms which is very
helpful. However, the author presumes a knowledge
of Greek, Latin, German and French, and often the
punch line is in one of these languages. The book
is *Synonyms of the New Testament,* by Richard Chene-
vix Trench, and is published by Wm. B. Eerdmans in
paperback. (Its Old Testament counterpart, *Synonyms
of the Old Testament,* by Robert Baker Girdlestone,
also published in paperback by Eerdmans, is wholly
in English, and thus much more useable to the average
student. But he cites a limited number of words.)

If there was a book of antonyms, I would go
out and buy it sight unseen. In some contexts, the
word you are studying might be vague or ambiguous,
whereas its antonym will be very clear. The meaning
of your word might simply be the opposite of its
antonym, which is very clear.

There are no 100% synonyms. Only when the context is
right for it, can you say that two words can be inter-
changed without any apparent change in the meaning of
the sentence in which they appear. Most of the time,
ἕτερος and ἄλλος are interchangeable. The same can be
said of ἀγαπάω and φιλέω. Yet, they are not exact
duplicates, and in some contexts, (Gal. 1:6-7 with the
first pair; John 21:15-19 with the second), their meanings *must* be distinguished.

CONCORDANCE TECHNIQUE

So, now you are ready to try your hand at it.

You have your T.T., your "Target Text," which is I Peter 2:3. You already have discovered the Greek word which the KJV has translated "tasted." And, you have discovered its lexical form, γεύομαι.

1. Look up γεύομαι in *The Englishman's Greek Concordance*. It is found on page 115. (I have copied this page and printed it as page 10:6.) Look at it. Find γεύομαι.

2. How many times does γευομαι appear in the New Testament? _____ If you had looked up the word in Young's *Concordance,* the count might not have been accurate. The Greek Testament which *The Englishman's Greek Concordance* used, is the one from which the KJV was translated. It is called the *Textus Receptus.* This edition of our New Testament is now about 450 years old. Since this *Englishman's Greek Concordance* was first published, new Greek manuscripts and versions have been discovered which bring us closer to the original "autographs." Therefore, the word count from this concordance may not be 100% accurate. If it is important to be accurate, also check the listing in Moulton and Geden's *A Concordance to the Greek Testament,* which is far more recent and accurate.

CAUTION: When you use *The Englishman's Greek Concordance,* you place upon yourself a serious psychological handicap which you must make every effort to overcome.

Turn to the sample page of *The Englishman's Greek Concordance* on page 10:6. Arbitrarily select the word γεωργός. Read down the 19 brief contexts of this word in the New Testament. You are not reading Greek, but the English of the KJV. The word in italics is the word that that particular version selected to translate γεωργός.

The translators may have made a mistake, or may have used a word which we don't use anymore or which we use differently today. When is the last time you used the word "husbandman" when you were talking to a friend?

So, you must discipline your mind to "X" the word in italics. That is, try to read the context without counting at all on what the English translation of the word you are studying happens to be. It is extremely difficult, but you must try very hard.

You must not prejudice your case by being influenced by the way the word has been translated in *The Englishman's Greek Concordance.*

CAUTION: The contexts in *The Englishman's Greek Concordance* are inadequate. You have been told over and over

γέννησις, *genneesis*.

Mat. 1:18. Now the *birth* of Jesus Christ was on
Lu. 1:14. gladness; and many shall rejoice at his *birth*.

γεννητός, *genneetos*.

Mat.11:11. Among *them that are born* of women
Lu. 7:28. Among *those that are born* of women

γένος, *genos*.

Mat.13:47. into the sea, and gathered of every *kind:*
17:21. Howbeit this *kind* goeth not out
Mar. 7:26. a Greek, a Syrophenician by *nation;*
9:29. This *kind* can come forth by nothing,
Acts 4: 6. of the *kindred* of the high priest,
36. a Levite, (and) of the *country* of Cyprus,
7:13. Joseph's *kindred* was made known
19. same dealt subtilly with our *kindred,*
13:26. children of the *stock* of Abraham,
17:28. For we are also his *offspring.*
29. then as we are the *offspring* of God,
18: 2. Aquila, *born* in (lit. by *birth* of) Pontus,
24. Jew named Apollos, *born* at Alexandria,
1Co.12:10. to another (divers) *kinds* of tongues;
28. governments, *diversities* of tongues.
14:10. many *kinds* of voices in the world,
2Co.11:26. (in) perils by (mine own) *countrymen,*
Gal. 1:14. many my equals in mine own *nation,*
Phi. 3: 5. of the *stock* of Israel, (of) the tribe of
1Pet.2: 9. ye (are) a chosen *generation,* a royal
Rev.22:16. I am the root and the *offspring* of David,

γερουσία, *gerousia*.

Acts 5:21. all the *senate* of the children of Israel,

γέρων, *gerōn*.

Joh. 3: 4. can a man be born when he is *old?*

γεύομαι, *gūomai*.

Mat.16:28. which *shall* not *taste* of death, till
27:34. *when* he *had tasted* (thereof), he would
Mar. 9: 1. here, which *shall* not *taste* of death,
Lu. 9:27. *shall* not *taste* of death, till they see
14:24. were bidden *shall taste* of my supper.
Joh. 2: 9. ruler of the feast *had tasted* the water
8:52. saying, he *shall* never *taste* of death.
Acts10:10. very hungry, and would *have eaten:*
20:11. had broken bread, and *eaten,* and talked
23:14. that we will *eat* nothing until we
Col. 2:21. Touch not; *taste* not; handle not;
Heb. 2: 9. *should taste* death for every man.
6: 4. *have tasted* of the heavenly gift, and were
5. *have tasted* the good word of God,
1Pet.2: 3. If so be ye *have tasted* that the Lord

γεωργέομαι, *geōrgeomai*.

Heb. 6: 7. for them by whom it *is dressed*, receiveth

γεώργιον, *geōrgion*.

1Co. 3: 9. with God: ye are God's *husbandry,*

γεωργός, *geōrgos*.

Mat.21:33. let it out to *husbandmen*, and went
34. sent his servants to the *husbandmen,*
35. the *husbandmen* took his servants,
38. when the *husbandmen* saw the son,
40. will he do unto those *husbandmen?*
41. (his) vineyard unto other *husbandmen,*
Mar.12: 1. let it out to *husbandmen*, and went
2. he sent to the *husbandmen*
— might receive from the *husbandmen*
7. those *husbandmen* said among
9. will come and destroy the *husbandmen,*
Lu. 20: 9. a vineyard, and let it forth to *husbandmen,*
10. sent a servant to the *husbandmen,*
— the *husbandmen* beat him,
14. when the *husbandmen* saw him,
16. shall come and destroy these *husbandmen,*
Joh.15: 1. my Father is the *husbandman.*
2Ti. 2: 6. The *husbandman* that laboureth
Jas. 5: 7. the *husbandman* waiteth for the

γῆ, *gee*.

Mat. 2: 6. thou Bethlehem, (in) the *land* of Juda,
20. go into the *land* of Israel: for they
21. came into the *land* of Israel.
4:15. The *land* of Zabulon, and the *land* of N.
5: 5. the meek: for they shall inherit the *earth.*
13. Ye are the salt of the *earth:* but if
18. Till heaven and *earth* pass, one jot or
6:10. Thy will be done in *earth,* as (it is)
19. for yourselves treasures upon *earth,*
9: 6. man hath power on *earth* to forgive
26. fame hereof went abroad into all that *land.*
31. abroad his fame in all that *country.*
10:15. for the *land* of Sodom and Gomorrha in
29. shall not fall on the *ground* without
34. I am come to send peace on *earth:*
11:24. more tolerable for the *land* of Sodom
25. O Father, Lord of heaven and *earth,*
12:40. three nights in the heart of the *earth.*
42. from the uttermost parts of the *earth* to
13: 5. where they had not much *earth:*
— they had no deepness of *earth:*
8. other fell into good *ground,*
23. received seed into the good *ground*
14:34. came into the *land* of Gennesaret.
15:35. multitude to sit down on the *ground.*
16:19. whatsoever thou shalt bind on *earth*
— whatsoever thou shalt loose on *earth*
17:25. of whom do the kings of the *earth* take
18:18. Whatsoever ye shall bind on *earth*
— whatsoever ye shall loose on *earth*
19. if two of you shall agree on *earth* as
23: 9. call no (man) your father upon the *earth:*
35. righteous blood shed upon the *earth,*
24:30. then shall all the tribes of the *earth*
35. Heaven and *earth* shall pass away,
25:18. received one went and digged in the *earth,*
25. went and hid thy talent in the *earth:*
27:45. there was darkness over all the *land*
51. the *earth* did quake, and the rocks rent;
28:18. given unto me in heaven and in *earth.*
Mar. 2:10. Son of man hath power on *earth* to

again how important the context is to any meaningful
Bible study. You cannot get the meaning of any word,
phrase, clause or sentence until you pick up the flow
of thought to, into, through, out of, and beyond the
object of your study.

The problem of reading the T.T. in English is a
psychological one. This is also a moral one. There
is no room for the lazy scholar in Biblical study.

So, you must look up each appearance in your Bible and
read before and after, far enough to pick up the thought,
and so you are able to feel comfortable in the way your
"X" fits into it.

As you progress in your Biblical knowledge, more and
more of these contexts will already be familiar to you.
This will reduce more and more your study time, as you
engage in this study.

CAUTION: Be sure to keep in mind that the same Greek
word, more often than not, will have more than one
meaning. Do not try to force a uniformity upon your
word. Only settle for a meaning which fits comfortably
into its context. Then when you come to your T.T., don't
impose all of the meanings the word is capable of convey-
ing, but only that one which fits most comfortably into
the context of the T.T.

Sometimes, this is going to threaten your theology. You
would be surprised about how major a role morality plays
in Bible study. Honesty is rare everywhere.

VISUALIZE THE EVENT

Your imagination must stay in high gear as you
read these various contexts. With historical material, it is easy. Start there. But you can do it in
other places also. As you picture the event on your
cranial television set, meaning flows into your void
"X," and if you are really getting the hang of it,
more often than not, an English word pops out of
nowhere and identifies this content.

If you're not satisfied, try some synonyms, using a
dictionary of synonyms if you have to. At this stage,
stick with English words you *know,* not sticking up your
nose at slang words. Later on, you might have to settle
for a more aristocratic word.

CAFETERIA ANARCHY VS. TYRANNY OF CONTEXT

The discovery that words have more than one
meaning too often presents to the student a temptation he does not possess the moral character to
resist. It is so easy to project our own preferences
and seize upon that meaning which suits *us*. Too
often the exegete is unable to cope with this unex-
pected source of power which the tools of exegesis
have placed in his hand. Coupled with ingenuity, he

finds himself able to reshape the Bible into his own image.

The many meanings a word might be able to convey do not constitute a cafeteria from which a student can select one according to his taste. We are enslaved to the "tyranny of the context."

An important hermeneutical rule, a most difficult one to administer objectively, exists which alleviates to some degree the tyranny of the context. Its fancy name is "The Analogy of Scripture." It is the most abused of all rules of interpretation.

It is based on the rather sound proposition that you ought to assume that the writer is not contradicting himself and that, therefore, the burden of proof rests with the person who would make such an allegation.

One might say, therefore, that in the light of the known beliefs of the writer, although option "y" rests slightly more comfortably in the context than option "z," option "z" is still what the author probably meant because it is the one which is more compatible with what we know he believes.

You can see right away what a "Pandora's box" we have opened. So, it is better for the "low roader" to err in the direction of the tyranny of the context, than in the direction of the analogy of the Scripture, even though in so doing he is in danger of introducing a contradictory statement. It would be the lesser of the two evils.

LEXICON LAST

Only after you have gone as far as you can without it, do you turn to your Greek dictionary, or lexicon. We will give you guidance about this in the next lesson. Meanwhile, we have some research to do.

LESSON 11

USE OF THE GREEK LEXICON

Before you look up a word in a lexicon to see what it means, it is best to first get your own point of view by studying the way the word and its cognates are used throughout the New Testament. After you have gotten your own meaning, then see what the lexicon says. This is why you have had all these beginning assignments.

A good Greek lexicon will give you much more than just the Biblical meaning of the word. It will tell you how it was used during Classical times and in other contemporary Hellenistic Greek writings. It will show how the Greek Church Fathers used the word. And of special interest, it will point out how the word was used in the LXX (remember: the Septuagint, or Greek translation of the Old Testament). Since the New Testament was written by Semitic people who had received their Greek theological vocabulary from the LXX, it becomes important to trace this vocabulary through the LXX and back into the Hebrew, from which it was taken.

The best and most up-to-date Greek lexicon is that done in German by Walter Bauer and translated into English by William F. Arndt and F. Wilbur Gingrich, entitled *A Greek - English Lexicon of the New Testament*. It defines all the Greek words that appear not only in the New Testament, but also in other early Christian and heretical literature.

OTHER LEXICONS

The following are some of the other available lexicons:

Liddell, Scott and Jones are editors of the comprehensive lexicon which serves all ancient Greek dialects. Joseph Henry Thayer first edited *A Greek - English Lexicon of the New Testament* in 1886, which though still in print, is replaced now by Arndt and Gingrich's.

If you are not planning to continue with Greek, you may wish to acquire one of the following in preference to Arndt and Gingrich's: *An Expository Dictionary of New*

Testament Words by W. E. Vine is very helpful and easy to understand. *Shorter Lexicon of the Greek New Testament* edited by F. W. Gingrich is an abridgment of the larger work by the same editor. It omits citations of non-New Testament appearances of words, morphological data and the extremely complicated abbreviational system of the original.

Another important work is the mammoth ten - volume *Theological Dictionary of the New Testament,* originally edited by Gerhard Kittel, and translated by Geoffrey Bromiley. It deals thoroughly with every significant word (and some not so significant) in the New Testament. Unfortunately, this tool is beyond your competence, although you may wish to take a volume down from the shelf and look it over.

However difficult Arndt and Gingrich might be, it is the best and most authoritative. For this reason, you will be studying and using it.

ABBREVIATIONS

The explanation of the elaborate abbreviational system in Arndt and Gingrich's *Lexicon* is found in the introduction, from pages xxix to xl, under six separate lists.

List 1 gives abbreviations of all the literature whose vocabulary is defined.

List 2 gives abbreviations of Semitic literature cited (LXX, Apocrypha, Pseudepigrapha, etc.).

List 3 gives abbreviations of collections of inscriptions and papyri.

List 4 gives abbreviations of writers and writings from Classical and Hellenistic times.

List 5 gives abbreviations of modern authors, literature, periodicals, etc.

List 6 gives general abbreviations.

The second edition adds supplementary lists of abbreviations from Greek papyri and from the Qumran literature on page xxx.

In order to make sense out of the definitions found in this lexicon, you must laboriously search through the lists and write out in full what has been abbreviated.

Unfortunately, these lists are incomplete. Apparently, the authors assume a considerable knowledge of Classical literature on the part of the users. For example, the book will refer by an abbreviation to a book by a certain author; but the lists do not have the abbreviation. The author of this textbook

is forced to confess that even after a considerable
search, he has not found out what some of the abbreviations mean.

PARTS OF SPEECH

All the words are listed in the alphabetical
order of their "lexical form." On finding this form,
you will want to pick out what part of speech the
word is. The following may be of help:

1. If there is no Greek immediately following the word,
   it is a verb.

2. If there is one of the Greek articles after the word,
   it is a noun.

3. If there are two other Greek words, but not an article,
   it is a pronoun or an adjective.

4. If there is "prep." after the word or after the first
   parenthesis, it is a preposition.

5. If there is "adv." after the word, it is an adverb.

6. If it is a conjunction, the word, "conjunction," will
   be written out after it.

EXAMPLE

Because the Arndt and Gingrich *Lexicon* is
complicated and difficult for beginners to understand,
you have been given a sample from the book. (See
page 11:4.) Turn the page and compare it step by
step with the following explanation. Since you will
have to "interpret" another word in the next worksheet, it is imperative that you understand what you
read!

If one would rewrite this definition of
γεύομαι, using no abbreviations, this apparently
brief definition would take on the size of an essay.
Let me have a go at it.

MORPHOLOGY AND
HISTORY

The future form of γεύομαι is γεύσομαι, and the past time
punctiliar form is ἐγευσάμην. The word appears often,
starting with Homer (eighth to sixth century before
Christ). It is also found among the papyri, in the Septuagint, in Philo of Alexandria and in Josephus, the last
two being contemporary to Jesus.

LITERAL MEANING

With the
Accusative

Its literal meaning is to "taste," "partake of," "enjoy"
something. As early as classical times (according to
Kuhner and Gerth, *Ausfurliche Grammatik d. griechische
Sprache*, Vol. 1, p. 356) and predominately since
Aristotle, the direct object of γεύομαι is in the
accusative case. (See Aristotle's *Poetics 22*.)
F. Preisigke observes the same in his *Sammelbuch Griech*,
page 1106, "οἱ συμπόσιον γευόμενοι" (those who participated in the "kegger"). Examples of this use are found

11:4

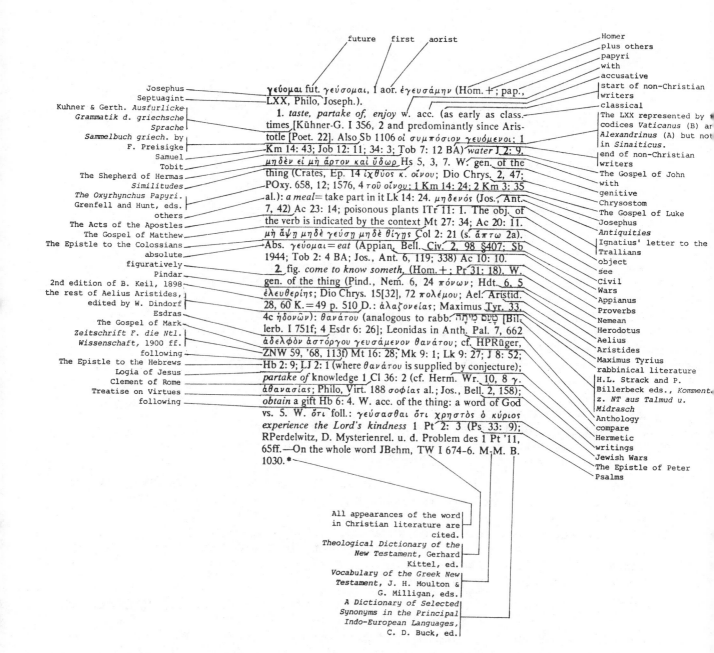

future   first   aorist

γεύομαι fut. γεύσομαι, 1 aor. ἐγευσάμην (Hom. +; pap., LXX, Philo, Joseph.).

1. *taste, partake of, enjoy* w. acc. (as early as class. times [Kühner-G. I 356, 2 and predominantly since Aristotle [Poet. 22]. Also Sb 1106 οἱ συμπόσιον γευόμενοι; 1 Km 14: 43; Job 12: 11; 34: 3; Tob 7: 12 BA) *water* J 2: 9. μηδὲν εἰ μὴ ἄρτον καὶ ὕδωρ Hs 5, 3, 7. W. gen. of the thing (Crates, Ep. 14 ἰχθύος κ. οἴνου; Dio Chrys. 2, 47; POxy. 658, 12; 1576, 4 τοῦ οἴνου; 1 Km 14: 24; 2 Km 3: 35 al.): *a meal*= take part in it Lk 14: 24. μηδενός (Jos., Ant. 7, 42) Ac 23: 14; poisonous plants ITr 11: 1. The obj. of the verb is indicated by the context Mt 27: 34; Ac 20: 11. μὴ ἅψῃ μηδὲ γεύσῃ μηδὲ θίγῃς Col 2: 21 (s. ἅπτω 2a). Abs. γεύομαι=*eat* (Appian, Bell. Civ. 2, 98 §407; Sb 1944; Tob 2: 4 BA; Jos., Ant. 6, 119; 338) Ac 10: 10.

2. fig. *come to know someth.* (Hom. +; Pr 31: 18). W. gen. of the thing (Pind., Nem. 6, 24 πόνων; Hdt. 6, 5 ἐλευθερίης; Dio Chrys. 15[32], 72 πολέμου; Ael. Aristid. 28, 60 K.=49 p. 510 D.: ἀλαζονείας; Maximus Tyr. 33, 4c ἡδονῶν): θανάτου (analogous to rabb. טָעַם מִיתָה [Billerb. I 751f; 4 Esdr 6: 26]; Leonidas in Anth. Pal. 7, 662 ἀδελφὸν ἀστόργου γευσάμενον θανάτου; cf. HPRüger, ZNW 59, '68, 113f) Mt 16: 28; Mk 9: 1; Lk 9: 27; J 8: 52; Hb 2: 9; LJ 2: 1 (where θανάτου is supplied by conjecture); *partake of* knowledge 1 Cl 36: 2 (cf. Herm. Wr. 10, 8 γ. ἀθανασίας; Philo, Virt. 188 σοφίας al.; Jos., Bell. 2, 158); *obtain* a gift Hb 6: 4. W. acc. of the thing: a word of God vs. 5. W. ὅτι foll.: γεύσασθαι ὅτι χρηστὸς ὁ κύριος *experience the Lord's kindness* 1 Pt 2: 3 (Ps 33: 9); RPerdelwitz, D. Mysterienrel. u. d. Problem des 1 Pt '11, 65ff.—On the whole word JBehm, TW I 674-6. M-M. B. 1030. *

Annotations (left):
- Josephus
- Septuagint
- Kuhner & Gerth. Ausfurlicke Grammatik d. griechsche Sprache
- Sammelbuch griech. by F. Preisigke
- Samuel
- Tobit
- The Shepherd of Hermas Similitudes
- The Oxyrhynchus Papyri. Grenfell and Hunt, eds.
- The Acts of the Apostles
- The Gospel of Matthew
- The Epistle to the Colossians
- absolute
- figuratively
- Pindar
- 2nd edition of B. Keil, 1898 the rest of Aelius Aristides, edited by W. Dindorf
- Esdras
- The Gospel of Mark
- Zeitschrift F. die Ntl. Wissenschaft, 1900 ff.
- following
- The Epistle to the Hebrews
- Logia of Jesus
- Clement of Rome
- Treatise on Virtues
- following

Annotations (right):
- Homer
- plus others
- papyri
- with
- accusative
- start of non-Christian writers
- classical
- The LXX represented by codices Vaticanus (B) and Alexandrinus (A) but not in Sinaiticus.
- end of non-Christian writers
- The Gospel of John
- with
- genitive
- Chrysostom
- The Gospel of Luke
- Josephus
- Antiquities
- Ignatius' letter to the Trallians
- object
- see
- Civil
- Wars
- Appianus
- Proverbs
- Nemean
- Herodotus
- Aelius
- Aristides
- Maximus Tyrius
- rabbinical literature
- H.L. Strack and P. Billerbeck eds., Komment z. NT aus Talmud u. Midrasch
- Anthology
- compare
- Hermetic
- writings
- Jewish Wars
- The Epistle of Peter
- Psalms

Annotations (bottom):
- All appearances of the word in Christian literature are cited.
- Theological Dictionary of the New Testament, Gerhard Kittel, ed.
- Vocabulary of the Greek New Testament, J. H. Moulton & G. Milligan, eds.
- A Dictionary of Selected Synonyms in the Principal Indo-European Languages, C. D. Buck, ed.

Taken from *A Greek-English Lexicon of the New Testament*. Walter Bauer ed., William Arndt and F. Wilbur Gingrich, translators, Second Edition revised and augmented by F. Wilbur Gingrich and Frederick W. Danker. Chicago: University Chicago Press, 1979. Used by permission of Walter de Gruyter & Co., Berlin.

in First Samuel 14:3; Job 12:11 and 34:3, and in the apocryphal book, Tobit 7:12 (as recorded in the Codices Alexandrinus and Vaticanus, but not Sinaiticus). In the Christian literature, water is partaken of, John 2:9. The Shepherd of Hermas (90-140 years after Christ) in his *Similitudes* 5, 3, 7, speaks of partaking of μηδὲν εἰ μὴ ἄρτον καὶ ὕδωρ (nothing except bread and water).

The word uses the genitive as object, also. In the non-Christian literature, Crates of Thebes (fourth century before Christ) does this in his *Epistulae* 14, when speaking of ἰχθύος καὶ οἴνου (partaking of fish and wine). Dio Chrysostom (first and second centuries after Christ) in 2:47, and two references in the *Papyrus Oxyrhynchus*, 658, 12 and 1567, 4, mention a partaking of wine in the genitive (τοῦ οἴνου). The genitive is found other places, including First Samuel 14:24 and Second Samuel 3:35 in the Septuagint. With the Genitive

In the Christian literature, Luke speaks of taking part in a meal (14:24), where "meal" is genitive. You have partaking in μηδενός ("nothing" in the genitive) in Acts 23:14 as also in the non-Christian Josephus, *Antiquities*, 7:42. Ignatius (110 years after Christ), in his first letter to the Trallians (11:1), mentions eating poisonous plants.

The object of the verb is indicated by the context in Matthew 27:34 and Acts 20:11. Paul, in Colossians 2:21, cites a popular Judaistic admonition: μὴ ἄψῃ μηδὲ γεύσῃ μηδὲ θίγῃς (do not touch, do not taste, do not handle). See what is said about this verse under ἅπτω, definition 2. a. in this lexicon.

The word is used absolutely, meaning "to eat." In the non-Christian literature, this use is cited in Appian's *Civil Wars* (second century after Christ) 2, 98, paragraph 407 and in F. Preisigke, *Sammelbuch Griech*, page 1944. Codex Vaticanus agrees with Codex Alexandrinus in the use of the word absolutely in the apocryphal book of Tobit (2:4), as does Josephus in his *Antiquities*, book 6, paragraphs 119 and 338. In Christian literature, the word is used absolutely in Acts 10:10.

The figurative use of γεύομαι, "to come to know something," also has an object in the genitive case, starting with Homer, and is found in many writings, including Proverbs 31:18. FIGURATIVE USE

In the non-Christian literature, such a use is found in Pindar's *Nemean 6:24* (fifth century before Christ), where one partakes of "labors" (πόνων), in Herodotus 6:5 (also fifth century before Christ), where one partakes of "freedom" (ἐλευθερίης), and in Dio Chrysostom 15 (32): 72 of "war" (πολέμου). Aelius Aristides (second century

after Christ) 28:60, which is in volume two of the edition of B. Keil, and again in 49, page 510, in the edition of W. Dindorf, mentions an assuming of "imposture"
(ἀλαζονείας, with γεύομαι meaning "assuming"). And
Maximus Tyrus (also second century after Christ) talks
about partaking of "pleasures" (ἡδονῶν), 33, 4c.

Compare this with H. P. Ruger's article in the periodical
Zeitschrift F. die Ntl. Wissenschaft, page 1900 following.
In the Christian literature, you have Matthew 16:28;
Mark 9:1; Luke 9:27, John 8:52; Hebrews 2:9; and the
Logia of Jesus 2:1 (where is is supplied by conjec-
ture) recording a partaking of "death" (θανάτου).
This is very much like the Rabbinic expression
מִיתָה טַעַם, according to H. L. Strack and P. Biller-
beck in *Kommentar zum Neuen Testament aus Talmud und
Midrash*, volume one, page 751-752. See also Fourth
Esdras 6:26. Leonidas of Tarentum (third century
before Christ) in his *Anthology Palatina, 7, 662,*
talks about a "brother without natural affection as
tasting death" (ἀδελφὸν ἀστόργου γευσάμενον θανάτου).

One can also use the word in a figurative sense with
"knowledge," as is seen in I Clement 36:2 (first century
after Christ). Compare this with the Hermetic Writings,
Hermetica 10:8, γ, edited by W. Scott, where "immortality"
(ἀθανασίας) is the object. Philo, in his *On Virtues 188*,
mentions the word in association with "wisdom" (σοφίας),
as do many others, including Josephus, *Wars 2, 158.*

One can "obtain a gift," (Hebrews 6:4) with the accusative case and obtain a "word of God" in the following
verse. Γεύομαι uses ὅτι ("that") to indicate its object
in γεύσασθαι ὅτι χρηστὸς ὁ κύριος (experience the Lord's
kindness) in First Peter 2:3, an allusion to the Septuagint in Psalm 33:9 (Psalm 34:9 in the English versions).
This verse in First Peter is treated in R. Perdelwitz's
Die Mysterienrel. und d. Problem des I Peter, 1911,
pages 65 and following.

REFERRAL

On γεύομαι as a whole, see Johannes Behm's article in
Gerhard Kittle's *Theological Dictionary of the New
Testament,* volume one, pages 674-676, and in Moulton
and Milligan's *Vocabulary of the Greek New Testament,*
and in C. D. Buck's *A Dictionary of Selected Synonyms
in the Principle Indo-European Languages.*

In the course of this article, every appearance of
γεύομαι in the early Christian literature has been cited.

HOW TO DO IT

Now that you have read my essay, I will show
you how I did it so that you can do it, too.

Preliminary
Material

The very first word is the lexical form. According to the help given on page 11:3, what part of

speech is it?_____ The next two Greek
words spell out the future and past punctiliar deponent
forms of the verb, information you do not need at this
point. Next, is a parenthesis with an abbreviation,
"Hom.," and a "plus sign." This tells you that Homer
was the first Greek writer known to use the word. (If
you did not know "Hom." is an abbreviation for "Homer,"
you would have had to refer to List 4 of the abbreviations, which gives the abbreviations of writers and
writings from Classical and Hellenistic times.) List
4 is also important because it gives the century or
years in which the writers lived.

    For instance, the list reads:

        Hom(er) .   .   .   . perh. VIII-VI B.C.

    This means Homer lived around the sixth to eighth
    century B.C.

    The "plus sign" means it is found in other Greek
works, also. Sometimes, various writers are mentioned
before the "plus sign." Notice the semi-colon which
follows. This tells you that a new segment of information is coming up.

    What is the next abbreviation? _____ What
do you think it means? _____ Sometimes,
"inscr." is written before "pap." Both of these abbreviations mean that the word has been found in
secular, non-literary writings.

    The next abbreviation is one you've seen before.
What does it stand for? _____ This, plus
the next two names, are a listing of Jewish writings
and writers. Unfortunately, Arndt and Gingrich did
not make a separate abbreviation list for them, and
so it is difficult to know which names are listed as
Jewish writers and writings in List 4. The following
can serve as a guideline:

    1. LXX
    2. Old Testament and Apocrypha
    3. Epistle of Aristeas
    4. Testaments of the Twelve Patriarchs
    5. Josephus
    6. Philo
    7. Enoch (Henoch)

    In summary, the information given before the
specific definitions, is:

    1. The lexical form of the word.
    2. The spelling of various forms of the word.

3. The first known Greek writer to use the word, plus other Greek writers.
4. The use of the word in secular, non-literary writings.
5. The use of the word by Jewish writers and writings.

Definition Proper   The definition(s) of the word comes next. It might be very brief, with only a word or two, or rather elaborate, with several definitions. When the definitions are long, the following breakdown is used to make divisions: an arabic numeral, English lower case letters, and finally, Greek lower case letters.

The literal meaning (often identified by "lit.") precedes the figurative meaning (identified by "fig."). What is the literal meaning of γεύομαι? _____
_____ After the English definition, is the abbreviation, "w. acc." This means that when the verb is used "with the accusative" (takes a direct object), it has that particular meaning. Sometimes, the Greek word τινος (or τινι, or τι), with or without a Greek preposition, is used. That word means "something," and is spelled accordingly to indicate the word's case: genitive, dative, or accusative, in that order. You are being told, in another way, that when the verb takes a direct object in that particular Greek case, then the word in italics is its definition. A preposition in front of a τι form indicates the verb will have a certain meaning when associated with that kind of prepositional phrase.

Now, another parenthesis follows. All the references within the parenthesis are considered as non-Christian. Yet, notice what is included. After a reference to a later usage is the abbreviation, "I Km 14:43." This is found in list number two on page xxx of the lexicon, and identifies it as I Samuel. What is the next reference?_____
How can these be considered non-Christian sources? The explanation is fairly simple. Since the editors are writing a lexicon of the New Testament and other early Christian literature, anything outside of this field is classified as non-Christian, and is placed within parentheses. These references will include Jewish writers, Old Testament writers, Hellenistic writers and Classical writers.

Every reference outside of the parentheses is classified as Christian. Included are references first to the New Testament, and then to early Christian Greek writers. These early writings by the Church Fathers are called _____ (see 9:4). In the example, Jn. 2:9 is a Christian New Testament writing, and "Hs. 5, 3, 7" is a Christian Patristic writing. The letter "H" represents "Hermas," an

Apostolic Father (See page 9:5) who wrote, among other things, *Similitudes,* represented by the lower case "s." The Greek word, γεύομαι, is found in chapter 5, section 3, paragraph 7.

Sometimes, the letters "v.l." appear after a New Testament reference. This abbreviation means "variant reading" (*varia lectio* - see abbreviation List 6, page vl in the lexicon). The sign means that the word is found in this location in one or more of the ancient manuscripts.

Intermingled among these references (both inside and outside of the parentheses) are Greek words and phrases intended to give you some understanding of the context of that particular citation. English often appears in italics. This gives you the editor's judgment of what the word meant *in that particular context.*

The editors do *not* intend that these various definitions of a single word are to be used like a cafeteria, down which line you peruse until you find a definition to your liking! (Reread pages 10:7-8.) These definitions have been meticulously sorted because of their contexts. You must be just as careful to respect the context of the particular word which you are defining.

Often, at the end of the definition, the reader   Final Matter
is referred to other works which treat the word in more detail. Some of the most common are:

    M-M. = Moulton and Milligan, *The Vocabulary of the Greek New Testament.*

    B.   = C. D. Buck, *Dictionary of Selected Synonyms in the Principal Indo-European Languages.*

    TW   = Gerhard Kittel, *Theological Dictionary of the New Testament.*

The very last mark, at the conclusion of our example, is a star, or asterisk (*).

    *   means every appearance of the word in the Christian literature has been cited.

    ** means every appearance in the New Testament (only) has been cited.

LESSON 12

COMMON SENSE RULES
FOR INTERPRETATION

Sooner or later--and the sooner, the better--
you are going to stop long enough in your Bible study
to ask yourself, "Am I doing it right? Are there
rules to go by for interpreting the Bible?" There
sure are! The subject is given the fancy name of
"Hermeneutics."

USE COMMON SENSE

Happily, it's hard to stir up a quarrel about
hermeneutics, because, since the Reformation, especially, just about everybody worth his salt espouses
the "Grammatico-Historical" system. I am no different. However, I prefer to call it the "Common Sense"
method.

"The grammatico-historical sense of a writer is such an
interpretation of his language as is required by the laws
of grammar and the facts of history."

-Milton S. Terry, *Biblical Hermeneutics,* page 203.

This man, Terry, whose book is about as definitive as any on the subject, says the following on
page 173 about common sense:

"It [grammatico-historical] applies to the sacred books
the same principles, the same grammatical process and
exercise of common sense and reason, which we apply to
other books."

So, my first rule is a rule about the rules.
If there ever was a place for common horse sense, it
can be found in the rules for interpreting the Bible.
I must advise you, therefore, ahead of time. Whatever rules I list which do not commend themselves to
your common sense as patently self-evident, you must
reject out of hand.

The same goes for anybody else's rules.

1
BE SIMPLE

1. Interpret the Bible as you would any other
book. Go with the simple and obvious meaning. Ingenuity in the exegete is a sin. Eschew the prevalent

"ear tickling" custom which produces "new" interpretations; interpretations which would be new to the very authors themselves.

Assume that if the writer is not playing games with us, he had a specific idea he wanted to get across. Although you may find a lot of ways to apply what he says, assume he had only one meaning when he said something.

Take whatever he says as literally as he wanted it to be taken; neither more, nor less.

> "'Literal' interpretation means the understanding which any person of normal intelligence would get, without any special spiritual gifts and without any 'code' or 'key.'"
>
> -William Sanford LaSor, "Interpretation of Prophecy," in *Hermeneutics*, edited by Bernard L. Ramm.

2
SUBMIT TO
"LAWS OF GRAMMAR"

2. Assume the writer employed the right combinations of words and forms to get his point across the way he wanted it. You have to take words and the way they are used in the way the language normally does. The reason this manual is written is because I believe that when people talk or write, even unconsciously, they employ grammatical principles which can be articulated and use words which can be defined. So, you use those grammatical principles and those dictionary definitions to determine what the writer meant when he wrote something.

Assume further that the author had his own unique way with the language, both in the nuances of word meanings, and in the way he put words together. You have already been introduced to the technical term, *Usus Loquendi* (page 9:2), when it applies to definitions of words. The same is true in respect to grammar.

Interpret idioms as idioms. We mentioned before (pages 5:4-5) how hard it is to get a handle on them. You can't manage them simply by comprehending their grammar, for they march to the tune of a different band. Nor can you memorize them all; the most visible ones, perhaps, but they cause the least of the trouble. It's the maybe-yes-and-maybe-no ones, which *almost* behave themselves, that are the true booby-traps. You've simply got to get the feel of them. There is no other way. More will be said about this in Lesson 22.

3
SUBMIT TO CONTEXT

3. The meaning of any text is limited and

controlled by its context. Your interpretation of
the text must fit into the flow of thought to, into,
through, out of, and away from it. So obvious is this
rule that we need not go into it. This is why it is
so important to read and reread whole books and large
sections of the Bible. Disregard the flow of thought
and you blow the whole thing. The "Mispah" benediction
is nothing to be repeated between fellowshiping Christians. Go read its context (Genesis 31:49).

This context extends to the whole book, its
structure and purpose. So, this law sort of merges
into the next rule.

4
SUBMIT TO
"FACTS OF HISTORY"

4. The meaning of any text is limited and
controlled by its external context. You are, really,
not explaining a text, as much as you are explaining
an historic event. Because this is such a neglected
principle, three lessons will be devoted to it.
Lesson 18 will be on the geographical context, Lesson
19 on the cultural context, and Lesson 20 on the
historical context.

5
RESPECT THE
"ANALOGY OF
SCRIPTURE"

5. Presume that the author is consistent. You
give any writer the benefit of doubt as you try to
construe him in a way which does not make him contradict himself.

You may not be successful every time, but at
least you try. This sets the burden of proof on that
interpretation which makes the author contradict himself. We have already identified this canon as the
"Analogy of Scripture" (page 10:8). You can really
see how, though it is a very important and necessary
principle, it can open up a "Pandora's box."

Two conditions must be met before the absolute
tyranny of the context can be alleviated. First, you
must know the writer well: what his convictions are,
how he looks out on life. Second, there has to be a
close "horse race" between the various interpretations.
Then, sometimes you will pass over that interpretation
which the context could judge to come in first, perhaps
even the one which "places," opting for the one which
merely "shows," for that one really represents the
writer's view.

How close to a "photo-finish" the race has to
be before the interpreter can take such liberties, I
honestly do not know. I have no guidelines. I only
know that it has to be close, and only employed by
the one who really knows the author.

By the canon of the analogy of Scripture, one

may interpret a verse, the meaning of which is obscure, by another verse that is more transparent. By obscure, I mean grammatically or lexically or historically obscure, *not* incompatible to you!

You also want to take a look at all that a writer has had to say about a subject. With this kind of background, you can more precisely assess any particular statement the author has made about that subject.

When Scripture quotes Scripture, to exegete one appearance of a statement and ignore the other is obvious folly.

Parallel word formations might be important when comparing Scripture with Scripture, but the real thing you are after are passages which are parallel in ideas.

All language is surprisingly resilient and bends under determined pernicious pressure. So, when a person *tries* to make a text mean some particular thing, he usually succeeds.

Too often, the most avid Bible student is the one most totally committed to a particular doctrinal system. People reading this book probably come mostly from this group.

Too often, the Bible is nothing more than a repository of doctrinal propositions supporting the already systematized theology of the student. To him, exegesis is that ingenious device which produces the many interpretive options of any given text, so that he may choose the one among them which is most compatible to his already established doctrine. The good exegete has got to learn how to "tip-toe through the tulips."

Here, the detached and uninvolved exegete often parts company with the exegete whose religious faith has brought him to the conclusion that this phenomenal library called the "Bible" finds its unity in a common Author, God, Himself.

To the latter, the analogy of Scripture embraces the whole of its literature, and he anticipates an emerging, coherent view of the world, its Creator, and the Creator's ingenious plan to reconcile it to Himself. And that coherent view, he must keep on telling himself, he does not already possess. Rather, it is in the process of being formulated in his mind as his understanding of what God's Word means grows.

So, he hangs his doctrine on a hook before he opens his Bible; for if he doesn't bring it *to* his Bible, he gets it *from* his Bible.

6. Everybody knows you have to treat a poem as a poem, and a fable as a fable. Every literary form has to be taken for what it is. The Bible winds up, in the providence of God, a library with many of the common "genre," and one or two of its own:

Didactic:
    Legal, as in Leviticus
    Wisdom, as in Proverbs

Homily:
    Prophetic, as in Isaiah
    New Testament Sermons, as in the Sermon on the Mount

Narration:
    History, as in Joshua and Acts
       Prediction, as in the Olivet Discourse
       Gospel, as in Mark (unique to the New Testament)
    Fiction, as in the Parables

Poetry, as in the Psalms

Epistle, as in Colossians

Apocalypse, as in Revelation

Each one has its own set of hermeneutical rules. The larger works on hermeneutics go into detail about these. Too heavy for the beginner, but a significant advance, is Ryken's *The Literature of the Bible,* published by Zondervan in 1974. However, the categories which he uses are quite a bit different from the ones I gave.

Special rules for each genre are added to the general rules I am citing, and do not violate them.

7. Interpret a text in the frame of its own philosophical presuppositions. For example, you can't interpret "Hamlet" unless, temporarily at least, you believe in ghosts.

Sympathy with a text--as opposed to feelings of hostility--is a prerequisite to a true interpretation of any text, be it by Paul or by Marx.

Who would understand what Marx has written must look out at the world through Marx's eyes.

Whether or not I believe in the deity of Jesus, the writer of the Fourth Gospel did! If I am to interpret it correctly, then that is the view I must adopt, at least for the time being. (As for me, personally, I have no such temporal limitations, ברוך השם. With Marx? That's another thing!)

There is a grossly over-worked and abused idea which, if true, affects how we interpret the Scriptures. We call it, "Progressive Revelation." It must not be exploited as a convenient "dispose-all" for Old Testament principles of behavior which we might regard today as unethical; say, capital punishment, slavery, or polygamy. For we have nothing to indicate that revelation is getting better and better; that III John is superior to Isaiah.

I hope I do not shock you when I say that Jesus is no better than Jehovah.

In its rational form, progressive revelation is predicated upon the indubitable fact that the Bible represents redemption to be an historical event. It further represents itself as a library, primarily, of redemptive history. And, when a book of the Bible got written down, that part of the Bible became a part of the mix of redemptive history.

As history progressed, the Divine library grew, and the emerging picture of redemption, with its accouterments (e.g., ethics and eschatology), was filled out.

When you apply the term, "Progressive Revelation" to the Bible, you should mean about the same as when you would apply the same term to a three-act play. We have a better understanding of any previous scene when we find out how everything gets unraveled in the last scene of the last act.

COMMENTARY LAST

"Why have I had to wait so long before being able to use a commentary?" This delay has been deliberate! Only after you have exhausted your other resources, can you turn to the commentaries with a clear conscience.

Often, the temptation is to just look in a commentary. However, this becomes habit-forming, and you have become a parrot rather than a student! You stop developing your own spiritual discernment until it is even difficult to evaluate what the commentary says. The purpose of this course is to discourage you from being a lazy Bible student.

God holds you responsible for what you teach (James 3:1)! "But that's what the commentary said" will not excuse your teaching of a misinterpretation. Only after you have done your best to understand the text without a commentary, are you in a position to best evaluate the findings in a commentary.

THEIR AUTHORITY

Mind vs. Spirit

Spiritual truth is more important and easier to find than dry grammatical, textual and historical data. Just open the Bible with a yielded, cleansed, and blank mind, and the Holy Spirit will fill you with spiritual truths which bless your soul and those to whom you minister. After all, this is the only thing that really matters!

Or is it? Just what is the purpose of the Bible? What is "spiritual truth" as compared with "plain truth"? What is a blessing? Is the Bible merely a catalyst to trigger euphoria? Or is the Bible also a repository of important information concerning the nature of God and of man's relationship to God? If the answer to the latter question is in the affirmative, then intensive homework into dry textual, grammatical and historical data is necessary to understand precisely what the Bible teaches. To gain such an end requires the teaching ministry of the Holy Spirit in the dry academic study. It is not either / or. It is the Holy Spirit *AND* hard study, and this should be the standard for judging the quality of a commentary. The author or editor should be meticulous, accurate, and balanced in his exposition, giving a place to both "dry" factual data and application. He must be taught by the Holy Spirit in both.

One vs. Several

A single commentary can be an evil thing. Like an eye, it takes two of them to be beautiful. A cyclops is a monster. As you consult your commentary time and time again, you will succumb gradually to its persuasiveness. It will become your dictator. When you aren't sure what can be taken for assured truth and what must be treated with caution, you will have the tendency to take everything--lock, stock, and barrel--as gospel truth. The best way to protect yourself against the persuasive force of a single commentary is to pit it against another. It is wise to buy two commentaries, not just one!

When the commentaries refuse to be pitted against one another, but rather line up in agreement, then it is possible you have found the correct interpretation. You *may* be on the right track. One commentary has little authority. Several commentaries saying the same thing have more authority. However, do not expect total agreement in everything. Sometimes, because something is so obvious, a commentator may not mention it. However, when one commentary advances an idea explicitly rejected by others, BEWARE! Generally speaking, there is merit in a consensus of opinion.

KINDS OF COMMENTARIES

In respect to Homework

There are differences in respect to the amount of homework the commentator did. Commentaries vary a great deal as far as thoroughness in research is concerned. Needless to say, the best are done by those best prepared and who did the most thorough research beforehand. Since no one has time to study all the commentaries, it is wise to study the more deserving of them.

In respect to Reader Level

There are differences in respect to the level of the reader. Some commentaries are addressed to the Biblical novice, while others aim to help Biblical scholars. The latter are much more difficult to read, since the writer assumes his readers have greater background knowledge.

In respect to Objective

There are differences in respect to the objective of the commentary. In the Introduction (Int. 7) it was mentioned that commentaries may be devotional, homiletical, expositional, exegetical, or critical. This lesson will deal with the use of the last three, which are the ones that comment on the original Greek.

What do the commentaries talk about?

"Non-commentary sections" include articles treating authorship, date, destination, integrity, authenticity, and historical backgrounds, and often precede the commentary proper. Essays of special interest and relevance to the particular book may follow the commentary section.

"Commentary section" includes material which can be arranged under fourteen headings to include almost anything that the better commentaries discuss. They are numbered below so you can identify the subject matter on the sample commentary pages that follow:

1. Grammar: matters dealing with the grammar of the text.

2. Lexical: matters dealing with the meaning of a word and occasionally with its etymology.

3. Historical: matters dealing with historical events or conditions at the time of the writing of the text.

4. Geographical: matter dealing with the geography of the origin or destination of the writing, or of the events of the text.

5. Cultural: matters dealing with the cultural anthropology of the events of the text.

6. Analogy: matters dealing with the analogy of Scripture, the citing of other Scriptures relevant to the text, or statements about Biblical theology.

7. Translation: the author's translation, or a translation quoted for approval or criticism.

8. Interpretation: matters dealing with what the text means.

9. Application: applying the text to the reader's needs.

10. Context: matters dealing with the context and how the text fits in.

11. Summary: summation of the thought of the text.

12. Illustration: illuminating examples introduced by the author to explain the meaning of the text.

13. History of Interpretation: the citing of early scholars, and particularly of the Patristics, to show how the text has generally been interpreted.

14. Referral: the citing of modern sources where the text (or subject) is treated in further detail.

Examples from
Good Commentaries

The sample pages which contain examples of
these fourteen items are found on pages 13:9-15,
and are from the following commentaries:

Bigg, Charles. *A Critical and Exegetical Commentary on the Epistles of St. Peter and St. Jude.* Edinburgh: T. & T. Clark, 1901.

Fronmüller, G. F. C. "The Epistles General of Peter," *Commentary on the Holy Scriptures,* by John Peter Lange. Grand Rapids: Zondervan Publishing Co., 1960.

Hart, J. H. A. "The First Epistle General of Peter," *The Expositor's Greek Testament,* ed. W. Robertson Nicoll. Grand Rapids: Wm. B. Eerdmans Publishing Co., 1970.

Lenski, R. C. H. *The Interpretation of the Epistles of St. Peter, St. John and St. Jude.* Minneapolis: Augsburg Publishing House, 1966.

Kelly, J. N. D. *A Commentary of the Epistles of Peter and of Jude. Harper's New Testament Commentaries.* New York: Harper & Row, Publishers, 1969.

Selwyn, Edward Gordon. *The First Epistle of St. Peter.* London: Macmillan & Co., 1947.

What is a good commentary?

Up until now, our study has been limited to a
small list of technical, standard research tools,
with little arbitrary choice as to which to employ.
It is an entirely different ball game with commentaries. So, perhaps here is the place to pause to
discuss the quality of commentaries and in so doing,
offer some guidance in library quality-control in
general.

Scholarly

When we ask about what a good commentary is,
in this context, we mean a good scholarly one. For
this is really the gate we are expending so much time
and mental energy to crash. There are on the market
a number of single-volume commentaries which under-
take to explain the Bible from Genesis through Revelation. As excellent as any one might be, such a
limitation of space disqualifies such a book for meeting our needs on the level of Biblical study we are
engaged in.

Old vs. New

Christians have been writing commentaries
throughout the whole lifespan of the Church. Biblical
exegesis is a discipline which moves like a glacier.

The best commentary isn't always the latest. Trying to keep up with the Joneses, Biblical exposition has grossly inflated contemporary efforts beyond their true value. Very little is going on in Hellenistic history and philology. The only excitement on the block is the discovery of the spin-offs resulting from the confrontation of Greco-Roman culture with Semitic culture, and the liberation of Biblical Greek from its Classical bondage, only to be enslaved once again; now by the Semites.

So, an old commentary can be the best. Age plays only a minor role when evaluating the quality of a commentary.

Really, we are talking about the person who writes the commentary. Though sometimes worse, it will never be any better than the person who writes it. It is the mark of the mature scholar to pay more attention to the author of a book than to its title. It doesn't seem very fair for the brand new writer; but he, himself, hopes that his second and third book will find a more ready acceptance, and in so doing, genuflects in the direction of the "system," that treats him so unfairly.

Commentary vs. Commentator

The commentator must first convince an editor. It is indeed rather shocking to learn of the extensive latitude in quality tolerated by differing publishing firms. Some of them preserve their integrity sufficiently to refuse to publish a bad book, even when convinced it will sell, yet at the same time will publish a good book when they know it won't. Oxford, Cambridge and T. & T. Clark are like that. And, there are others, but not many. So, if you know your publishers, they can be of some help, but it isn't a very good test by itself.

Commentator vs. Editor and Publisher

A large percentage of the commentaries you will be using will be one in a series of commentaries, composing a set covering the whole Bible, or occasionally, the New or Old Testament.

In most of these, various books of the Bible are done by different scholars. More often than not, the scholarship is a bit spotty. And, nowhere would all the contributors be of equal competency. Often, you cannot buy a single volume of the set, but must buy all of it, the worse with the better.

What makes a good commentator? As far as morality goes, he has to be honest and industrious. He must not be lazy and he must have disciplined himself to be objective, as well. Anybody can say, "I call them as I see them." But, only the objective scholar

Qualifications

can do a good job of "calling them *as they really are.*" This, he sometimes must do, even when he devoutly wishes that he could say something else. And, he diciplines himself so that he doesn't cop-out by saying nothing when the evidence is against his wishes. When you read his commentary, you have a hard time detecting his special brand of theology.

As far as his homework is concerned, he is competent. For one thing, he knows his history. And by this, we include the cultural anthropology and geography of the Bible. And, I cannot see how a New Testament scholar can be adequate in this department if he does not have a working knowledge of the Rabbinic literature. He knows the languages well in which the Bible was written. And, he understands well the current state of this art. He is broadmind-ed in his investigation, knowing what his contempo-raries are thinking and what directions they are heading. He is not isolated in some "golden ghetto," committing academic incest with his compatriots who share his own views to a "T."

Primarily, he is a biblicist. By this, I mean he takes the Bible simply for what it says and ex-plains it in the light of its own presuppositions. Whether or not he is a biblicist by conviction (as I happen to be), he writes like one. He explains the convictions of the writer, never correcting them.

> Though I was never adequately endowed in this area, what modicum of humility I possess recoils at the preposterous presumption that I might improve anything Moses or Isaiah or Jesus or Paul said. The priest arranging the loaves of bread on the "presence table," if he should forget even for a moment where he is, should be summarily removed from office. The first prerequisite of the Bible commentator is that of awe. He writes with his shoes off, for he is painfully aware of the character of the ground upon which he is standing.

HOW CAN I TELL?

Every Bible student, be he a "high-roader" or a "low-roader," wants to use the best commentaries. But how is he to know? Not by the publisher's blurb on the dust jacket, for sure!

Outside Help

He can learn about new books in the book review section in the academic journals. There is a lot of latitude in the quality of the book reviewer between journals, so compare them. Who is more thorough, more objective, more knowledgeable? Who evaluates a book on the basis of the theological compatability between the book and the editorial policy of the journal?

Then, there are published bibliographies; many of them, and more and more each year. These include older books, also. The one I personally like the best is compiled by David M. Scholer, *A Basic Bibliographic Guide for New Testament Exegesis,* published by Eerdmans in 1973. But, there are many other very good ones, such as *The Minister's Library,* by Cyril Barber, published by Baker in 1974, and already supplemented in 1976.

Look for footnote frequency. As you begin reading more and more worthwhile books, you will be glancing down at the bibliographic footnotes. Certain titles and authors will be cropping up frequently enough for you to get acquainted with them. It will occur to you that if many of the writers you respect enough to read respect those commentaries enough to quote them, they must be very good books, like Lightfoot on *Galatians.*

1. Know your authors and publishers. They will give an indication of the book's worth. I buy everything F. F. Bruce writes, for example. I pay special attention to T. & T. Clark, Oxford and Cambridge publications.

A Do-it-Yourself Kit

2. Use before you buy. Take advantage of the libraries near you. Don't assume they don't have it. What libraries buy depends largely upon the frequency of inquiries. If too far away, pressure your church library to buy serious Bible study tools along with missionary biographies and Christian novels. When visiting the big city, set some time aside for library browsing. I have made it a habit never to buy a book until I have wanted it three times.

3. Compare what several books say about the same verse. You will develop good judgment about which is better.

4. Be sure you identify the purpose of the commentary. Don't ask it to do what it was not designed to do. Don't expect Matthew Henry to exegete a *crux interpretum.*

5. Your own growing experience with study in various subjects and books will aid you in recognizing a good book when you see it.

6. And, your previous research in a given text gives you the best possible grounds to evaluate commentaries which comment on it. Remember, the rule is "commentary last."

Other Commentary
Sources

There are other excellent commentary sources than formal book commentaries which give excellent comments on shorter passages:

Theologies

Monographs on special themes, like "The Lord's Prayer," "Parables," or books on problems, like Goodspeed's *Problems of New Testament Translation,* or Field's *Notes* (if you can find a copy), or books of essays

Bible dictionaries and encyclopedias

Grammars and lexicons, especially Kittel's *Theological Dictionary of the New Testament*

"Festschriften" (books of essays written in honor of a famous scholar by other famous scholars), annuals, and academic journals

However, for the fledgling student, his hands are full just getting a handle on the formal commentaries.

(Hort). The simile, which is very appropriate for those who are ἀναγεγεννημένοι, recalls Matt. xviii. 3. In St. Peter's view Christians are always babes, and therefore also always recently born. This is in substance the explanation of Dr. Hort and von Soden. Kühl insists that ἀρτιγέννητα must mean that the readers had been quite recently converted, and finds in the word a confirmation of his view that the readers of the Epistle did not belong to Churches founded by St. Paul, and that the Epistle was written before Romans. But this is too large a conclusion from so slender a premiss. Even if the readers had been converted by St. Paul, their Christianity was still young. But in respect of Eternity, as von Soden well says, the beginning of the new life must always seem a thing of yesterday.

ἐπιποθήσατε . . . σωτηρίαν. "Desire the sincere milk of the word that ye may grow thereby" (A.V.). "Long for the spiritual milk, which is without guile, that ye may grow thereby unto salva-tion" (R.V.). The words εἰς σωτηρίαν are undoubtedly genuine; see Tischendorf's note. Λογικὸν γάλα is understood by the great majority of commentators, as by the A.V., to mean "milk of the word," on the grounds that St. Peter is recalling the λόγος of i. 23 (just as in ἄδολον he recalls the δόλον of the preceding verse), and that λόγος in the New Testament always means "word." Of those who thus translate the phrase, some regard "milk of the word" as meaning "the milk which is the word" ("lac uerbi est periphrasis "uerbi ipsius," Bengel); others, "the milk which is contained in the word," that is to say, specially Christ (so Kühl, Weiss, Keil, von Soden). This latter point seems unimportant, if we consider what St. Peter has said touching the relation of Christ to Scripture.

Dr. Hort insists that λογικός in the Stoic writers (even in Aris-totle; see Bonitz, Index), in later Greek, and commonly in Philo, means rational, and can mean nothing else; further, that in Rom. xii. 1 (the only other passage in the Greek Bible where the word is found) it bears this sense, and that Eusebius uses the word with the same meaning. It may be observed, however, that St. Paul does not use the phrase λογικὸν γάλα, and that his λογικὴ λατρεία corre-sponds to St. Peter's πνευματικὰς θυσίας; that the usage of St. Paul can never be compared with that of St. Peter without great caution and reserve; that λόγος, in the sense of the word of God, or scripture, is unknown to secular Greek; and that λογικός, "belonging to the word," is at any rate strictly analogous to λογικός, "belonging to the human reason." Finally, as it is certainly the habit of St. Peter to pick up and repeat his words, it would seem that the balance of argument is in favour of the translation of the A.V. "Ἄδολος does not mean "unadulterated," nor exactly "veracious," as in Aesch. Ag. 95, χρήματος ἁγνοῦ μαλακαῖς ἀδόλοισι παρηγορίας, but "guileless," as the pattern of sincerity, and as forbidding all δόλος, cf. ii. 22. Γάλα is probably a reminiscence of Isa. lv. 1; if so, there is an

additional reason for taking λογικόν as above. In any case the word is suggested to St. Peter quite simply by ἀναγεγεννημένοι and βρέφη. The passage marks better than any other the difference between St. Peter, the Epistle to the Hebrews, and St. Paul. In St. Peter's eyes the Christian is always a babe, always in need of mother's milk, always growing, not to perfection, but to deliverance.

In Heb. v. 12, vi. 2, milk is the catechism, the rudiments of the faith, including repentance, faith, baptisms, laying on of hands, resurrection, judgment, and is contrasted with "the solid meat" of the perfect, who have a formed character (διὰ τὴν ἕξιν), can judge for themselves, and do not need a guide. This is an adaptation of the teaching of Philo (de migr. Abr. 9 (i. 443), ἕτερος νηπίων καὶ ἕτερος τελείων χῶρός ἐστιν: 6 (i. 440), ἐν ταύτῃ τῇ χώρᾳ καὶ γένος ἐστὶ οσι τὸ αὐτομαθές, τὸ αὐτοδίδακτον, τὸ νηπίας καὶ γαλακτώδους τροφῆς ἀμέτοχον: 16. 39, οὐ θέλεις ἤδη, ὡς τὰ παιδία, ἀπογαλακτισθῆναι καὶ ἅπτεσθαι τροφῆς στερεωτέρας; It takes up the old philosophic distinction between the βίος πρακτικός and θεωρητικός, and regards the Christian as moving up naturally and properly through instruction, obedi-ence, law, discipline, into knowledge and freedom. This was the view adopted by Clement of Alexandria and Origen, and indeed by the whole of the later Church. It represents a via media between St. Peter and St. Paul. The latter draws the same distinction as Hebrews between γάλα and βρῶμα (1 Cor. iii. 1, 2), but regards the "babes in Christ" as οὐ πνευματικοί, σάρκινοι, or σαρκικοί. Here also the distinction is probably based, if not on Philo, on some cognate Rabbinical teaching. St. Paul is vexed with "the babe," who is in fact the weaker brother, the formalist, and needs not to be carried further along the same line, but to be put upon a different line. Neither to St. Paul nor to Hebrews is "milk" the biblical milk of Isaiah, nor is "the babe" the little child of the Gospels. St. Peter not only differs from them both, but he differs as being more scriptural and evangelical. This point, which is in many ways of the gravest importance, has not received the attention it deserves.

3. εἰ ἐγεύσασθε ὅτι χρηστὸς ὁ Κύριος. "If ye have tasted that the Lord is good." "Milk" suggests a quotation from Ps. xxxiii. (xxxiv.) 9, γεύσασθε καὶ ἴδετε ὅτι χρηστὸς ὁ Κύριος. The words καὶ ἴδετε are omitted as not quite suiting the milk. A.V., R.V. translate "the Lord is gracious," but we need an adjective that will suit the figure of speech. "In the Psalm ὁ Κύριος stands for Jehovah, as it very often does, the LXX. inserting and omitting the article with Κύριος on no apparent principle. On the other hand, the next verse shows St. Peter to have used ὁ Κύριος in its commonest, though not universal, N.T. sense of Christ. It would be rash, however, to conclude that he meant to identity Jehovah with Christ. No such identification can be clearly made out in the N.T." (Hort). But

Taken from *A Critical and Exegetical Commentary on the Epistles of St. Peter and St. Jude* by Charles Bigg, in The International Critical Commentary, edited by S. R. Driver, A. Plummer and C. A. Briggs, published by T. & T. Clark, and is used by permission.

13:10

raiment." The figures of laying aside and putting on clothes was peculiarly apposite because the early Christians were wont to lay aside their old garments and to exchange them for white and clean apparel when they were baptized and regenerated. It is necessary to observe that the exhortation to laying aside is only addressed to those who had the new man, while the unbelieving and unregenerate had first to receive another mind [μετάνοια, after-thought, after-wisdom, a change of disposition must precede baptism and new-birth.—M.]. The vices to be laid aside bear upon the relation to our neighbour and exert a deadly influence on brotherly love. κακία [*nocendi cupiditas*] denotes here, in particular, malicious disposition toward others, aiming at their hurt, injury and pain, and assuming various manifestations, cf. 1 Cor. xiii. 5. The accomplishment of such evil intent necessitates lying, cunning and other artifices; its concealment requires hypocrisy and dissembling. The sense of dependence on those before whom dissimulation is practised, the sight of their happiness, the shame felt in the conscience in the presence of the virtuous—excite envy, and envy engenders all manner of evil, detracting and injurious speaking. [*Malitia malo delectatur alieno; invidia bono cruciatur alieno; dolus duplicat cor; adulatio duplicat linguam; detractatio vulnerat famam.*—Augustine.—M.]. 'Thus,' observed Flacius, 'one vice ever genders another.' Huss says of κακαλαλιά that it takes place in various ways, either by denying or darkening a neighbour's virtues, and either by attributing to him evil or imputing to him evil designs in doing good.

VER. 2. **As newborn babes.**—This goes back to ch. i. 23. The connection is similar to ch. i. 14. They had been addressed as children of obedience, now their young and tender state is mentioned as a reason why they should seek strength in the word of God. 'Newborn babes' was a current expression among the Jews for proselytes and neophytes. As the desire and need of nourishment predominate in the former, so they ought to predominate in babes in Christ. The expression so far from being derogatory, sets forth the tenderness of their relation to God, and implies the idea of guilelessness, cf. Is. xl. 11; Lk. xviii. 15, etc.

Long for—word.—ἐπιποθεῖν denotes intense and ever recurring desire. While the regenerate experience a longing after the word of God, by which they had been begotten, similar to the desire of newborn babes for their mother's milk, Ps. cxix. 31. 72; xix. 11, still the hereditary sin which yet cleaves to them renders it necessary that they should be constantly urged to the diligent use of the divine word in order to partake of it.—Milk, in opposition to solid food, 1 Cor. iii. 2; Heb. v. 12; vi. 1, signifies the rudiments of Christian doctrine, not only its simple representation adapted to the capacity of the weak but also the more easily intelligible articles of Christianity. In this place, however, where no such antithesis exists, the figure comprises the sum-total of Christianity, the whole Gospel. Milk is the first, most simple, most refreshing, most wholesome food, especially for children; so is the word of God, cf. Is. lv. 1. The most advanced Christians ought to consider themselves children, in respect of what they are to be hereafter. "Christ, the crucified, is milk for babes, food for the advanced." Augustine. Clement of Alexandria suggests the partaking of the incarnate *Logos*.—λογικόν is best explained by the Apostle's peculiarity to elucidate his figures by additional illustrations, cf. ch. i. 13. 23. It is milk contained in and flowing from the word, spiritual milk, which, as Luther explains, is drawn with the soul. The rendering '*reasonable*' is against the *usus loquendi* of the New Testament, and equally inadmissible in Rom. xii. 1. [Alford renders 'spiritual' after Allioli and Kistemaker.—M.] The nature of this milk is further defined by ἄδολον, which means unadulterated, pure, cf. 2 Cor. iv. 2; ii. 17. [ἄδολον seems rather to be in contrast with δόλον in v. 1.—M.] It is consequently doctrine that is not compounded with human wisdom and thus rendered inefficacious. For the word of God has the property that it exerts purifying, liberating, illuminating and consoling influences only in its purity and entireness. Irenæus says of the heretics: "They mix gypsum with the milk, they taint the heavenly doctrine with the poison of their errors."

ἐν αὐτῷ, receiving it into your innermost soul, making it your full property. Growth in holiness depends on the constant assimilation of the word. "The mother who gave them birth, nourishes them also."—Harless.

VER. 3. **If, otherwise ye have tasted.**—7
A conditional statement is often by emphasis ac- 1
cepted as real. Grotius renders the sense well;
"I know that you will this, as surely as you—cf.
Rom. viii. 9; 2 Thes. i. 6." This form of speech 6
contains also an invitation to self-examination.
Calov perceives a connection with ver. 1. "The 10
more you eradicate the bitter root of malice, the
more also do you taste the sweetness of the good-
ness of the Lord." Cf. Song of Sol. ii. 3; v. 13; 6
Sir. xxiii. 27. The expression, to taste with reference to the figure of milk, and with full allusion to Ps. xxxiv. 9, denotes experience of the 6
essential virtue of a thing as perceived by the 8
sense of taste. It is transferred very properly
to the experiences of the soul which enters into
and unites with the object in order to know it in
all its bearings. Cf. Heb. vi. 5; ii. 9. [Alford 6
says, "The infant once put to the breast desires 12
it again."—M.]

[Wordsworth quotes the words of Augustine
(*Serm.* 353), addressed to the newly *baptized:*
"These words are specially applicable to you,
who are yet fresh in the infancy of spiritual re-
generation. For to you mainly the Divine Ora-
cles speak, by the Apostle St. Peter, Having
laid aside all malice, and all guile, as new- 13
born infants desire ye the "*rationabile et in-
nocens lac, ut in illo crescatis ad salutem,*" if ye have
tasted that the Lord is gracious (*dulcis.*) And we
are witnesses that ye have tasted it . . . . Che- 9
rish, therefore, this spiritual infancy. The infancy of the strong is humility. The manhood
of the weak is pride."—M.]

That the deed is good.—[Friendly, Germ.] χρηστός applied to tender, pleasant-tasting solids and liquids, to the sweet flavour of old wine, Luke v. 39; then to persons, kindly, friendly, condescending, Eph. iv. 32; Luke vi. 35. Ὁ κύριος is the Lord Jesus, ver. 4, who invites us to Him-

54 — ΠΕΤΡΟΥ Α   II.

II. 1 ῥῆμα τὸ εὐαγγελισθὲν εἰς ὑμᾶς.   ἀποθέμενοι οὖν πᾶσαν
κακίαν καὶ πάντα δόλον καὶ ὑπό κρίσιν καὶ φόνους[1] κ̀ πάσας
2 καταλαλιὰς ὡς ἀρτιγέννητα βρέφη τὸ λογικὸν ἄδολον

[1] φόνους is an error (peculiar to Codex Vaticanus) for φθόνους.

CHAPTER II.—Vv. 1-10. Continuation of practical admonition with appeal to additional ground-principles illustrating the thesis of i. 10.

Ver. 1. *Put away then all malice—all guile and hypocrisy and envy—all back-biting.* οὖν resumes διὸ (i. 13). The faults to be put away fall into three groups, divided by the prefix *all*, and correspond to the virtues of i. 22 (ὑπόκρισιν ἀνυπόκριτον). The special connection of the command with the preceding Scripture would require the expression of the latent idea, that such faults as these are inspired by the prejudices of the natural man and belong to *the fashion of the world*, which is *passing away* (i. John ii. 17).—ἀποθέμενοι, *putting off.* Again participle with imperative force. St. Peter regards the metaphor of removal as based on the idea of washing off filth, *cf.* σαρκὸς ἀπόθεσις ῥύπου (iii. 21). St. James (i. 21, διὸ ἀποθέμενοι πᾶσαν ῥυπαρίαν καὶ περισσείαν κακίας) which seems to combine these two phrases and to deduce the familiarity of the spiritual sense of *filth* (*cf.* Apoc. xxii. 11, ῥυπαρὸς κ̀γιος). St. Paul has the same word but associates it with the putting off of clothing (Col. iii. 5 ff.; Eph. iv. 22; Rom. xiii. 12—all followed by ἐνδύσασθαι).—κακίαν, probably *malice* rather than *wickedness*. Peter is occupied with their mutual relations and considering what hinders brotherly love, not their vices, if any, as vice is commonly reckoned. So James associates the removal of κακία with *courtesy*; and St. Paul says *let all bitterness and anger and wrath and shouting and ill-speaking be removed from you with all malice* (Eph. iv. 31; *cf.* Col. iii. 8). κ. is generally eagerness to hurt one's neighbour (Suidas)—the feeling which prompts *backbitings* and may be subdivided into *guile, hypocrisy, and envy*.—δόλον, *Guile* was characteristic of Jacob, the eponymous hero of the Jews, but not part of the true Israelite (ἴδε ἀληθῶς Ἰσραηλίτης ἐν ᾧ δόλος οὐκ ἔστιν John i. 47). It was also rife among the Greeks (μεστοὺς . . δόλου, Rom. i. 29) as the Western world has judged from experience (Greek and grec = cardsharper; compare characters of Odysseus and Hermes). δ. is here con-

trasted with *obedience to the truth* (i. 22). in v. 22, iii. 10.—ὑπόκρισιν is best explained by the saying Isaiah prophesied about you hypocrites. . . . *This people honours me with their lips but their heart is far away from me* (Mark vii. 6 f. = Isa. xxix. 13). It stands for ḤNP *profane, impure* in Symmachus' version of Ps. xxxv. 16; so ὑποκριτὴς in LXX of Job (xxxiv. 30, xxxvi. 13), and Aquila (Prov. xi. 9), etc. In 2 Macc. vi. 25, ὑ is used of (unreal?) —not secret) *apostasy* perhaps in accordance with the earlier sense of ḤNP, which only in post-Biblical Hebrew and Aramaic = *hypocrisy*. In His repeated denunciations of the hypocrites Jesus repeated the Pharisees description of the Sadducees *that live in hypocrisy with the saints* (Ps. Sol. iv. 7). Polybius has ὑ. in the classical sense of oratorical delivery, and once contrasted with the purpose of speakers (xxxv. 2, 13).—καταλαλιὰς, *detractiones* (Vulgate), of external slanders in ii. 12, iii. 11. For internal calumnies, *cf.* Jas. iv. 11; 2 Cor. xii. 20 illustrates one special case, for φλυαρῶσις καταλαλιαί correspond to εἰς ὑπὲρ τοῦ ἑνὸς φυσιοῦσθε κατὰ τοῦ ἑτέρου of 1 Cor. iv. 6 (*cf.* i. 12).

Ver. 2. *as . . . inasmuch as you are new-born babes: cf.* ἀναγεγεννημένοι (i. 23). The development of the metaphor rests upon the saying, *unless ye be turned and become as the children* (ὡς τὰ παιδία) *ye shall not enter into the kingdom of heaven* (Matt. xviii. 3).—βρέφος (only here in metaphorical sense) is substituted for παιδία (preserved by St. Paul in 1 Cor. xiv. 20) as = *babes at the breast.* Ἀπαιδίον might have lost its traditional innocence but not a βρέφος (= either *child unborn* as Luke i. 41, or *suckling* in classical Greek). For the origin of the metaphor, which appears also in the saying of R. Jose, "the proselyte is a child just born," compare Isa. xxviii. 9, *Whom will he teach knowledge? . . Them that are weaned from the milk and drawn from the breasts*, which the Targum renders, *To whom was the law given? . . . Was it not to the house of Israel which is beloved beyond all peoples?* —τὸ . . . γάλα. The quotation of ver. 3 suggests that the *milk* is Christ;

55 — ΠΕΤΡΟΥ Α   1-5.

γά λα ἐπιποθήσατε ἵνα ἐν αὐτῷ αὐξηθῆτε[1] εἰς σωτηρίαν 3, 4
εἰ ἐγεύσα σθε ὅτι χρηστὸς ὁ Κς̄   πρὸς ὃν προσερχόμε νοι
λίθον ζῶντα ὑπ' ἀ θρώπων μὲν ἀποδε δοκιμασμένον παρὰ δὲ
Θῶ ἐκλεκτὸν ἔντι μον· καὶ αὐτοὶ ὡς λίθοι ζῶντες οἰκοδο-5
μεῖσθε οἶκος πνευματικὸς εἰς ἱεράτευμα ἅγιον ἀνενέγκαι

[1] The variant ἀξιωθῆτε for αὐξηθῆτε illustrates the possibilities of variation and consequently of emendation: at the same time it directs attention to the omni-potence of God and the relative impotence of man.

compare St. Paul's explanation of the tradition of the Rock which followed the Israelites in the desert (1 Cor. x. 4) and the *living water* of John iv. 14. Milk is the proper food for babes; compare Isa. lv. 1, *buy . . milk* (LXX, στέαρ) *without money* (*cf.* i. 18). This milk is *guileless* (*cf.* δόλον of ver. 1) *pure or un-adulterated* (*cf.* μηδὲ δολοῦντες τὸν λόγον τοῦ θεοῦ, 2 Cor. iv. 2). The interpretation of λογικόν (pertaining to λόγος) is doubtful. But the use of λόγος just above (i. 23) probably indicates the sense which St. Peter put upon the adjective he borrowed (?) from Rom. xii. 1, τὴν λογικὴν λατρείαν. There and elsewhere λ. = *rationabilis, spiritual*; here belong-ing to contained in the Word of God, delivered by prophet or by evangelist. St. Paul in his use of λ. and of the meta-phor of *milk* (solid food, 1 Cor. iii. 1 ff.) follows Philo and the Stoics.—ἵνα . . . σωτηρίαν, *that fed thereon ye may grow up* (*cf.* Eph. iv. 14 f.) *unto salvation; cf.* Jas. i. 21, "receive the ingrafted word which is able to save your souls".

Ver. 3. St. Peter adopts the language of Ps. xxxiv. 9, omitting καὶ ἐδέτε so inap-propriate to γάλα. Χρηστὸς (identical in sound with χριστός) = *dulcis* (Vulg.) or *kind* (*cf.* Χρηστότης θεοῦ, Rom. ii. 4, xi. 22). Compare Heb. vi. 4 f. γευσαμένους τῆς δωρεᾶς τῆς ἐπουρανίου . . . καὶ καλὸν γευσαμένους θεοῦ ῥῆμα.

Vv. 4-10. Passages of scripture prov-ing that Christ is called stone are first utilised, then quoted, and finally ex-pounded. The transition from *milk* to the *stone* may be explained by the pro-phecy *the hills shall flow with milk* (Joel iii. 18), as the stone becomes a mountain according to Dan. iii. 21 f.; or by the legend to which St. Paul refers (1 Cor. x. 4); compare also ποτίσαι of Isa. xliii. 20, which is used in ver. 9. This collection of texts can be traced back through Rom. ix. 32 f. to its origin in the saying of Mark xii. 10 f.; Cyprian (Test. ii. 16 f.) gives a still richer form.

Ver. 4. πρὸς ὃν προσερχ. from

Ps. xxxiv. 6, προσελθόντες πρὸς αὐτὸν (Heb. and Targum, *they looked unto Him*; Syriac, *look ye* . .). Cyprian uses Isa. ii. 2 f.; Ps. xxiii. 3 f. to prove that the stone becomes a mountain to which the Gentiles *come* and the just ascend.—λίθον ζῶντα, a paradox which has no obvious precedent in O.T. Gen. xlix. 24 speaks of the Shepherd the stone of Israel, but Onkelos and LXX substitute ʾBN *thy father* for ʾBN *stone*. The Targum of Isa. viii. 14, how-ever, has ʾBN *a striking stone*, for ʾBN which might be taken as meaning *reviving or living stone*, if connected with the foregoing instead of the follow-ing words. The LXX supports this con-nection and secures a *good* sense by in-serting a negative; the Targum gives a *bad* sense throughout. ὑπ' . . . ἔντιμον, *though by men rejected, yet in God's sight elect precious.* ἀποδεδοκ. ἐκλ. ἔντ. from Isa. xxviii. 16 (see ver. 6). ἀνθρώπων is probably due to Rabbinic exegesis "read not ʾBN *builders* but ʾBN *sons of men*". St. Peter insists upon the contrast between God's judg-ment and man's in the sermon of Acts ii.

Ver. 5. Fulfilment of the saying, *Destroy this temple and in three days I will raise it* (John ii. 19). Christians live to God through Jesus Christ (Rom. vi. 11). For this development of the figure of building, *cf.* especially Eph. ii. 20 ff.—οἰκοδομεῖσθε, indicative rather than imperative. "It is remarkable that St. Peter habitually uses the aorist for his imperatives, even when we might expect the present; the only exceptions (two or three) are preceded by words re-moving all ambiguity, ii. 11, 17, iv. 12 f." (Hort).—οἶκος.—ἅγιον, *a spiritual house for an holy priesthood.* The con-nection with *priesthood* (Heb. x. 21) and the offering of sacrifices points to the special sense of the House of God, *i.e.*

Word; by adding ἄδολον he brings out the thought that this milk is unlike that found in any other λόγος: it is without the least guile to mislead or to deceive. All other (human) word (teaching, doctrine, spoken or written) is not "guileless." This divine Word is; "guileless" states the moral quality of this Word-milk. It is perfectly safe for babes to take although they, being just born, have no ability to be careful as to what they drink. We do not think that ἄδολον means "unadulterated." As far as the two adjectives are concerned, why should we suppose that only the first and not also the second indicates that "the milk" is figurative, spiritual milk — if such an indication were necessary, which it is not?

"Long for this milk!" Peter writes and uses the decisive aorist imperative exactly as he did in 1:13, 17, 23. These aorists are used because they are stronger than present imperatives would be. Call them constative if you will. The implication is: long for this milk and for none other. Even Christians often hanker after the fleshpots of Egypt and grow tired of the simple, wholesome, saving Word, which is manna for the soul. To cease longing for the divine milk is the most serious sign of spiritual decline, which soon ends in spiritual death. A starved babe pales and dies. Note Ps. 119:20: "My soul breaketh for the longing that it hath unto thy judgments at all times."

"In order that in connection with it you may be made to grow unto salvation" does not mean that the readers cease to be newborn babes and grow up to be men. Paul speaks of childhood and manhood in this way by making full-grown manhood the ideal. Not so Peter. As he states no contrast between milk and solid food, so he has no advance from babes to men. We are ever babes, ever long for this divine milk, and so grow unto salvation, the end of our faith,

salvation of souls (1:9). Ἐν means "in connection with" this milk.

We should not extend the idea of the verb αὐξηθῆτε as though it indicates a growth from babyhood to old age. It is an aorist passive and deals only with babes, who grow in the sense of being alive and hearty and thus as babes attain eternal salvation. God makes them grow thus; while the aorist is constative it has its termination only in salvation and not in any stage of growth. Peter's thought is quite simple and should not be made complex.

3) When Peter attaches the condition of reality:—"if you did taste that the Lord is benignant," he asks his readers to recall their experience with the Lord and counts on the fact that they have found the Lord χρηστός, kind or benignant, bestowing only what is wholesome and pleasant. There is no play on words between χρηστός and Χριστός, for Peter uses Κύριος, and the adjective that is derived from χράομαι has nothing to do with χρίω, "to anoint, the Anointed." He alludes to Ps. 34:9: "Oh, taste and see that the Lord is good!" Peter is not quoting; he simply appropriates the psalmist's statement to express his own thought. What is true of Yahweh is equally true of Christ.

Having tasted that the Lord is benignant does not make the Lord "the milk" as some suppose. They overlook the passive verb "be made to grow," which implies an agent, namely this beneficent Lord. It would be a strange conception to picture the Lord as milk. Nor does Peter say, nor does the psalmist say that we are to taste the Lord but that we are to taste "that he is good," beneficent in bestowing this precious milk of the Word upon us, in making us grow unto salvation. Do we know of anyone else who has such food for us? What we taste is his benignity, which we experience in his Word. "Taste" is a suitable word for both "milk" and benignity.

THE FIRST EPISTLE OF PETER   ii. 2-3

honey (always linked with milk in our main texts, as in Ex. iii. 8) discourages confidence. Actually, the comparison of religious teaching with milk is found in 1 Cor. iii. 2; Heb. v. 12, and is used by Philo (*Agric.* 9; *Migr. Abr.* 29), and a very striking parallel is provided by the Qumran hymns (vii. 21, where 'the children of grace' are pictured as drinking in true doctrine as infants drink milk at the breast). So, too, in the Christian but markedly Semitic Odes of Solomon (viii. 16: cf. xix. 1-5) the enlightenment which the Lord bestows is likened to milk from His breasts. All this evidence tends to suggest that the writer did not need to look beyond his Jewish environment for his imagery.

When children feed on good milk, they **grow up** to physical maturity; the Christian who drinks in the gospel is nourished **by it for salvation**, i.e. the glory and blessedness which God has prepared for His elect at the End (see on i. 5). The Greek original for **by it** (*en autōi*) literally means 'in it' or even 'in him': It would have been more natural to write 'through it' (*di autou*), but he prefers the ambiguous *en autōi* because he does not distinguish between the word which is the Christian's **milk** and Christ. His thought has already shifted to Him, and as a spur he evokes his readers' experience: **seeing 'you have tasted that the Lord is good'**. For **seeing** the Greek has *ei* (lit. 'if'), where the particle is not conditional but, as frequently in the NT (cf. i. 17; Mt. vi. 30; Lk. xii. 28; Rom. vi. 8; etc.), states as a supposition what is actually the case. The sentence is a loose quotation from Ps. xxxiv. 8, where the LXX gives, 'Taste and see that the Lord is good'. In the original 'the Lord' of course denotes Yahweh, but the Christian understanding of the Psalter naturally transferred the title to Christ. The verse brings out the full significance of the spiritual nourishment by which Christians are sustained. If in a sense it is God's word, in a deeper sense it is Christ Himself, whom they receive in word and sacrament. For a fine parallel, cf. Od. Sol. xix. 1: 'A cup of milk was presented to me, and I drank it in the sweet graciousness of the Lord'. The adjective (*chrēstos*) should not be translated 'kind' or 'gracious', a meaning which would be appropriate in other contexts; as applied to foods it had the special sense 'delicious to the taste' (e.g. Jer. xxiv. 2-5; Lk. v. 39), which is the one required here.

86

ii. 3-4   THE ELECT PEOPLE OF GOD

Our writer's citation of Ps. xxxiv. 8 is not haphazard; the whole psalm was present in his mind as he wrote the letter, and must have been familiar to his readers. He will have recourse to it again in the next verse; in iii. 10-12 he will quote verses 12-16, and there are close verbal correspondences between i. 15-18 and the LXX of verses 4, 9 and 22. Its theme is broadly the same as that of the letter: if in distress you seek the Lord, He will deliver you from all your troubles (4), for 'though the afflictions of the righteous are many, the Lord will rescue them out of them all' (19). In appealing to 8, however, is he thinking in general terms of the satisfaction his readers have derived from the gospel, or of something more specific? Because of its obvious aptness Ps. xxxiv came to be closely associated with the euchar- ist, being sung during the communion (*Apost. const.* viii. 13. 16; Cyril of Jerusalem, *Cat. myst.* v. 20; Jerome, *Ep.* lxxi. 6; Liturgy of St. James; Mozarabic Liturgy), and 8 in particular was applied by the fathers to partaking of it. In what follows the writer will be dwelling on the priestly aspect of the Christian community and on its 'spiritual sacrifices'. In this context (note also the suppression of 'and see' in the LXX) it is hard to evade the conclusion that the psalm was already being understood in a eucharistic sense and that he is reminding the Asian Christians of the blessings they have received through sacramental fellow- ship. If accepted, this interpretation runs counter to the theory that the bulk of 1 Peter is a baptismal liturgy; if it were, the imperative in Ps. xxxiv. 8 ('Taste . . .') would surely have been preserved as a fitting invitation to the communion which fol- lowed baptism, whereas the alteration to **you have tasted** insinuates that the readers are already communicants.

The writer now comes to his main thought, that as Christians they form an élite community assured of God's protection. His opening words, **to whom coming**, are a further echo of Ps. xxxiv, verse 5 of which reads in the LXX, 'Come to him (*proselthate pros*: the same verb and preposition) and be en- lightened'. The idea he is working up to is that of triumph in the midst of apparent disaster. So, suddenly switching from his picture of Christ as the Christian's spiritual sustenance, he represents Him as the **living stone, rejected indeed by men but chosen and honoured in God's sight**. This description

87

Taken from *A Commentary on the Epistles of Peter and of Jude* by J.N.D. Kelly in the New Testament Commentary series, published by A & C Black (Publishers) Limited, and is used by permission.

156 FIRST EPISTLE OF ST. PETER [II. 2]

θῆτε εἰς σωτηρίαν, ³εἰ ἐγεύσασθε ὅτι χρηστὸς ὁ Κύριος· ⁴πρὸς

-tive of strong desire (ἐπι-) and vigorous action (aor. imp.), such as are seen in a child being suckled. The word is common in LXX, especially the Psalms, and expresses intense and yearning desire (usually with a preposition, ἐπί, εἰς, or πρός), cf. Ps. xlii.1, "As the hart panteth after (ἐπιποθεῖ ἐπί) the water-brooks, so panteth my soul after thee, O God", and cxix.174, "I have longed for thy salvation, O Lord". Intensity of desire is also indicated by its use in classical authors, e.g. Herod. v. 93, Plato, Protag. 329 D. Intensity rather than addition seems to be the force of ἐπί in verbs compounded with it.

ἵνα ἐν αὐτῷ αὐξηθῆτε] that you may thrive on it and grow up. αὐξάνεσθαι is a common word in Greek for the growth of children; cf. Herod. v. 92. 5, μετὰ ταῦτα ὁ παῖς ηὔξετο, Eur. Suppl. 323, ἐν γὰρ τοῖς πόνοισιν αὔξεται [sc. σὴ πατρίς], "your country thrives on trouble", a passage which likewise illustrates the use of ἐν after αὐξάνεσθαι. I have added the words "and grow up", in order to provide a link with the εἰς σωτηρίαν which follows. Hort thinks that St. Peter's words are "founded on" Eph. iv. 15, but the hypothesis seems unnecessary. The image of the suckled child still governs the passage.

εἰς σωτηρίαν] omitted in some late MSS., but probably genuine. For the connexion of this passage with Jas.i.21 see Essay II, pp. 389 ff. The words support the view taken above that γάλα represents the grace of God, for there is no suggestion (as in 1 Cor. iii. and in Heb. v. 12, vi. 2) that the milk is a diet to be outgrown. Bigg's note on the contrasted uses of the milk image by St. Peter, St. Paul, and the Epistle to the Hebrews respectively is instructive.

3. εἰ ἐγεύσασθε ... Κύριος] The present tense of γεύομαι is never found in N.T., though the future occurs once; in all other passages the word is in the aorist tense, indicating a single or initial act of some kind. The verb governs a dependent clause introduced by ὅτι once in LXX (Prov. xxxi. 18), but never in N.T. except here, nor apparently ever in classical authors. The construction is to be explained here by the fact that the phrase is adapted from Ps. xxxiv. 8, γεύσασθε καὶ ἴδετε ὅτι χρηστὸς ὁ κύριος, the καὶ ἴδετε not being used owing to its not being required by the imagery of the suckled child,[1] or having fallen out in liturgical use. The meaning of the passage hardly lies on the surface. If the fact of the quotation is ignored, the passage would be an admonition to "go on growing in grace, provided your first taste of the Christian life has proved satisfactory"—a qualification which one cannot imagine coming from the pen of a N.T. writer. The emphasis must, therefore, lie on the ἐγεύσασθε rather than on its object, the meaning being, "go on growing in grace, now that you have once begun", in fact that it is a quotation. In that case, the underlying idea is closely similar to that of Heb. vi. 4-6, "For it is impossible for those who were once enlightened, and have tasted (γευσαμένους) of the heavenly gift, and were made partakers of the Holy Ghost, and have tasted (γευσαμένους) the good word of God, and the powers of the world to come, if they shall fall away, to renew them again unto repentance". The first γευσαμένους governs the genitive, the second the accusative, and the order of the words (καλὸν γευσαμένους θεοῦ ῥῆμα) is such that they might fairly be translated, "having tasted that the word of God is good". We may compare also St.

[1] If Rendel Harris is right in seeing in Acts xxvi. 23 (εἰ παθητὸς ὁ Χριστός, εἰ πρῶτος κτλ.) the tiles of catenae of O.T. proof-texts, this phrase εἰ ἐγεύσασθε κτλ. might be in the same category. Or it may have been the title of a hymn.

II. 4] FIRST EPISTLE OF ST. PETER 157

Bernard (letter to Prior Guiges), "So having tasted how sweet the Lord is he [sc. the Christian] passeth to the third stage and loveth God not for his own sake, but for the sake of God Himself". The three stages are (i) love of self, (ii) love of God for self's sake, (iii) love of God for God's sake.

The force of the passage would be best brought out, therefore, if we rendered it by, "if you have responded to the Psalmist's words, 'taste and see that the Lord is good'", i.e. if you have taken the initial step of adherence to Christ. εἰ then means "seeing that" (Lat. siquidem), as in i. 17, a usage recognized by Winer, Grammar, p. 562, who gives a number of classical and N.T. examples. Cf. also St. Paul's similar argument in Eph. iv. 17-24, especially verse 20, ὑμεῖς δὲ οὐχ οὕτως ἐμάθετε τὸν Χριστόν· εἴγε αὐτὸν ἠκούσατε καὶ ἐν αὐτῷ ἐδιδάχθητε. And this is rendered the more likely, in view of the fact that "the whole Psalm was present to St. Peter throughout the Epistle" (Bigg); cf. verse 10 with i. 17 and with verses 13-17 quoted verbatim in ii. 4; verse 5 with i. 17 and with verse 23, λυτρώσεται . . ἐλπίζοντες ἐπ' αὐτόν with i. 18, 13; and verse 20 with the Epistle passim. We may perhaps conjecture that the Psalm was already in use in the Church in Asia Minor, perhaps as part of a "catechumen-document" or of a "persecution-document", or as a baptismal hymn.

It is interesting to observe that Ps. xxxiv. came into regular use in the early Church at the Eucharist; cf. the passages quoted in Bingham, Antiquities, Book XV, ch. v. § 10, e.g. Apost. Const. VIII. xiii., Cyril, Cat. Myst. v. 17 (who shews that it was verse 8 which brought this about), Jerome, Epist. xxviii. (who adds Ps. xlv.). If baptism was already in the first century connected with the great Feast of the Redemption, which culminated in the Eucharist, the "first communion" of the converts may have been present to the author's mind here. For γεύσασθαι in this connexion cf. Acts xx. 11. Lohmeyer (Theol. Rundschau (1937), p. 296) is not prepared to rule out a Eucharistic reference in this verse itself: cf. Add. Note H, pp. 295-7.

χρηστός] used of things tasted in Jer. xxiv. 3 (figs), Lk. v. 39 (wine).

ὁ Κύριος] i.e. Christ, as shewn by the next verse; cf. iii. 15, Κύριον δὲ τὸν Χριστὸν ἁγιάσατε. In the Psalm it means God (Jehovah), as usual in LXX. The application of the title to Christ probably comes from the language of the original community at Jerusalem, i.e. Aramaic, and was none the less acceptable owing to the fact that the Hellenistic world was familiar with the word in a religious connotation. Cf. A. D. Nock, in Essays on the Trinity and the Incarnation, p. 85.

4. πρὸς ὃν προσερχόμενοι] The words effect a swift transition from the individual to the institutional aspect of religion, which is nevertheless kept personal throughout. For a general discussion of verses 4-10 see Add. Notes E, F, G, H, pp. 268-98. This opening phrase recalls Matt. xi. 28, δεῦτε πρός με; with which cf. various forms of ἔρχομαι πρός in Jn. vi. προσερχόμενοι in N.T. takes the dative, cf. Heb. iv. 16, vii. 25, xi. 6. But it is used absolutely in Heb. x. 1, 22, and the construction with πρός is quite common in classical Greek. Hort thinks that the root of the word present in προσήλυτος may have been in St. Peter's mind; but Philo (de Monarchia i. 7 [II. 219 M]) in this connexion uses the dative. His suggestion that Ps. xxxiv. 6, προσέλθατε πρὸς αὐτὸν καὶ φωτίσθητε has influenced the expression is perhaps more probable, as (1) the Psalm has just been quoted, (2) φωτίσθητε was germane to a baptismal context, and may have suggested the allusions to φῶς in verse 10, (3) the second part of the verse, καὶ τὰ πρόσωπα ὑμῶν οὐ μὴ καταισχυνθῇ is very like Is. xxviii. 16b

Taken from *The First Epistle of St. Peter* by Edward Gordon Selwyn, published by Macmillan, London and Basingstoke, and is used by permission.

```
┌─────────────────────────┐
│                         │
│     LESSON  14          │
│                         │
│   THE HEBREW ALPHABET   │
│                         │
└─────────────────────────┘
```

We are still on the "low road"! As in Greek, the student of this course will not learn how to do Hebrew exegesis. Such a privilege is reserved for the "high-roaders." In fact, we will not study Hebrew as thoroughly as we have studied Greek.

However, the student can catch a glimpse of the formation of the Hebrew language. He can also learn enough of its alphabet and terminology to understand what the Hebrew lexicons and the better Hebrew commentaries are saying. The material in these next three chapters is far more extensive than should be expected of the student to comprehend and retain. It is here for a quick going-over and for future reference.

IT IS DIFFERENT

Hebrew is even stranger than Greek! So, you will find it a little more difficult to memorize the alphabet and its pronunciations. The vowel arrangement on the page will also take a bit of getting used to. One reads a Hebrew book from "back to front" and a line from right to left.

PARTS OF SPEECH

There is one way, however, where it is about the same as English and Greek. It has nouns, pronouns, verbs, adjectives, prepositions, conjunctions, participles, and an article.

APPEARANCE

What did Hebrew look like? Hundreds of years before Moses, some Phoenician genius happened on to an efficient method of picturing linguistically significant sounds: an alphabet. It replaced the older and more cumbersome methods of employing different characters for each syllable or word.

In the Semitic family, the consonants are more important linguistically than are the vowels. The first alphabet only recorded the consonants, and left it up to the reader's memory to supply the appropriate vowel sounds. I would guess the first verse of the Bible would have looked something like the following illustration when it was first written down:

THE ALPHABET

You will be required to memorize the alphabet so that you are able to pronounce its sounds and write its characters. After you have memorized its first two letters, you will discover the etymology of our word "Alphabet." You must memorize the Hebrew alphabet for the same reasons that required you to memorize the Greek alphabet.

Form	Final Form	Translitered as	Name	Prounounced as in
א		ʾ	ʾAleph	(Silent)
בּ (ב)		b (bh or ḇ)	Beth	ball (like ו)
גּ (ג)		g (gh or ḡ)	Gimel	gone (same)
דּ (ד)		d (dh or ḏ)	Daleth	dog (same)
ה		h	He	hat
ו		w or v	Vav	very
ז		z	Zayin	zeal
ח		ḥ or ch	Heth	Bach (the compose
ט		ṭ	Teth	ten
י		y	Yodh	yet
כּ (כ)	ך	k (kh or ḵ)	Kaph	king (like ח)
ל		l	Lamedh	long
מ	ם	m	Mem	men
נ	ן	n	Nun	new
ס		s	Samech	sign
ע		ʿ	ʿAyin	(Silent)
פּ (פ)	ף	p (ph or p̄)	Pe	pea (phone)
צ	ץ	ṣ or ts	Tsadhe	hits
ק		q	Qoph	unique
ר		r	Resh	run
שׂ		ś	Sin	so
[שׁ		[š or sh	[Shin	[ship
תּ (ת)		t (th or ṯ)	Tav	toe (then)

The two "silent" consonants have no pronunciation value,
but there is a difference in the way they affect the
sounds of the vowels that follow them. The א makes no
sound at all. You only pronounce the vowel that follows
it. When you say an ע, however, you tighten your throat,
as if you were gargling, before you pronounce the following vowel. It almost makes a "g" sound.

Although the chart lists שׁ and שׂ separately, many grammars
and lexicons do not treat them as separate letters. Since
they make a different sound, you will learn them as though
they were separate, but related, letters.

The unique situation of the six letters that have dots in
their middle will be explained later. Just know for now
that there is a "softer" sound when there is no dot in them.

The five final forms are the way those letters look when
they come last in a word. They are no different in sound.

ITS VOWELS

After Hebrew ceased as a living language and
most of the people had forgotten what it sounded like,
scholars became dissatisfied with a written language
which contained only consonants. So, sometime during
the last half of the first millennium A.D., Jews,
called Massoretes, invented vowel signs which they
sprinkled in among those consonants. So respectful
were they, however, of the sacred consonantal text,
that they managed this without budging a single consonant. Most of these vowels were placed under the
consonant which preceded them. The "u" was in among,
and the "o" was on top. The Massoretes put these in
as they remembered what the sounds of the words were.
They also threw in a few other signs, like a consonant
change indicator and accentuation, for good measure.

Occasionally the meaning of a word is actually
changed by the vowels that go with it. One has to be
careful not to grant the same canonical authority to
the Massoretes as to Moses and the prophets. Nor
should one be too critical of the modern Old Testament
scholar who thinks he has just cause to alter one or
two of the signs the Massoretes had introduced. I
have never heard of a fundamentalist arguing for the
divine inspiration of the Massoretes.

Alas, the Massoretes were too late with one word, and a
most important word at that; the special name the Jews
had for God. I guess we never really will know for sure
how it originally sounded. Very early, the Jews began
to get uneasy when they mentioned this special name. It
was like getting too close to the Ark of the Covenant.
So, when they came across the word in the Sacred Text,
they would substitute a more common name for God in
pronouncing it. The most sacred name was יהוה, YHVH.
They substituted אדני, Adonai, whose vowel sounds they
knew, every time they came to the divine name.

The substituted name means "Lord." So, the Jews began to consider these two separate words as meaning "Lord." The translators of the King James Version wanted to continue with the custom, but also wanted to distinguish someway between the two Hebrew words. They solved the problem by writing "Lord" when the Hebrew was אדני, and "LORD" when the Hebrew was יהוה.

This worked fine except when the Old Testament inconsiderately put the two words together: אדני יהוה, "Lord Jehovah," in which case they translated, "Lord GOD." So pay attention. Every time you see LORD or GOD, all in capital letters, the King James Version is translating the Jewish Sacred Name!

When the Massoretes came to give vowel signs to יהוה, they put the vowel signs of אדני, a faint "e," an "o," and an "a," under the sacred consonants. Later, Christians who did not know any better, simply joined the consonants of the Sacred Name with the vowels of the word for "Lord" and came up with a new word, sounding something like, "Yahova." En route to the English, the "Y" got hardened to "J," and the word wound up as "Jehovah." The only thing you can be certain about is that "Jehovah" is *not* the way the word should be spelled or sounded. The most intelligent guess at this late date is that it should sound something like "Ya," (the German "yes") and "wet" (without the "t"); "Yawe." And, if you want to be fancy, scrape your tonsils just a bit between the "a" and the "w."

Don't worry that only the consonants were preserved and that it might open the door for all kinds of readings. Remember that newspapers and books in Israel today are normally published only in these consonants and modern Israelis are not complaining. TH PRSN WH CN NT RD THS SNTNC HS RCKS N HS HD. ND TH PRSN WH HD LTS F PRCTC CLD RD T FF S QKCLY S WTH TH VWLS.

Full vowels

Here is the chart of the vowels that the Massoretes invented. It must be memorized. Here is good news. It is the last item you are required to memorize for this course.

Vowel Class	Short		Sounds Like	Long		Sounds Like
a	_	pathah	⟶	ָ	kamets	f<u>a</u>ther
e	ֶ	seghol	m<u>e</u>t	ֵ	tsere	th<u>e</u>y
i	ִ	hirek	⟶	ִי	hirek yodh	mach<u>i</u>ne
o	ָ	kamets hatuph	⟶	וֹ or ֹ	holem	r<u>o</u>ll
u	ֻ	kubbuts	⟶	וּ	shurek	t<u>u</u>ne

You probably noticed that "kamets" and "kamets hatuph" look exactly alike. Do not let that bother you, for although they are distinct vowels and we will not be learning how to distinguish them, they make about the same sound. That's all we will be concerned with on the "low road."

All of the short vowels, as well as "kamets" and "tsere," are placed under the consonant they follow (הַ, "ha"). "Shurek" and "holem" (whether written as ֹ or וֹ) are placed after the consonant they follow (בּוּ, "boo"). "Hirek yodh" is placed both under and after (סִי, "see").

There are also what are called "half vowels" or   Half Vowels
"reduced vowels" in Hebrew. The ringleader of this gang is called "shewa," which looks like a colon set under a letter (ְ). It is only given about half of an "eh" sound when pronounced. It is not a real vowel but rather an indicator that no vowel is present.

We have some "half vowels" in English. For example, we fully pronounce the "a" in "battle," but when we say "lapel," we almost skip over the "a" in our hurry to pronounce the second syllable. This is the same pronunciation value to give to "shewa."

There are three other "half vowels," which occur instead of "shewa" under certain consonants. These, along with the "shewa," must be learned as a part of the vowel chart:

ְ	shewa:	half of an "eh" sound, sometimes no sound
ֲ	hateph pathah:	half of an "a" sound
ֱ	hateph seghol:	half of an "e" sound
ֳ	hateph kamets:	half of an "o" sound

PRACTICE READING

Genesis 1:1 - 2:21 is printed for you to practice reading on, like you did with the first chapter of John (pages 1:9 - 11). The better you are able to sound out words, the better you will be able to use the basic Hebrew research tools for word studies. The cassette tape of Hebrew and Greek sounds, available from Multnomah Press, pronounces these verses for you.

Notice the page numbers of the following pages. If you are puzzled, refer to 14:1.

ד אֵ֣לֶּה תוֹלְד֧וֹת הַשָּׁמַ֛יִם וְהָאָ֖רֶץ בְּהִבָּֽרְאָ֑ם בְּי֗וֹם עֲשׂ֛וֹת יְהֹוָ֥ה

ה אֱלֹהִ֖ים אֶ֥רֶץ וְשָׁמָֽיִם׃ וְכֹ֣ל ׀ שִׂ֣יחַ הַשָּׂדֶ֗ה טֶ֚רֶם יִֽהְיֶ֣ה בָאָ֔רֶץ וְכׇל־

עֵ֥שֶׂב הַשָּׂדֶ֖ה טֶ֣רֶם יִצְמָ֑ח כִּי֩ לֹ֨א הִמְטִ֜יר יְהֹוָ֤ה אֱלֹהִים֙ עַל־הָאָ֔רֶץ

ו וְאָדָ֣ם אַ֔יִן לַֽעֲבֹ֖ד אֶת־הָֽאֲדָמָֽה׃ וְאֵ֖ד יַֽעֲלֶ֣ה מִן־הָאָ֑רֶץ וְהִשְׁקָ֖ה

ז אֶֽת־כׇּל־פְּנֵֽי־הָֽאֲדָמָֽה׃ וַיִּ֩יצֶר֩ יְהֹוָ֨ה אֱלֹהִ֜ים אֶת־הָֽאָדָ֗ם עָפָר֙

מִן־הָ֣אֲדָמָ֔ה וַיִּפַּ֥ח בְּאַפָּ֖יו נִשְׁמַ֣ת חַיִּ֑ים וַֽיְהִ֥י הָֽאָדָ֖ם לְנֶ֥פֶשׁ חַיָּֽה׃

ח וַיִּטַּ֞ע יְהֹוָ֧ה אֱלֹהִ֛ים גַּן־בְּעֵ֖דֶן מִקֶּ֑דֶם וַיָּ֣שֶׂם שָׁ֔ם אֶת־הָֽאָדָ֖ם אֲשֶׁ֥ר

ט יָצָֽר׃ וַיַּצְמַ֞ח יְהֹוָ֤ה אֱלֹהִים֙ מִן־הָ֣אֲדָמָ֔ה כׇּל־עֵ֛ץ נֶחְמָ֥ד לְמַרְאֶ֖ה

י וְט֣וֹב לְמַֽאֲכָ֑ל וְעֵ֤ץ הַֽחַיִּים֙ בְּת֣וֹךְ הַגָּ֔ן וְעֵ֕ץ הַדַּ֖עַת ט֥וֹב וָרָֽע׃ וְנָהָר֙

יֹצֵ֣א מֵעֵ֔דֶן לְהַשְׁק֖וֹת אֶת־הַגָּ֑ן וּמִשָּׁם֙ יִפָּרֵ֔ד וְהָיָ֖ה לְאַרְבָּעָ֥ה

יא רָאשִֽׁים׃ שֵׁ֥ם הָֽאֶחָ֖ד פִּישׁ֑וֹן ה֣וּא הַסֹּבֵ֗ב אֵ֚ת כׇּל־אֶ֣רֶץ הַֽחֲוִילָ֔ה

יב אֲשֶׁר־שָׁ֖ם הַזָּהָֽב׃ וּֽזְהַ֛ב הָאָ֥רֶץ הַהִ֖וא ט֑וֹב שָׁ֥ם הַבְּדֹ֖לַח וְאֶ֥בֶן

יג הַשֹּֽׁהַם׃ וְשֵֽׁם־הַנָּהָ֥ר הַשֵּׁנִ֖י גִּיח֑וֹן ה֣וּא הַסּוֹבֵ֔ב אֵ֖ת כׇּל־אֶ֥רֶץ

יד כּֽוּשׁ׃ וְשֵׁ֨ם הַנָּהָ֤ר הַשְּׁלִישִׁי֙ חִדֶּ֔קֶל ה֥וּא הַֽהֹלֵ֖ךְ קִדְמַ֣ת אַשּׁ֑וּר

טו וְהַנָּהָ֥ר הָֽרְבִיעִ֖י ה֥וּא פְרָֽת׃ וַיִּקַּ֛ח יְהֹוָ֥ה אֱלֹהִ֖ים אֶת־הָֽאָדָ֑ם

טז וַיַּנִּחֵ֣הוּ בְגַן־עֵ֔דֶן לְעׇבְדָ֖הּ וּלְשׇׁמְרָֽהּ׃ וַיְצַו֙ יְהֹוָ֣ה אֱלֹהִ֔ים עַל־הָֽאָדָ֖ם

יז לֵאמֹ֑ר מִכֹּ֥ל עֵֽץ־הַגָּ֖ן אָכֹ֥ל תֹּאכֵֽל׃ וּמֵעֵ֗ץ הַדַּ֙עַת֙ ט֣וֹב וָרָ֔ע לֹ֥א

יח תֹאכַ֖ל מִמֶּ֑נּוּ כִּ֗י בְּי֛וֹם אֲכׇלְךָ֥ מִמֶּ֖נּוּ מ֥וֹת תָּמֽוּת׃ וַיֹּ֙אמֶר֙ יְהֹוָ֣ה

יט אֱלֹהִ֔ים לֹא־ט֛וֹב הֱי֥וֹת הָֽאָדָ֖ם לְבַדּ֑וֹ אֶֽעֱשֶׂה־לּ֥וֹ עֵ֖זֶר כְּנֶגְדּֽוֹ׃ וַיִּ֩צֶר֩

יְהֹוָ֨ה אֱלֹהִ֜ים מִן־הָֽאֲדָמָ֗ה כׇּל־חַיַּ֤ת הַשָּׂדֶה֙ וְאֵת֙ כׇּל־ע֣וֹף הַשָּׁמַ֔יִם

וַיָּבֵא֙ אֶל־הָ֣אָדָ֔ם לִרְא֖וֹת מַה־יִּקְרָא־ל֑וֹ וְכֹל֩ אֲשֶׁ֨ר יִקְרָא־

כ ל֧וֹ הָֽאָדָ֛ם נֶ֥פֶשׁ חַיָּ֖ה ה֥וּא שְׁמֽוֹ׃ וַיִּקְרָ֨א הָֽאָדָ֜ם שֵׁמ֗וֹת לְכׇל־

הַבְּהֵמָה֙ וּלְע֣וֹף הַשָּׁמַ֔יִם וּלְכֹ֖ל חַיַּ֣ת הַשָּׂדֶ֑ה וּלְאָדָ֕ם לֹֽא־מָצָ֥א

כא עֵ֖זֶר כְּנֶגְדּֽוֹ׃ וַיַּפֵּל֩ יְהֹוָ֨ה אֱלֹהִ֧ים ׀ תַּרְדֵּמָ֛ה עַל־הָֽאָדָ֖ם וַיִּישָׁ֑ן

כב וַיִּקַּ֗ח אַחַת֙ מִצַּלְעֹתָ֔יו וַיִּסְגֹּ֥ר בָּשָׂ֖ר תַּחְתֶּֽנָּה׃

א

כ וַיֹּאמֶר אֱלֹהִים יִשְׁרְצוּ הַמַּיִם שֶׁרֶץ נֶפֶשׁ חַיָּה וְעוֹף יְעוֹפֵף עַל־הָאָרֶץ עַל־פְּנֵי רְקִיעַ הַשָּׁמָיִם:

כא וַיִּבְרָא אֱלֹהִים אֶת־הַתַּנִּינִם הַגְּדֹלִים וְאֵת כָּל־נֶפֶשׁ הַחַיָּה ׀ הָרֹמֶשֶׂת אֲשֶׁר שָׁרְצוּ הַמַּיִם לְמִינֵהֶם וְאֵת כָּל־עוֹף כָּנָף לְמִינֵהוּ וַיַּרְא אֱלֹהִים כִּי־טוֹב:

כב וַיְבָרֶךְ אֹתָם אֱלֹהִים לֵאמֹר פְּרוּ וּרְבוּ וּמִלְאוּ אֶת־הַמַּיִם בַּיַּמִּים וְהָעוֹף יִרֶב בָּאָרֶץ: וַיְהִי־עֶרֶב וַיְהִי־בֹקֶר יוֹם חֲמִישִׁי:

כג

כד וַיֹּאמֶר אֱלֹהִים תּוֹצֵא הָאָרֶץ נֶפֶשׁ חַיָּה לְמִינָהּ בְּהֵמָה וָרֶמֶשׂ וְחַיְתוֹ־אֶרֶץ לְמִינָהּ וַיְהִי־כֵן:

כה וַיַּעַשׂ אֱלֹהִים אֶת־חַיַּת הָאָרֶץ לְמִינָהּ וְאֶת־הַבְּהֵמָה לְמִינָהּ וְאֵת כָּל־רֶמֶשׂ הָאֲדָמָה לְמִינֵהוּ וַיַּרְא אֱלֹהִים כִּי־טוֹב:

כו וַיֹּאמֶר אֱלֹהִים נַעֲשֶׂה אָדָם בְּצַלְמֵנוּ כִּדְמוּתֵנוּ וְיִרְדּוּ בִדְגַת הַיָּם וּבְעוֹף הַשָּׁמַיִם וּבַבְּהֵמָה וּבְכָל־הָאָרֶץ וּבְכָל־הָרֶמֶשׂ הָרֹמֵשׂ עַל־הָאָרֶץ:

כז וַיִּבְרָא אֱלֹהִים ׀ אֶת־הָאָדָם בְּצַלְמוֹ בְּצֶלֶם אֱלֹהִים בָּרָא אֹתוֹ זָכָר וּנְקֵבָה בָּרָא אֹתָם:

כח וַיְבָרֶךְ אֹתָם אֱלֹהִים וַיֹּאמֶר לָהֶם אֱלֹהִים פְּרוּ וּרְבוּ וּמִלְאוּ אֶת־הָאָרֶץ וְכִבְשֻׁהָ וּרְדוּ בִּדְגַת הַיָּם וּבְעוֹף הַשָּׁמַיִם וּבְכָל־חַיָּה הָרֹמֶשֶׂת עַל־הָאָרֶץ:

כט וַיֹּאמֶר אֱלֹהִים הִנֵּה נָתַתִּי לָכֶם אֶת־כָּל־עֵשֶׂב ׀ זֹרֵעַ זֶרַע אֲשֶׁר עַל־פְּנֵי כָל־הָאָרֶץ וְאֶת־כָּל־הָעֵץ אֲשֶׁר־בּוֹ פְרִי־עֵץ זֹרֵעַ זָרַע לָכֶם יִהְיֶה לְאָכְלָה:

ל וּלְכָל־חַיַּת הָאָרֶץ וּלְכָל־עוֹף הַשָּׁמַיִם וּלְכֹל ׀ רוֹמֵשׂ עַל־הָאָרֶץ אֲשֶׁר־בּוֹ נֶפֶשׁ חַיָּה אֶת־כָּל־יֶרֶק עֵשֶׂב לְאָכְלָה וַיְהִי־כֵן:

לא וַיַּרְא אֱלֹהִים אֶת־כָּל־אֲשֶׁר עָשָׂה וְהִנֵּה־טוֹב מְאֹד וַיְהִי־עֶרֶב וַיְהִי־בֹקֶר יוֹם הַשִּׁשִּׁי:

ב וַיְכֻלּוּ הַשָּׁמַיִם וְהָאָרֶץ וְכָל־צְבָאָם: וַיְכַל אֱלֹהִים בַּיּוֹם הַשְּׁבִיעִי מְלַאכְתּוֹ אֲשֶׁר עָשָׂה וַיִּשְׁבֹּת בַּיּוֹם הַשְּׁבִיעִי מִכָּל־מְלַאכְתּוֹ אֲשֶׁר עָשָׂה:

ג וַיְבָרֶךְ אֱלֹהִים אֶת־יוֹם הַשְּׁבִיעִי וַיְקַדֵּשׁ אֹתוֹ כִּי בוֹ שָׁבַת מִכָּל־מְלַאכְתּוֹ אֲשֶׁר־בָּרָא אֱלֹהִים לַעֲשׂוֹת:

א

א בְּרֵאשִׁ֖ית בָּרָ֣א אֱלֹהִ֑ים אֵ֥ת הַשָּׁמַ֖יִם וְאֵ֥ת הָאָֽרֶץ: וְהָאָ֗רֶץ א

הָיְתָ֥ה תֹ֙הוּ֙ וָבֹ֔הוּ וְחֹ֖שֶׁךְ עַל־פְּנֵ֣י תְה֑וֹם וְר֣וּחַ אֱלֹהִ֔ים מְרַחֶ֖פֶת

ג עַל־פְּנֵ֥י הַמָּֽיִם: וַיֹּ֥אמֶר אֱלֹהִ֖ים יְהִ֣י א֑וֹר וַֽיְהִי־אֽוֹר: וַיַּ֧רְא אֱלֹהִ֛ים

ה אֶת־הָא֖וֹר כִּי־ט֑וֹב וַיַּבְדֵּ֣ל אֱלֹהִ֔ים בֵּ֥ין הָא֖וֹר וּבֵ֥ין הַחֹֽשֶׁךְ: וַיִּקְרָ֨א

אֱלֹהִ֤ים ׀ לָאוֹר֙ י֔וֹם וְלַחֹ֖שֶׁךְ קָ֣רָא לָ֑יְלָה וַֽיְהִי־עֶ֥רֶב וַֽיְהִי־בֹ֖קֶר י֥וֹם

אֶחָֽד:

ו וַיֹּ֣אמֶר אֱלֹהִ֔ים יְהִ֥י רָקִ֖יעַ בְּת֣וֹךְ הַמָּ֑יִם וִיהִ֣י מַבְדִּ֔יל בֵּ֥ין מַ֖יִם

ז לָמָֽיִם: וַיַּ֣עַשׂ אֱלֹהִים֮ אֶת־הָרָקִיעַ֒ וַיַּבְדֵּ֗ל בֵּ֤ין הַמַּ֙יִם֙ אֲשֶׁר֙

ח מִתַּ֣חַת לָרָקִ֔יעַ וּבֵ֣ין הַמַּ֔יִם אֲשֶׁ֖ר מֵעַ֣ל לָרָקִ֑יעַ וַֽיְהִי־כֵֽן: וַיִּקְרָ֧א

אֱלֹהִ֛ים לָֽרָקִ֖יעַ שָׁמָ֑יִם וַֽיְהִי־עֶ֥רֶב וַֽיְהִי־בֹ֖קֶר י֥וֹם שֵׁנִֽי:

ט וַיֹּ֣אמֶר אֱלֹהִ֗ים יִקָּו֨וּ הַמַּ֜יִם מִתַּ֤חַת הַשָּׁמַ֙יִם֙ אֶל־מָק֣וֹם אֶחָ֔ד

י וְתֵרָאֶ֖ה הַיַּבָּשָׁ֑ה וַֽיְהִי־כֵֽן: וַיִּקְרָ֨א אֱלֹהִ֤ים ׀ לַיַּבָּשָׁה֙ אֶ֔רֶץ וּלְמִקְוֵ֥ה

יא הַמַּ֖יִם קָרָ֣א יַמִּ֑ים וַיַּ֥רְא אֱלֹהִ֖ים כִּי־טֽוֹב: וַיֹּ֣אמֶר אֱלֹהִ֗ים תַּֽדְשֵׁ֤א

הָאָ֙רֶץ֙ דֶּ֔שֶׁא עֵ֚שֶׂב מַזְרִ֣יעַ זֶ֔רַע עֵ֣ץ פְּרִ֞י עֹ֤שֶׂה פְּרִי֙ לְמִינ֔וֹ אֲשֶׁ֥ר

יב זַרְעוֹ־ב֖וֹ עַל־הָאָ֑רֶץ וַֽיְהִי־כֵֽן: וַתּוֹצֵ֨א הָאָ֜רֶץ דֶּ֠שֶׁא עֵ֣שֶׂב מַזְרִ֤יעַ

זֶ֙רַע֙ לְמִינֵ֔הוּ וְעֵ֧ץ עֹֽשֶׂה־פְּרִ֛י אֲשֶׁ֥ר זַרְעוֹ־ב֖וֹ לְמִינֵ֑הוּ וַיַּ֥רְא אֱלֹהִ֖ים

יג כִּי־טֽוֹב: וַֽיְהִי־עֶ֥רֶב וַֽיְהִי־בֹ֖קֶר י֥וֹם שְׁלִישִֽׁי:

יד וַיֹּ֣אמֶר אֱלֹהִ֗ים יְהִ֤י מְאֹרֹת֙ בִּרְקִ֣יעַ הַשָּׁמַ֔יִם לְהַבְדִּ֕יל בֵּ֥ין הַיּ֖וֹם

טו וּבֵ֣ין הַלָּ֑יְלָה וְהָי֤וּ לְאֹתֹת֙ וּלְמ֣וֹעֲדִ֔ים וּלְיָמִ֖ים וְשָׁנִֽים: וְהָי֤וּ

טז לִמְאוֹרֹת֙ בִּרְקִ֣יעַ הַשָּׁמַ֔יִם לְהָאִ֖יר עַל־הָאָ֑רֶץ וַֽיְהִי־כֵֽן: וַיַּ֣עַשׂ

אֱלֹהִ֔ים אֶת־שְׁנֵ֥י הַמְּאֹרֹ֖ת הַגְּדֹלִ֑ים אֶת־הַמָּא֤וֹר הַגָּדֹל֙ לְמֶמְשֶׁ֣לֶת

הַיּ֔וֹם וְאֶת־הַמָּא֤וֹר הַקָּטֹן֙ לְמֶמְשֶׁ֣לֶת הַלַּ֔יְלָה וְאֵ֖ת הַכּֽוֹכָבִֽים:

יז וַיִּתֵּ֥ן אֹתָ֛ם אֱלֹהִ֖ים בִּרְקִ֣יעַ הַשָּׁמָ֑יִם לְהָאִ֖יר עַל־הָאָֽרֶץ: וְלִמְשֹׁל֙

יח בַּיּ֣וֹם וּבַלַּ֔יְלָה וּֽלֲהַבְדִּ֔יל בֵּ֥ין הָא֖וֹר וּבֵ֣ין הַחֹ֑שֶׁךְ וַיַּ֥רְא אֱלֹהִ֖ים

יט כִּי־טֽוֹב: וַֽיְהִי־עֶ֥רֶב וַֽיְהִי־בֹ֖קֶר י֥וֹם רְבִיעִֽי:

HOW WORDS ARE
FORMED

Three consonants

Normal root words had three consonants (with appropriate accompanying vowels, of course). Inflections of the verb were indicated by adding consonants to the beginning, the end, and sometimes inside the three basic consonants. These new letters brought their own vowels along, also.

a three-consonant word:	קָטַל	"he killed"
added consonant at the beginning:	יִקְטֹל	"he will kill"
added consonant at the end:	קָטַלְתָּ	"you killed"
added letter inside:	קוֹטֵל	"killing"

Sometimes, inflections were shown only by vowel change. Since the vowels were not written in originally, one can imagine the possible variation of interpretation. Other times, one of the original three consonants was dropped.

Syllables

There are four basic rules which will make identification and reading of the Hebrew syllable much easier:

1. Every syllable must begin with a consonant. (But sometimes the conjunction וְ [16:3] becomes a vowel beginning a word.)

2. Every syllable must have a vowel.

3. No syllable can have more than one vowel.

4. Only the final syllable of a word may end in more than one consonant, and then not in more than two.

Thus, the two basic syllables which make up a word are as follows, where C means consonant, and V means vowel:

1. "Open": $\underset{V}{C}$ or   2. "Closed": $\underset{V}{CC}$

And, at the end of the word, it may be "doubly closed": $\underset{V}{CCC}$

The English "to" written the Hebrew way would look like $\underset{O}{T}$)

The English "ton" written the Hebrew way would look like $\underset{O}{NT}$)

The English "tong" written the Hebrew way would look like
גְ‍נְ‍טֹ

An "open" syllable written in Hebrew looks like
סָ, סֶ, סוֹ

A "closed" syllable written in Hebrew looks like
סָר, סֶר, סוּר, סוֹר

SHEWA

The shewa (ְ - see page 14:5) is placed under every consonant without a full vowel of its own except:

1. If the consonant is "quiescent." Sometimes י, ו, ה, and א lose their consonantal character and "quiesce," i.e., they become silent.

2. If the consonant is the final letter of a word.

Simple Shewa

The simple shewa is written ְ and sometimes you ignore it, and sometimes you give it a faint neutral sound (see page 14:5). "Low roaders" will not learn when, but the following rules will help:

Ignore the shewa when:

  1. it is under the last consonant of a word: אַתְּ
  2. it comes after a short unaccented vowel: יִקְטֹל
  3. it precedes a consonant with a dot in it: וַיִּבְדֵּל
  4. it precedes another shewa: תְּקְטְלִי

Pronounce the shewa when:

  1. it is under the first consonant of a word: קְטֹל
  2. it comes after a "metheg" accent (ָ‍ ֽ): קָטְלָה
  3. it is under a consonant with a dot in it: תְּקַטְּלִי

Compound Shewa

There are four "guttural" consonants; א, ע, ה, and ח, and sometimes a fifth, ר, so named because they are "throat letters." These have several peculiarities. One is that they take a compound shewa rather than a simple shewa. These compound shewas were introduced with simple shewa on page 14:5.

NOUNS

The Hebrew noun has two genders (masculine and feminine) and three numbers (singular, plural and dual) Normally the dual is used for the names of objects that go in pairs, like eyes, feet and ears. The normal gender and number indicators are found in the suffixes:

Masculine singular	no indicator	סוּס	"horse"
Masculine plural	ִים	סוּסִים	"horses"
Masculine dual	ַיִם	סוּסַיִם	"pair of horses"

Feminine singular	הָ	סוּסָה	"mare"
Feminine plural	וֹת	סוּסוֹת	"mares"
Feminine dual	תַיִם	סוּסָתַיִם	"pair of mares"

The noun also has a case system, which they call "state," and is divided into "absolute" and "construct" states. Absolute construction is thought of as the normal form and is used with subjects, complements and objects of the prepositions. Direct objects are usually distinguished by the use of the particle, אֵת, which appears just before the direct object. This sign is never translated.

Besides the absolute construction, Hebrew has a construct construction, which is used to show possession or other relationships which we express in English with the word "of." The following is an example:

English: "Word   ofGod"   "of" is connected with "God"

Hebrew: "Wordof   God"   "of" is connected with "Word"

"Wordof" is in the construct state and "God" is in the absolute state. This relationship is shown by the position of the nouns (the absolute always follows the construct) and sometimes by a change in the spelling of the word which is in construct.

If one wanted to say "God of the Word," in which state would "God" be? _____ In which state would "Word" be? _____ Notice the difference in order and in spelling in the following example:

בְּנֵי הָאָב   "The sons of the father"

אֲבִי הַבָּנִים   "The father of the sons"

Notice that the definite article (הַ) only is attached to the word which is in the absolute state, but it makes both words definite. The Hebrew is very particular about this.

VERBS

The Hebrew verb has person (first, second and third), number (singular and plural), gender (masculine and feminine), state (or kind of action) and stems. Since person, number and gender are not new to the student, there is no need for explanation.

State

The state of the verb describes the kind of action that is involved, but not the time. Generally, when the verb asserts something to be:

complete,   it is called "perfect"

incomplete,   it is called "imperfect"

continuous,   it is called "participle"

commanded,   it is called "imperative"

Stems

The verb system uses seven normal "stems," although there are others at its disposal. The verb קָטַל, in third person singular, masculine, perfect has been chosen to contrast the spelling and translation of these stems:

	SIMPLE	INTENSIVE	CAUSATIVE
ACTIVE	QAL קָטַל "he killed"	PIEL קִטֵּל "he brutally killed"	HIPHIL הִקְטִיל "he made someone kill"
PASSIVE	(NIPHAL) (נִקְטַל) "he was killed"	PUAL קֻטַּל "he was brutally killed"	HOPHAL הָקְטַל "he was made to kill"
REFLEXIVE	NIPHAL נִקְטַל "he killed himself"	HITHPAEL הִתְקַטֵּל "he brutally killed himself"	HISHTAPHEL הִשְׁתַּקְטֵל "he made himself kill"

The simple passive is in parentheses because there is no specific simple passive in the perfect or imperfect. The niphal stem fills in here.

Also, the hishtaphel stem was only recently discovered and is only used with one verb in the Old Testament. This verb, חָוָה, is used 170 times in the Bible, and means "to bow down." So, the rareness of this stem, and the absence of a simple passive perfect is the reason I said there were seven normal stems. The other two are added here to make the chart look nice.

Tense

There is no tense in Hebrew: no form to indicate past, present, or future. The perfect state speaks of completed action, the imperfect of incomplete or linear action, but both can refer to past, present, or future. The only way you can tell the time in Hebrew is by the context.

Isaiah 52:12 reads: "Behold: my servant will act wisely; he will be raised, he will be lifted up, he will be greatly exalted." Although all of the verbs are translated in the future tense, the first two are imperfect, and the other two are perfect! Although the forms cannot tell you the time orientation, it is clear in context that they all do refer to the future.

The Hebrew language can vividly describe action but is all thumbs when it comes to philosophical inquiry. It did not go much for signaling inferred relationships by subordinate clauses. It rather strung events together, using one "and" after another as links in this chain. After all, why get so pernickety about distinguishing purpose and result? The action is the same, isn't it?

STYLE

An Action Language

Although the verb had no built-in form to indicate time, the Hebrew did indicate time orientation with adverbs such as לְפָכִים "formerly," עוֹד "still," and אַחַר "later." But what was more important was whether the action was complete or not. But as I mentioned before, the time orientation is usually clear in context, so don't criticise the translators for putting tense in your English Bible--you cannot write English without it.

Time

Only rarely did the Hebrew poet--they dearly loved poetry--play with the accidental sound of words like we enjoy doing. And when they did, they did it differently. Once in a while, they would arrange their words so that the beginning letters fit the order of their alphabet. "Acrostic" is the name you give to this.

Its Poetry

Most translations let the reader in on the Bible's most elaborate acrostic. Turn to Psalm 119 and see if yours does.

But, making up patterns with accidental word sound, stresses and vowel lengths was too superficial for the Hebrew poet. Rather, he balanced off statements about reality in elaborate patterns.   Word sounds have nothing to do with the trans-cultural values of:

He makes me lie down in green pastures,
He leads me beside still waters.

Don't think of poetry as only existing in Psalms, though. Because poetry is a vivid type of communication, having to do with rhythms and wordplays, it was the medium of communication for most of the prophets, too. Most modern versions, such as the NIV, RSV, and the Jerusalem Bible, show you the poetic structure of such books as Isaiah, Jeremiah, and Ezekiel by using special indentations. This structure of balanced statements in these books is called "parallelism."

Most scholars speak of three sorts of parallelism: synonymous, antithetical, and synthetic, although this last category really just contains everything that doesn't fit in the first two.

In synonymous parallelism, the same thought is in two statements to make it more vivid, such as in Psalm 1:2:
>"But his delight is in the law of the Lord,
>And in his law he meditates day and night."

Antithetical parallelism contrasts two thoughts, usually connected with the adversative conjunction "but," as in Psalm 1:6:
>"For the Lord watches over the way of the righteous, but the way of the wicked will perish."

Synthetic parallelism does not have this formal relationship, and often the two lines of poetry simply continue one line of thought, as in Psalm 1:3:
>"He is like a tree planted by rivers of water, which yields its fruit in its season."

Its Word Order   The Hebrew sentence usually went from verb to pronoun object or indirect object to noun subject to noun object. For instance, "The student turned his term paper in to me," would come out, "Turned in to me the student his term paper." deviation from this word order usually meant some kind of emphasis.

Its Slow Pace   One final characteristic, reflecting a tempo of life style perhaps forever gone, is the Hebrew lack of urgency to get a thing said. Any modern editor would feel duty-bound to blue-pencil out much of t Old Testament.

As you allow yourself to be lulled by the casual pace of the Hebrew rhythms, you cannot help conjuring up in your mind's eye a group seated before a bedouin tent being entertained into the dusk by the traveler who earns his night's lodging and meals by his gossip and his tales. As one, relishing the taste of a morse procrastinates a swallow, so he goes on and on with hi

"He lifted up his eyes and saw"

"He answered and said"

"He fed them food with which they were fed"

"He captured captives"

OTHER MARKINGS

Accents   You are not required to memorize all the names and functions of the accents (be thankful; there are nearly three dozen of them), but you should recognize them and distinguish them from the vowel pointings. Every word has at least one accent mark.

Accents originally had three purposes:

1. To mark the "tone-syllable," i.e., to indicate the
   syllable to be stressed in pronunciation, like
   the accent does in Greek. In Genesis 1:1 (see
   page 14:6), notice that the first four words have
   an accent mark on the last syllable. The next,
   הַשָּׁמַיִם, has it on the next to last syllable.

2. As punctuation marks, i.e., they divide the verse
   into its logical constituent parts. The two major
   stops are:

   a. Silluq (ֽ), which always appears under the last
      word of a verse, as in Genesis 1:1, 2, etc.
      This is the greatest stop in a verse and is
      regularly followed by the sign (׃) called Soph
      Pasuq, equivalent to our period.

   b. Athnah (֑), the second greatest stop, which
      divides the verse into two logical parts. Can
      you find it in Genesis 1:1?

3. As musical signs for chanting the Scriptures in the
   Synagogue.

When two or more short words are closely asso-   Maqqeph
ciated in meaning, like a preposition and its object,
they are often joined together by a hyphen-like line
called "Maqqeph" (־). For grammatical purposes, they
are considered virtually as one word. In this case,
only the last word retains its accent while the first
word loses its.

A preposition and its object are so joined in Genesis
   1:2, in the middle of the second line: עַל־פְּנֵי.

At the end of the third verse (page 14:6, again) a verb
   is so joined to its complement: וַיְהִי־אוֹר

The Daghesh is the dot placed inside of a letter   Daghesh
which I have been promising I would talk about.

There are two kinds:

1. Daghesh Lene: This is the dot that appears in the six
   letters, בּ, גּ, דּ, כּ, פּ, תּ, which gives them a hard
   pronunciation. These letters will only have Dagesh
   Lene when they do not immediately follow a vowel sound.
   Therefore, they always have the dot at the beginning
   of a sentence or clause, always in the middle of a
   word after a closed syllable (see pages 15:1-2), and
   usually at the beginning of a word.

2. Daghesh Forte: This is a dot in a consonant to indicate
   that that consonant is doubled. The Hebrews preferred
   to do this than write the letter twice. So, in Genesis 1:2, the final word, הַמָּיִם is equivalent to
   הַמְמָיִם or ham-ma-yim.

Dagesh Forte can appear in all the letters (includir
the six above) with the exception of the gutturals
(א, ה, ח, ע) and the letter, ר.

Kethiv and Qere

"Kethiv" means "written," and "Qere" means
"read," i.e., "to be read." In the printed Hebrew
Bibles, if a correction needed to be made, even for
an obvious error, it was made in the margin or footnote, and the uncorrected reading was left in the
text, marked with (°) or (*). This was due to the
extreme reverence which the Massoretes felt for the
text, and acted as a safeguard against tampering
with it.

The uncorrected reading in the text is the
Kethiv ("it is written"), and the corrected reading
in the margin or footnote is the Qere ("to be read").

Most Kethiv-Qere readings are corrections of
simple misspellings. Rather than tamper with the
text, the proper spelling was inserted into the
margin.

The first such example in the Bible is found in Genesis
8:17. The text contains the reading הוצא when this
meaningless form should be הַיְצֵא An early scribe had
mistaken the י for a ו (an easy error to commit!).

Sometimes a reading was just too racy or was
theologically objectionable to the Massoretes, so
they changed the reading without changing the text.
This way, the objectionable reading would not be
heard in the synagogue, yet the scholars would still
know the contents of the original text.

In Deuteronomy 28, the text describes how in the days
of Israel's disobedience, Yahweh will bring judgment
on them. In verse 30, men's fiancees will be ravished
by other men. The word for "ravish" (שָׁגַל) was too
explicit for the Massoretes, who substituted the Qere
שָׁכַב, simply meaning "to go to bed with."

In the case of the Sacred Name יהוה, as mentioned in
14:3-4, it was considered too sacred to mention. Since
this was universally known among the Hebrews, the printed
texts do not give a Qere for it, but the reader is expecte
to read אֲדֹנָי in its place. This is termed a "perpetual
Qere," along with several other words in the Hebrew
Bible.

If you have secured the Hebrew and Greek cassette tape
from Multnomah Press, notice how Mr. Frydman, the "voice"
on the Hebrew side of your cassette, employs this very
Qere consistently.

THE HEBREW TOOLS

The set of Hebrew research tools is very much
like the set of Greek research tools. After practice
with the Greek tools and after learning the Hebrew
alphabet, it takes little adjustment to get on to
the tools for Old Testament study.

Lexical Forms

The Hebrew language will also have lexical
forms:

For the noun, the lexical form will be singular number,
absolute state, and either masculine or feminine
gender.

For the adjective, the lexical form will be singular
number and masculine gender.

For the verb, the lexical form will be Qal stem,
perfect state, third person, masculine gender,
and singular number.

You will find these lexical forms in the *Hebrew
Analytical Lexicon,* as well as in Strong's *Exhaustive
Concordance* and Young's *Analytical Concordance.*

You must pay special attention to the instructions about the use of the *Hebrew Analytical Lexicon,*
because it will present a particular difficulty which
was not encountered in the *Analytical Greek Lexicon.*

LETTER CLUSTERS

The problem is caused by a strange phenomenon
in the Hebrew language which I call "letter clusters."
It is as if "I saw him in the bank" were written
"Isawhim inthebank." It makes this six-word sentence
look like it was made up of only two words. At this
point, you have no way of knowing how many words are
in these clusters. How do you go about parsing
"Isawhim"? And, where do the divisions come between
the words?

You have to look up the whole letter cluster
in the *Hebrew Analytical Lexicon* as if it were one
word. This book will tell you what words compose

the cluster, give the lexical form of each and parse any inflected form found there. The following are the kinds of words which join on nouns or verbs or prepositions to compose a letter cluster.

The Article Like Greek, Hebrew has no indefinite article. A word without the Hebrew article is usually translated with the English indefinite article or without any article at all, according to the context. (All of the examples in this section will be taken from the first chapter of Genesis, printed on page 14:6.)

אוֹר (1:3) is translated "light" or "a light"

Unlike Greek (or English), the Hebrew article (הַ) never stands alone. It is always attached to the front end of a word, as a prefix. It also doubles the first letter of the word, unless that letter is a guttural, or ר. Because these do not double, the vowel under the article is changed. "Low roaders" will not learn these vowel change rules.

הַשָּׁמַיִם (1:1) is translated "the heavens"

הָאָרֶץ (1:1) is translated "the earth"

Notice the doubling of the שׁ in the first example is indicated by Daghesh Forte.

In the *Analytical Hebrew Lexicon,* the definite article will always be noted as "pref. הַ."

The Interrogative Also unlike Greek or English, Hebrew does not have question marks. So, they used the same letter as the article, only with a different vowel (הֲ), to indicate a question. Again, gutturals will affect this vowel.

הֲיִהְיֶה (not in Genesis) is translated "will it happen?"

In the *Analytical,* the interrogative will always be noted as "pref. הֲ."

Note that not all words that begin with ה are definite or interrogative. For example, הָיְתָה in 1:2 is Qal perfect, third person, feminine singular of הָיָה.

Prepositions:

Inseparable Prepositions There are three prepositions which, like the article, never stand alone, but are attached to words as prefixes:

בְּ : "in, with, by means of"

כְּ : "as, like, according to"

לְ : "to, for, at"

When these prepositions are prefixed to an indefinite noun, they normally take a shewa. But, if
the word already begins with a shewa, the preposition
takes a hirek.

    בְּרֵאשִׁית (1:1) is translated "in (the) beginning"

    בִּרְקִיעַ (1:14) is translated "in (the) firmament"

When these prepositions join a definite noun,
the ה drops off, and is replaced by the preposition,
while the vowel that was under the ה remains unchanged.

    הָאוֹר (1:4), "the light," becomes לָאוֹר (1:5), "to the light"

In the *Analytical*, these prepositions will be
noted as "pref. בְּ, כְּ, or לְ."

The preposition, מִן ("from, out of"), can be   **Preposition מִן**
written separably or inseparably. When it is written
separably, it is easy to spot and is normally connected
to the word it modifies with a maqqeph (־, see 15:6).
When it is prefixed to a word to form a letter cluster,
the נ disappears and the first letter of the word is
doubled. "Low roaders" will need the *Analytical* for
this one!

    מִתַּחַת (1:7) = מִן־תַּחַת, "from beneath"

In the *Analytical*, this preposition is referred
to as "pref. ·מִ."

The Hebrew "and" (וְ) is also an inseparable   **The Conjunction**
prefix. In fact, almost all words in the Old Testa-
ment that begin with this letter are words which
have the conjunction prefixed to them. If you looked
up the word וְהָאָרֶץ (1:2) in the *Analytical*, you would
not find it listed. Instead, it would say:

    "NOTE.- *All forms beginning with Vav (the few following*
    excepted) will be found in the alphabetical order of the
    analysis according to the letter which next follows Vav
    in each form."

So, you would look up the word הָאָרֶץ in order to parse
the word in the text.

    The *Hebrew Analytical Lexicon* will do more than parse
    all of these clusters. It also gives the rules and vowel
    changes for adding prefixes. If you are interested,
    look up the paragraph that immediately follows the letter
    that represents the appropriate prefix, i.e., ה for the
    definite article.

Hebrew also has inseparable suffixes. The most   **Pronoun Suffixes**
common are pronoun suffixes which attach to nouns.   **On Nouns**

These suffixes show similar relationship to the noun as the Greek genitive and English possessive do. But, where Greek and English use separate words, Hebrew sticks the pronoun right onto the noun.

אָבִי = πατέρ μου = "my father"

Now, you can start to have real fun as you find words with both inseparable prefixes and suffixes:

לְמִינוֹ = לְ+מִין+וֹ, "after its kind" (1:11)

On Verbs

Pronoun suffixes attached to verbs indicate the object of the verbal action. English uses word order to indicate this; the Greek uses accusative and dative cases. Actually, the Hebrew can indicate the object of the action in three ways:

1. Verb + direct object indicator (אֵת, see 15:3) + noun. קָטַל אֶת־דָוִד, "he killed David"

2. Verb + direct object indicator with attached pronoun. קָטַל אֹתִי, "he killed me"

3. Verb with attached pronoun. קְטָלַנִי, "he killed me"

In the case of a noun or a verb with an attached pronoun suffix, the *Analytical* will parse the noun or verb first, and then will parse the suffix. In the above cases, the suffix would be referred to as, "with suff. 1 pers. sing.," for it is first person, singular, with "common" gender (gender is not distinguished in the first person pronoun).

On Prepositions

These suffixes attach to the inseparable prepositions to form the smallest letter clusters in the Hebrew Bible:

לִי is a two-word cluster meaning "to me."

EXAMPLES

To illustrate how the *Analytical Hebrew Lexicon* works, we will work through two examples, one a noun and the other a verb, both found on the Hebrew page 14:6. (The text page, 16:5, has the appropriate material from the *Analytical* reproduced in two columns.) We will look first at לְמֶמְשֶׁלֶת, found in Genesis 1:16 (line 21 of page 14:6).

1. Find לְמֶמְשֶׁלֶת on page 16:5. (If you get stuck, it is the last word in the left-hand column.)

2. Let's analyse the information given about it. (I will "decode" the abbreviations this time, but for the worksheets you will need to consult the tables on page 8 of the *Analytical*.)

Left column (לְמִישׁוֹר—לְמֶמְשֶׁלֶת)

- לִמְלוּכָה ˣ — pref. ל bef. (:) ✗ noun fem. sing. — מלך
- לְמַלְכִּי — pref. ל ✗ Kh. (לְ)מַלְכִּי, K. (לְ)מַלִּיכוּ, see מַלּוּךְ — מלך
- לִמְלָלוֹתִי — pref. ל ✗ pr. name masc. — מלל
- לְמֶלַח ˢ — pref. id. ✗ noun masc. sing. — מלח
- לְמֶלְחָה ˢ — pref. ל bef. (:) ✗ noun fem. sing. — מלח
- לַמִּלְחָמָה — pref. ל f. {לְהַ n.f.s.d.11a, with su... — לחם
- לְמִלְחָמָה — pref. ל q. v. } fr. חֵמָת d. 13a (§42.r.5) —
- לְמִלִּין — pref. id. ✗ noun fem. with pl. masc. term. from מִלָּה dec. 10 — מלל
- לַמֶּלֶךְ — ן pref. ל for לְהַ ✗ noun masc. sing. dec. 6a — מלך
- לַמֹּלֶךְ — pref. id.} ן pr. name of an idol; ן bef. (:) — מלך
- לְמֶלֶךְ — pref. id. ✗ noun masc. s. d. 6a; Chald. d. 3a — מלך
- לִמְלֹךְ — pref. ל bef. (:) ✗ Kal inf. constr. — מלך
- לְמַלְכָּא — Chald., pref. ל ✗ noun masc. sing., emph. of מֶלֶךְ (§59) dec. 3a — מלך
- לְמַלְכָּהּ — ן pref. id. ✗ noun masc. sing., suff. 3 pers. sing. fem. from מֶלֶךְ dec. 6a; ן bef. (:) — מלך
- לְמַלְכּוֹ — pref. id. ✗ id. with suff. 3 pers. sing. masc. — מלך
- לְמָלְכוֹ — pref. id. ✗ Kal inf., suff. 3 pers. sing. masc. — מלך
- לְמַלְכוּת — pref. ל f. {לְהַ noun fem. sing. dec. 10; Ch.} pref. ל q. v. constr. of מַלְכוּ dec. 8c — מלך
- לְמַלְכוּתוֹ — pref. id. ✗ id. with suff. 3 pers. sing. masc. — מלך
- לְמַלְכֵי — ן pref. id. ✗ noun masc. pl. constr. from מֶלֶךְ dec. 6a; ן bef. (:) — מלך
- לְמַלְכִּיָּה, לְמַלְכִּיאֵל — pref. id. ✗ pr. name masc. — מלך
- לַמְּלָכִים — pref. ל for לְהַ ✗ noun m. pl. of מֶלֶךְ d. 6a — מלך
- לְמַלְכֵּינוּ — pref. ל bef. (:) ✗ id. pl., suff. 1 pers. pl. — מלך
- לְמֹלֶכֶם — ן pref. ל ✗ pr. name of an idol; ן bef. (:) — מלך
- לְמַלְכֵּנוּ — pref. id. ✗ noun masc. sing., suff. 1 pers. pl. from מֶלֶךְ dec. 6a — מלך
- לְמַלְכַּת — pref. id. ✗ n. fem. s., constr. of מַלְכָּה d. 12a — מלך
- לְמַלְכֶת — pref. ל bef. (:) ✗ noun fem. sing. — מלך
- לִמְלַמְּדַי — ן pref. id. ✗ Piel part. pl. masc., suff. 1 pers. sing. from מְלַמֵּד dec. 7b — למד
- לְמַלְקוֹשׁ — pref. ל ✗ noun masc. sing. — לקשׁ
- לְמַמְלָכָה — pref. id. ✗ noun fem. sing., constr. לֶכֶת with suff. (לְכְתּוֹ (§42. rem. 5) — מלך
- לְמַמְלְכוֹת — ן pref. id. ✗ id. pl. constr. st. — מלך
- לְמֵימַר — Chald., pref. id. ✗ for מֵאמַר Peal inf. (§53) — אמר
- לְמִמְשְׁלוֹת — pref. id. ✗ pl. of the foll. — משׁל
- לְמֶמְשֶׁלֶת — pref. id. ✗ noun fem. sing. dec. 13a (used as the constr. of מֶמְשָׁלָה §42. rem. 5) — משׁל

Right column (לְמַעֲנִי—לְמִשְׁמֶרֶת)

- לְמִשְׂגָּב — pref. ל ✗ noun masc. sing., dec. 8a (suff. מִשְׂגַּבּוֹ §37. No. 3c) — שׂגב
- לְמִשַׁגֶּנֶת — pref. id. ✗ Hiph. part. sing. fem. — נשׂג
- לְמֹשֶׁה — pref. id. ✗ pr. name masc. — משׁה
- לְמַשּׂוּאוֹת — pref. id. ✗ noun fem., pl. of [מַשּׂוּאָה] d. 10 — שׂוא
- לִמְשׁוּבָתִי — pref. ל bef. (:) ✗ noun fem. sing., suff. 1 pers. sing. from מְשׁוּבָה dec. 10 — שׁוב
- לִמְשׁוֹךְ — pref. id. ✗ Kal inf. constr. (§8. rem. 18) — משׁך
- לִמְשׁוֹל — pref. id. ✗ Kal inf. constr. (§8. rem. 18) — משׁל
- לִמְשׁוּסָה — pref. id. Kh. מְשׁוּסָה, K. מְשִׁסָּה noun fem. sing. dec. 10 — שסס
- לִמְשֹׁחַ — ן pref. id. ✗ Kal inf. constr. — משׁח
- לְמָשְׁחָה — pref. ל ✗ id. with fem. term. (§8. rem. 10); noun fem. Nu. 18.8 — משׁח
- לְמַשְׁחִית — pref. id. ✗ noun masc. sing. — שׁחת
- לְמָשְׁחֲךָ — pref. ל bef. (:) ✗ Kal inf. [מְשֹׁחַ], suff. 2 pers. sing. masc. (§16. rem. 10 & 11; but others read מָשְׁחֲךָ from (מָשַׁח) — משׁח
- לְמָשִׁיב — pref. ל ✗ Hiph. part. sing. masc. dec. 3b — שׁוב
- לְמָשִׁיחַ — pref. ל bef. (:) ✗ n. m. s., constr. of [מָשִׁיחַ] d.3a — משׁח
- לִמְשִׁיחוֹ — pref. id. ✗ id., suff. 3 pers. sing. masc. — משׁח
- לִמְשִׁיחִי — pref. id. ✗ id., suff. 1 pers. sing. — משׁח
- לְמִשְׁכָּב — pref. ל ✗ noun masc. sing. dec. 2b — שׁכב
- לְמִשְׁכַּב — pref. id. ✗ id., constr. st. — שׁכב
- לְמַשְׂכִּיל — pref. id. ✗ Hiph. part. sing. masc. dec. 1b — שׂכל
- לַמִּשְׁכָּן — pref. ל for לְהַ ✗ noun masc. sing. dec. 2b — שׁכן
- לְמִשְׁכַּן — pref. ל ✗ id. constr. st. — שׁכן
- לְמִשְׁכְּנוֹתָיו — pref. id. ✗ id. pl. fem., suff. 3 pers. sing. m. — שׁכן
- לִמְשֹׁל — ן pref. id. ✗ noun masc. s. d. 4a; ן bef. (:) — משׁל
- לִמְשָׁל־ — וְ pref. ל bef. (:) ✗ Kal inf. constr., or (Job 17. 6) subst. masc. (§8. r. 18) — משׁל
- לְמִשְׁלַח — pref. ל ✗ noun m. s., constr. of [מִשְׁלָח] d. 2b — שׁלח
- לְמִשְׁלוֹים — ן pref. ל bef. (:) ✗ noun m., pl. of מָשָׁל d. 4a — משׁל
- לְמִשְׁלָם — pref. id. ✗ pr. name masc. — שׁלם
- לִמְשֶׁלֶמְיָהוּ — ן pref. id. ✗ pr. name masc. — שׁלם
- לְמִשְׁמוֹת — pref. id. ✗ noun fem., pl. of מְשַׁמָּה dec. 10 — שׁמם
- לְמַשְׁמִיעִים — pref. ל ✗ Hiph. part. m., pl. of מַשְׁמִיעַ d.1b — שׁמע
- לְמִשְׁמַע — pref. id. ✗ n. m. s., constr. of [מִשְׁמָע] d.2b — שׁמע
- לְמִשְׁמָר — pref. id. ✗ noun masc. sing. dec. 2b — שׁמר
- לְמִשְׁמָרוֹת — pref. id. ✗ pl. of the foll. (§44. rem. 5) — שׁמר
- לְמִשְׁמַרְתּ / לְמִשְׁמֶרֶת — pref. id. ✗ noun fem. sing. (suff. (מִרְתּוֹ) dec. 13a — שׁמר

x Eze. 16. 13.
y Eze. 47. 11.
z Ps. 107. 34.
a Job 18. 2.
b Jos. 10. 30.
c 1 Sa. 2. 10.
d Est. 4. 14.
e 1 Ki. 10. 29.
f Ps. 47. 7.
g Pr. 5. 13.
h Je. 49. 28.
i Is. 10. 10.
k Job 29. 23.
l 2 Ch. 22. 9.
m Ezr. 5. 11.
n Ps. 136. 9.

c Da. 9. 24.
d Ex. 29. 29.
e 1 Sa. 15. 1.
f Ru. 4. 15.
g 1 Sa. 24. 7.
h Ps. 132. 17.
i Ex. 21. 18.
k Je. 24. 9.
l Ge. 36. 43.
m Job 17. 6.
n Ge. 1. 18.
o Joel 2. 17.
pp Eze. 14. 8.
q Je. 7. 25.
r Je. 48. 34.
s 1 Ch. 16. 42.
t Is. 11. 3.
u Is. 11. 3.
v Ex. 16. 34.
w Eze. 38. 7.

Taken from the *Analytical Hebrew and Chaldee Lexicon* published by Zondervan, and is used by special arrangement with Samuel Bagster & Sons Ltd., London.

```
pref. id.  = prefix as above (6 lines up it is לְ)
noun       = the word is a noun
fem.       = feminine in gender
sing.      = singular in number
dec. 13a (used as the constr. of מֶמְשָׁלָה §42 rem. 5)
           = although most of this matter refers
             to a chart in the front part of the
             Analytical, we need to notice the
             abbreviation "constr.," which tells
             us the noun is construct in state.
```

3. The same questions you asked of Greek pronouns
   (page 8:3) you ask of Hebrew nouns, except you ask
   what *state* it is rather than what *case* it is
   (possibilities: absolute or construct):
   a. What is its state?_____ _____
   b. What is its number?_____
   c. What is its gender?_____

4. The Hebrew word following all these abbreviations is
   usually the lexical form, although in this case it
   is the root under which the lexical form would be
   listed, like in the *Analytical Greek Lexicon*
   (page 7:6). The actual lexical form is the word
   מֶמְשָׁלָה which occurs in the note just before מָשַׁל.

Let's try a verb form next, וְלִמְשֹׁל, from Genesis
1:18 (line 23 of page 14:6).

1. Because the word begins with וְ (see 16:3), we assume
   this is the conjunction and look up לִמְשֹׁל on page 16:5.

2. Let's analyse the information. (Again, I will "decode
   the abbreviations for us.)
```
וִn         = footnote n (Ge. 1:18--our verse)
              gives us a verse with this form
              having a וְ on the front
pref. לְ    = prefixed לְ
bef. (.)    = the לְ, normally pointed with . is
              before a . (see page 16:3)
Kal         = Qal stem
inf. contr. = infinitive construct
or (Job 17:6) = the rest of the note deals with
                Job 17:6
מָשַׁל       = the lexical form or root
```

3. We can summarize this information by asking and
   answering the verb-type questions listed on page 16:8
   a. What is its stem?_____
   b. What is its state?_____
   c. Since this is an infinite construct, it has no
      person, gender or number, so we skip questions
      3, 4, and 5, and ask,
      Does it have a pronoun suffix?_____
   d. We do not ask the conjunction וְ or the prefix
      preposition לְ any questions, we just note that

they are there, making this form a three-word
cluster.

As we discovered with לְמֶמְשֶׁלֶת, the *Analytical*
does not always give us the lexical form. Sometimes
it gives only the cognate root under which the
lexical form would be listed. Further, it does not
point the lexical form or root with the proper vowels,
thus making it very difficult to go from this section
of the *Analytical* directly to another lexicon. In
fact, it is nearly impossible. You must first look
up the cognate root and its listings to see the
proper vowel pointing before you can do any work
outside the bounds of the *Analytical*.

Actually, there is a reason for the lack of points in
the right column: money! When you consider that each
piece of type was set by hand when the *Analytical* was
first published--imagine, each consonant and vowel a
separate piece!--you can sympathize with the desire to
keep costs down by eliminating all but the most
necessary setting. Be thankful that this book was ever
produced at all, rather than critical of its shortcomings.

A further problem exists once you turn to the
cognate listings in the *Analytical*. The Hebrew
vocabulary is built for the most part on the three
consonants of the verbal root, with extra letters or
different vowels added to make nouns, adjectives, and
even other verbs. Thus, it is often easier to spot
family relationships in Hebrew than in Greek. However,
because the Semitic languages were always borrowing
words from each other's vocabularies and adopting the
sounds into their own spellings, Hebrew often came up
spelling different words with the same letters! That
is because Hebrew had only 22 letters with which to
approximate the sounds of the 30 or more letters
floating around among the other Semitic tongues.
Unfortunately for us, the *Analytical* does *not* differ-
entiate between these "homomorphs," that is, words
which are spelled the same, yet are actually quite
different words. Don't despair, however, for we
will learn how to tell them apart in the next lesson.
For now, simply know that you *cannot ever* trust the
Analytical Hebrew Lexicon for cognate studies the
way you could the *Analytical Greek Lexicon*; it will
only confuse you as it confuses the roots.

The following are the questions you should ask
of verbs, nouns, adjectives and pronoun suffixes.
Although the participle, imperative, infinitive
absolute and infinitive construct are separate
parts of speech, they will be treated here and
in the *Analytical* as a state or tense of the verb.

"High roaders" will learn more about these as
they continue in their studies.

ASK A VERB SIX QUESTIONS:

1. What is its *stem*? Options: Qal, Niphal, Piel, Pual,
   Hithpael, Hiphil, Hophal or Hishtaphel.
2. What is its *state?* Options: perfect[1], imperfect[2],
   participle, imperative, infinitive absolute or
   infinitive construct.
3. This applies only to perfect and imperfect states,
   and the imperative: What is its *person*? Options:
   first, second or third person for perfect and imperfect; second or third for imperative.
4. This applies to all but the infinitives: What is
   its *gender*? Options: masculine or feminine.
5. This applies to all but the infinitives: What is
   its *number*? Options: singular or plural.
6. This applies to all but the infinitive absolute:
   Does it have a pronoun suffix? Options: yes or no.

[1]The *Analytical* will call the perfect, "preterite."
[2]The *Analytical* will call the imperfect, "future."

ASK A NOUN THREE QUESTIONS:

1. What is its *number*? Options: singular, plural or
   dual.
2. What is its *state*? Options: absolute*, construct or
   pronominal*.
3. What is its *gender*? Options: masculine or feminine.

*The *Analytical* will only mention if a noun is in the
construct state. If it says nothing about state and
has no suffix, it is absolute. If it says nothing
about state but has a suffix, it is pronominal.

ASK AN ADJECTIVE TWO QUESTIONS:

1. What is its *gender*? Options: masculine or feminine.
2. What is its *number*? Options: singular, plural or
   dual.

ASK A PRONOUN OR PRONOUN SUFFIX THREE QUESTIONS:

1. What is its *person*? Options: first, second or third.
2. What is its *number*? Options: singular or plural.
3. What is its *gender*? Options: masculine or feminine.

Note: The *Analytical* will also mention "case" in
relationship to Hebrew words. However, there are no
case inflections in Hebrew, so case is merely a name
used to describe the position of the word in the sentence, not its form. That is why I have not mentioned
case in analyzing Hebrew words. It makes no difference
at this point.

LESSON 17

THE HEBREW LEXICON

THE LEXICA

You have already had instruction in the Greek
lexicon and practice in its use (Lesson 11). We now
do the same with a Hebrew lexicon. The best one
available is *A Hebrew and English Lexicon of the Old
Testament,* based on the *Lexicon* of William Gesenius
by Francis Brown, S. R. Driver and Charles A. Briggs.
Although it is extremely difficult, we will practice
using it.

The other lexicons are easier to use than Brown,
Driver, and Briggs' and are more up-to-date. However,
none of them is as thorough in the organization of
definitions, nor in the completeness of Biblical
references. *Lexicon in Veteris Testameni Libros,* by
Koehler and Baumgartner (Grand Rapids: Wm. B.
Eerdmans Publishing Co.) is currently the best full-
sized lexicon for etymologies and cognate studies.
However, its definitions were originally done in
German and translated by a German into English, thus
leaving much to be desired in the way of precision
and clarity. An English abridgment, *A Concise Hebrew
and Aramaic Lexicon of the Old Testament*, by William
Holladay (also published by Eerdmans), is far better
for definitions, yet not nearly as complete as Brown,
Driver, and Briggs. Several Hebrew word study books
geared to English readers have appeared in the last
few years. Actually, these are reprints of outdated
18th and 19th century dictionaries which are best
left out-of-print due to the giant steps Hebrew
lexicography has taken throughout this century.

One final lexical tool should be mentioned. It
is a projected ten-volume set edited by Botterweck and
Ringgren (again, published by Eerdmans) called the
Theological Dictionary of the Old Testament. This
massive work, of which three volumes are currently
available in English, goes far beyond definitions as
it studies the whole range of secular and religious
uses of major Hebrew words and their Semitic
"relatives" throughout the ancient Near East, and then
applies these concepts to major Biblical passages.
You may want to work with this set sometime in the

Note: Only the first reference to an abbreviation is "decoded."

All OT references cited

Driver, "Journal of Philology," Volume 11, (1882), page 215.

König, *Hebrew Grammar*, Volume 2, page 182.

Psalm

Gesenius' *Hebrew Grammar*, section 130, note 1.

suffixed form

Isaiah

plural construct form

2 Chronicles

that is

et cetera

the same text as

Daniel

Genesis

verse

noun feminine

etymological infor

compare

absolute form

spelled as lexical

Micah

construct form

Jeremiah

2 occurrences not specified

I Kings

Sennacherib

following

parallel in usage

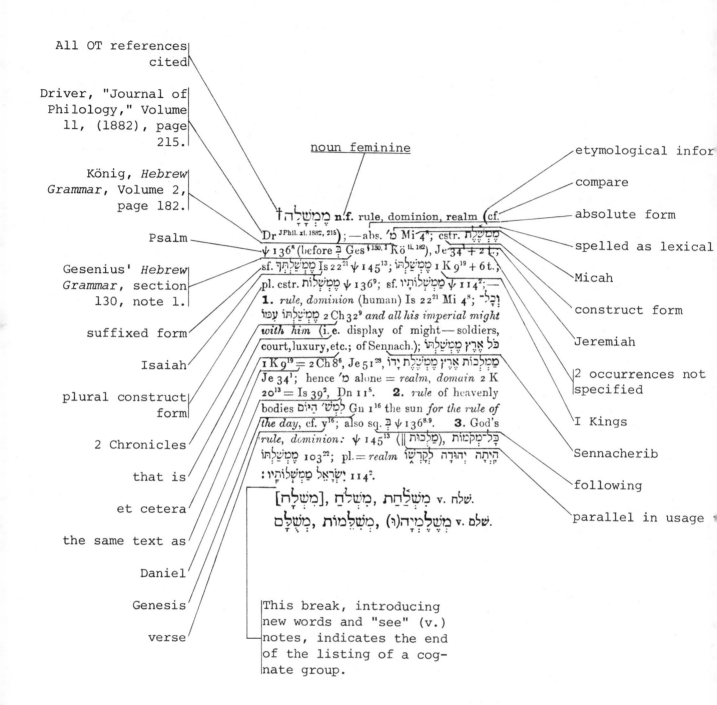

This break, introducing new words and "see" (v.) notes, indicates the end of the listing of a cognate group.

Taken from *A Hebrew and English Lexicon of the Old Testament*, based on the *Lexicon* of William Gesenius, edited by Francis Brown, S. R. Driver and Charles Briggs, published by Oxford: At the Clarendon Press and is used by permission, page 606, basis of Lesson 17.

future, but be aware that its theological orientation is liberal, even though its data and research are very valuable.

Aramaic Sections

The Old Testament is largely Hebrew. However, it has some sections in Aramaic, a close cognate to Hebrew (see page 1:3, and Daniel 2:4b-7:28; Ezra 4:8-6:18, 7:12-26; Jeremiah 10:11). These Aramaic words are defined in a separate section at the end of the lexicon, starting on page 1078 in Brown, Driver and Briggs, page 396 in Holladay, and page 1047 in Koehler-Baumgartner.

AN EXAMPLE

Let's study the word מֶמְשָׁלָה we worked on in Lesson 16. First, we would need to turn in the *Analytical* to this root מֹשֵׁל to be sure we had the correct spelling of the lexical form. This would be on page DXXI, (not reproduced here). Here we would find the spelling מֶמְשָׁלָה as listed in parentheses in the *Analytical's* parsing of the word לְמֶמְשֶׁלֶת (see page 16:5). If we looked up this word alphabetically in Brown, Driver and Briggs (BDB) on page 577, we would find no definition, but the statement:

מֹשֵׁל v. מֶמְשָׁלֶת, מֶמְשָׁלָה, מִמְשָׁל

Why? Remember in 16:7 we stated that Hebrew words are built off of the verb? Well, BDB *arranged* its lexical order around the verb rather than on the basis of the alphabet. Thus, if you want to find a word's definition, you have to look for it underneath its verbal root. The verbal root for מֶמְשָׁלָה, we are told, is מֹשֵׁל ("v" means "see the listing under this root").

However, when we turn to מֹשֵׁל, we see that there are on pages 605 and 606 no less than *seven* words with the consonants מֹשֵׁל, and various vowels!

Type size becomes important at this point. Remember on page 16:7 we said that many words are spelled the same, yet are different words, because of the limited Hebrew alphabet? BDB puts the major roots in large script, with their cognate family in alphabetic order underneath them in a smaller script. Further, each distinct root has its own Roman numeral, to distinguish it from the other roots. We see, then, that there are three "families" of מֹשֵׁל, and our word is a member of the third, whose root meaning is "rule." So, once we find a word, we are already in position to do cognate studies. And, in BDB, we do not have the confusion of these roots (as though they were all the same) that we do in the *Analytical*.

We will now interpret this entry, reproduced on page 17:2, as we did in Lesson 11 with the *Lexicon* of Bauer, Arndt, Gingrich and Danker.

Etymology   מֶמְשָׁלָה is treated in this entry in all of its Old Testament occurrences. It is a feminine noun. Its basic ideas are "rule, dominion, realm," as developed by Driver in the "Journal of Philology," volume 11 (1882), page 215.

Morphology   Its absolute form occurs in Micah 4:8, and its construct form מֶמְשֶׁלַח in Psalm 136:8. The construct occurs here even before the preposition בְּ, as discussed in Gesenius' *Hebrew Grammar,* section 130, and in Konig's *Hebrew Grammar,* volume 2, page 182. The construct form also is found in Jeremiah 34:1 and two other places.

      With a second person, masculine, singular suffix, it (מֶמְשֶׁלְתְּךָ) is found in Isaiah 22:21 and Psalms 145:13; with a third person masculine, singular suffix, it (מֶמְשַׁלְתּוֹ) is found in I Kings 9:19 and six other places. The plural construct form (מֶמְשְׁלוֹת), is found in Psalm 136:9, and the suffixed plural form (מֶמְשְׁלוֹתָיו) is found in Psalm 114:2.

Meanings   This Hebrew word has three basic categories of meanings.

      1. It means human rule or dominion in Isaiah 22:21 and Micah 4:8. In 2 Chronicles 32:9, also, the phrase וְכָל־ מֶמְשַׁלְתּוֹ עִמּוֹ, "and all his imperial might with him," indicates a display of might--soldiers, court, luxury, and so forth, referring to Sennacherib. כֹּל אֶרֶץ מֶמְשַׁלְתּוֹ found in I Kings 9:19, the same as 2 Chronicles 8:6 and Jeremiah 51:28, with מַמְלְכוֹת אֶרֶץ מֶמְשֶׁלֶת יָדוֹ in Jeremiah 34:1, show us that מֶמְשָׁלָה alone can mean "realm or domain," such as in 2 Kings 20:13, which is the same as Isaiah 39:2, and Daniel 11:5.

      2. This word is also used of the "rule" of heavenly bodies. In Genesis 1:16, לְמֶמְשֶׁלֶת הַיּוֹם in reference to the sun means "for the rule of the day;" compare this to verse 16. Following the preposition בְּ, as in Psalm 136:8 and 9, it has the same meaning.

      3. The third category deals with God's rule or dominion. In Psalm 145:13, our word is parallel in meaning to מַלְכוּת. The phrase כָּל־ מְקֹמוֹת מֶמְשַׁלְתּוֹ appears in Psalm 103:22 with the same meaning. In its plural form, it means "realm," as illustrated by the phrase הָיְתָה יְהוּדָה לְקָדְשׁוֹ יִשְׂרָאֵל מַמְשְׁלוֹתָיו from Psalm 114:2.

      If you wanted to do a cognate study on מֶמְשָׁלָה, you would deal with every word between its cognate root מָשַׁל III. and the beginning of the next entry. You can tell when a new cognate group starts in BDB in two ways. The first is the type size: a large-type word indicates a new root. The second indication is a listing of lexical forms with the "v." or "see this root" note at their end. This is the case here, as seen in our sample page on page 17:2.

Finding words in the lexicons by Koehler-Baumgartner and Holladay is much easier: both are in strict alphabetical order. The cognate studies will require some page flipping, though. Only Koehler-Baumgartner will give you this information. If you are studying a word which is a member, but not the "clan leader," of a family, they give you its root immediately after the lexical form.

On the other hand, at the end of the entry discussing the etymology, meanings, and usage of a cognate root, following the abbreviation "Der.," (for "derivatives"), they will list the various family members. Most scholars prefer Koehler-Baumgartner's cognate work to BDB because they had the advantage of fifty years of work in Akkadian, the discoveries at Tel el Amarna, the discovery of Ugaritic at Ras Shamra, and the Dead Sea Scrolls, all of which happened since the last edition of BDB and have had great bearing on our understanding of Biblical Hebrew. *All* prefer *anything* to the cognate work of the *Analytical*.

THE EXTERNAL
CONTEXT

I worry a lot about this book. It concentrates so much on the *text* of the Bible, one might get the impression that Bible study is limited to the examination of the text. Actually, Bible study is not so much an examination of a text as it is an examination of an historical event. The text you examine was addressed to somebody for some reason at some particular time and place.

Too many Bible teachers regard Palestine like the land of Oz, floating about, unmoored, in the sky. Palestine is a very real place and constitutes a very real stage on which very real people did very real things as they found themselves performing in God's redemption drama.

That very real place, with those real people, creating very real history, must be understood before that book which contains them can be understood as it ought to be.

The German term, often overused and certainly abused, *sitz im leben*, identifies the actual, historical, life situation in which a revelation occurs. I call it "external context" and break it down into geography, culture and history.

This external context must be studied as carefully as the textual context. And the proverb is equally true about it:

> *A text,*
> *Taken out of its external context*
> *Becomes a pretext.*

This *sitz im leben* is not equally pertinent in every part of your Bible. In some places it has less significance although it would be difficult to find a place where it had no input at all. For instance, this external context is more important to the understanding of 1 and 2 Corinthians than it is to Romans; and is indispensable with Philemon, but not so much with the Epistle to the Hebrews.

GEOGRAPHY YOU MAY NOT KNOW

Geography is the easiest of the three. We will start there. Did you know that you go down-hill to the top of Mt. Nebo? That Jericho is an oasis in the desert? That there are no natural harbors there? That the Sea of Galilee is too salty to be used for irrigation and is hundreds of feet lower than the Mediterranean? That it rains as much in Jerusalem as it does in London?

And by geography, I don't mean so much mountains, rivers and seas, as I do human geography of countries, roads, cities and farms. What do you know about such things?

What kind of land is it where water is so critical and yet rivers, lakes and seas are so inconsequential? Where wadies, not rivers, are important? Where so much happens on such a little wrinkled postage-stamp land--so wrinkled as to vary more than a mile in elevation and be savagely cloven in twain by the biggest crack on the earth's surface? Where a land's most fertile plain was pirated all the way from Ethiopia, grain by grain, through the largess of the Nile? What is this ever so short and ever so thin thread from which dangles the whole of heavy Africa, and up and down which thread ever scurry merchant caravans and armies going forth to war? What is this Earth's navel which always has been an out-of-the-way place, this barren land which manages to spawn nothing but rocks and the loftiest thoughts man has ever dreamt, this "David country," this "Jesus country"?

How much detail in those sacred events that happened there was generated by the lay of the land? And why, when You had your pick of any place on earth, did you homestead *there*, O God?

THE LAY OF THE LAND

Look at Palestine as the bottom half of the east coast of the Mediterranean Sea, and then look at it as four long strips lying north and south, side by side. The westernmost strip is the coastal plain which diminishes as you go farther north. Next to it is the strip we call the Cis-Jordan Mountains, which break in two toward the top with a veering off into the sea just below the break. Then comes the strip we call the great rift valley, almost ramrod straight and enclosing the lakes Hula and Gennesaret and the Dead Sea with the Jordan River connecting the three. Finally, with ill-defined eastern edges, the last strip, the Trans-Jordan highlands, noticeably higher than the Cis-Jordan Mountains, forms a level, integral part of the great granite block called Arabia which extends on and on eastward.

So it is harder to go east and west than it is
to go north and south, and it is very hard to keep a
country together when you have a large ditch running
through the middle, splitting it in two.

HUMAN GEOGRAPHY

See the land complying with the timeless
dichotomy between the hill people and the bottom land
people, together with the social stratification that
accompanies this. Then regard Israel as the people
of the hills and the Philistines and Phoenicians and
Canaanites as the upper class, wealthier people of
the bottom land.

Fear the forest and the sea; love donkeys and
the desert and olive oil. Love rain and celebrate
its arrival in the fall and celebrate again when it
lasts until late spring. See how rain gets scarcer
as you go east and especially when you go south.
Value cisterns, build one, own it, and defend it with
your life. It is more yours than the land on which
you build it.

HOW DO YOU STUDY
BIBLE GEOGRAPHY?

How does one go about learning biblical geography? First, you have to convince yourself that
the subject is important to you and to your understanding of the Bible.

Then, get in the habit of looking up in an atlas
any strange place-names you run across. This will
take discipline because it will slow up your reading
so much, especially at the start.

The atlas in the back of your Bible will be
most frustrating because every time you look up something in it, you lose your place in the Bible. And
that, more often than not, is excuse enough for not
continuing the practice.

You would do better to get a separate Bible
atlas, one that opens up flat, and that has a good
index of place-names in it. They are not too expensive. Both the Hammond and Holman publishers have
reasonable ones. The Oxford one is excellent, but
the paperback edition doesn't open up flat. A very
good but expensive atlas which faithfully maps
individual, biblical events is called *The Macmillan
Bible Atlas* by Yohanan Aharoni and Michael Avi-Yonah
(revised edition, 1978).

Try to keep distances in mind (a person normally
traveled about twenty miles a day). Heights, however,
are almost impossible to visualize from a map.

Don't try to memorize grocery lists of place-
names. You will learn these soon enough if you are
faithful to use an atlas.

Another important habit to get into is to look at photographs of the Holy Land, again, with an open atlas before you. Notice where in the Holy Land the picture was taken. Look up the place in your atlas and then try to imagine from the photograph how that area looked. There are excellent photographs in coffee table books about the Bible, in Bible atlases, and in the many articles in the *National Geographic Magazine*. When you look at these photographs, you must try to think away the roads and buildings. And if the picture was taken in the area of Hebron and north, but not in the Negev, you have to think forests back into the picture.

You will also want to read some Bible geography books. There are two which deserve your careful reading and which complement each other. Denis Baly does a superb job in describing the lay of the land in his *The Geography of the Bible* (Harper and Row, revised edition, 1974). And Yohanan Aharoni in his *The Land of the Bible* (Westminster, 1967) accurately describes the importance of geography in historical events, even though he ignores the New Testament.

MORE THAN PALESTINE

Of course, your major interest is in Palestine proper. However, the geography of the lands surrounding Palestine actually affects the geography of Palestine, especially the human geography of Palestine. So you must study about Mesopotamia, Egypt and the Sinai.

Furthermore, many highly significant biblical events occurred outside the boundaries of Palestine, such as the Patriarchs in Mesopotamia and Egypt, Moses and the Exodus in Egypt and the Sinai, the captivities in Mesopotamia, etc. And Paul requires a study of Italy, Greece, Turkey and the whole of the Levant.

Just as Bible study is an ongoing thing, so is the study of its geography. It is an habitual aspect of your continuing Bible study.

SEE IT FOR YOURSELF

With air travel getting so reasonable, many people are finding it possible to visit the Holy Land. When it comes to geography, there is no substitute for seeing it firsthand. If you take seriously what you read in this chapter, and follow my advice about launching an ongoing study of Bible lands, your desire to go to Palestine will become so overpowering that you will manage somehow to get there.

It is best for first-timers to go with a tour group. Choose one very carefully. Make certain your tour director is an expert in Biblical geography. To be

knowledgeable about Biblical content is hardly enough.
And as a lot, the official guides are not dependable.

Take a good look at your fellow tourists. Do they really
want to learn Biblical geography badly enough to suffer
a little to do it or are they on a shopping tour?

And if you can only be away for two weeks, don't go. Wait
until you have at least four weeks. You will be surprised
about how little more it will cost. Costs vary considerably
between tour groups, not only because of the differences
in the quality of hotels, but also on how many freeloaders
you are paying for who go along for nothing.

Study until you know the land like the back of your hand;
not until then should you see if firsthand. Don't
contribute to the ignorant, blank stares of the tourist
group. He who would know the Bible lands when he returns
home must learn them before he departs.

WHY STUDY CULTURE?

Did you know that there are a lot of "old wives' fables" going around about how the people of the Bible lived and thought? Take, for instance, the fable about the Jews in Jesus' day going around Samaria rather than through it, or that there was a gate in ancient Jerusalem called "the Eye of the Needle," etc.?

These stories are generated from a strongly felt need to fill a vacuum. Because our instincts are *right* when they tell us that they did things differently, and to know "how" helps to understand the Bible. Actually, not only did they do things differently, they didn't think exactly as we do now, especially about their value system. And one's value system has more influence on what one does than anything else.

Take, for instance, the interesting contrasts between the way the angels were "entertained unawares" first by host Abraham, and then, in contrast, by host Lot (Genesis, chapters 18-19).

It may look incredibly silly to us for Abraham to run out, prostrate himself before three perfect strangers, and demean himself with:

"If I have found favor in your eyes, my lord, do not pass your servant by. Let a little water be brought, and then you may all wash your feet and rest under this tree. Let me get you something to eat, so you can be refreshed and then go on your way--now that you have come to your servant" (Genesis 18:4-5).

And then, to top it off, he orders his wife to drop what she is doing and prepare a feast for them!

However, no one back then would have seen anything at all strange in Abraham's behavior. He was simply responding to his value system by conforming to the customs of hospitality which were indigenous to his desert culture. For a man's status was determined to a large degree by his ability to show hospitality. Hospitality was a cultural compulsion almost never broken.

But contrast this successful exercise of hospitality with Lot's abortive effort, now in the city of Sodom. See how Lot's insistence on entertaining these same strangers comes with the same kind of demeaning language:

> "'My lords, please turn aside to your servant's house. You can wash your feet and spend the night and then go on your way early in the morning.'...He insisted so strongly that they did go with him and entered his house. He prepared a meal for them, baking bread without yeast" (Genesis 19:2-3).

An essential part of the law of hospitality is the protection the host *must* give to his guests. That Lot would go to such extremes as to offer to sacrifice his own daughters for the safety of his guests only shows the awful compunction he was under. But what would have impressed a person from this culture most, when he hears this frightful story, is Lot's total devastation when his guest had to save *him*!

And when the psalmist says, "Thou preparest a table before me in the presence of my enemies," to a person of that culture, the listener conjures up a fugitive, relaxed in the tent of his powerful host, casually eating from his host's bounty. At the same time his enemies who have pursued him, now made impotent by the law of hospitality enforced by that strong host, are partaking of the same meal. It is a song to snuggle up by and go fast asleep.

If you are to be a faithful servant whose service includes the teaching of God's word, you must always be conscious that you are not only teaching an historical event which has geographical moorings, but also a book which records events in cultures different from your own. You must make the effort to crawl inside the skins of the actors and look at the historical events through their eyes. How did the prophet regard the statements he was making, and how did his audience respond to them? For what was being said is intricately entwined with the culture of those actors. You won't understand what was preached or written any better than you understand that culture.

Man, of course, is essentially the same, no matter what culture you find him in. So he can understand the essential message of the Bible and the Bible can meet his needs. For he can get the Bible's basic message without a sophisticated understanding of the culture of the Bible. I am talking about the average Christian. However, I expect that the user of this book aspires to be a skillful effective *teacher* of that Bible. Such a high aspiration places his prerequisites on a much higher plane, a plane which includes understandings of the Biblical culture.

But where can one secure information about the SOURCES
cultural anthropology of ancient Israel? Unfortunately, adequate, reliable and convenient tools, which
you can keep within reach and which describe cultural
patterns relevant to the text you happen to be examining,
do not exist.

About the handiest sources are the commentaries.
But almost to a man, their authors are linguistic
experts whose lack of competence in cultural anthropology is patently obvious. Books devoted to a
formal description of the cultures of the Bible are
rare, brief and most frustrating when one tries to
use them on any given text. One must resort to
their haphazard Biblical indices. Really, these
books ought to be used in the manner for which they
were designed: to be read through. That way, the
student soaks up the culture and it becomes background understanding which remains available whenever he looks at a relevant text.

The best book I know about is Ronald DeVaux's
Ancient Israel (McGraw-Hill, 1961, 592 pp). But it
is so thoroughly saturated with the "Documentary
Hypothesis" that it is most difficult to use. Second
best is a pair of books, *Everyday Life in Old Testament
Times* by E. W. Heaton, and *Everyday Life in New
Testament Times* by A. C. Bouquet (both by Scribners).
A very excellent, but thin book, written by Ludwig
Köhler (Abingdon, 1953), is *Hebrew Man*.

There are a number of excellent titles which
devote themselves to some particular aspect of the
culture of ancient Israel. For example, warfare is
treated thoroughly in Yigael Yadin's *The Art of Warfare
in Biblical Lands* (McGraw-Hill, 1965, 2 vols.). There
is Donald A. Leggett's book, *The Levirite and Goel
Institutions in the Old Testament* (Mack, 1974, 351
pages). Navigation during the first century is
explained beautifully in James Smith's *The Voyage and
Shipwreck of St. Paul* (Baker, 1978, a reprint of an
1880 classic, 293 pages). Joachim Jeremias gives an
exhaustive and masterly description of life in
Jerusalem in the first century in his *Jerusalem in
the Time of Jesus* (Fortress, 1967, 405 pages). And
Sherman-White's *Roman Society and Roman Law in the
New Testament* (Oxford, 1963, 206 pages) is a perfect
gem.

One discovers cultural goodies in the strangest
places: in the rabbinic literature, in archaeological
reports, in descriptions of modern Bedouin culture,
in coffeetable picture books about the Bible, and
in many articles in *The National Geographic*. Many
can be found in James B. Pritchard's twin-volume,

magnum opus: *Ancient Near Eastern Texts* and *The Ancient Near East in Pictures* (Princeton University Press). These books might be too expensive for your pocket book, about $50 a piece; but you can bring pressure on your public or church library to buy them. And do not despise the lowly picture. You can learn a lot from a picture if you look at it hard enough.

THE BIBLE AS A SOURCE

The best book, by far, for learning the biblical cultures is the Bible itself. Cultural data is found on every page, especially in the area of axiology. Develop an alertness for these details.

May I suggest an ongoing study for you that will reward your investment in time many times over? First, get a list of the normal catagories of cultural anthropology, like:

I.   Family -- courtship, marriage, divorce, concubinage, incest, woman's role, economic values, domestic routine, meals, house/tent, family size, kinship, inheritance, etc.
II. Government -- clan, tribe, village, city, country, crime/punishment, taxation, lawmaking, etc.
III. Education -- formal/informal, sexual distinction, schools, teacher/tutor, literacy, etc.
IV. Occupation -- farmer, stockman, merchant, potter, dyer, metalsmith, carpenter, tax agent, tanner, banker, apprenticeship, guilds, etc.
V.   Economics -- money, barter, credit, property, transportation, profit, interest, etc.
VI. Play -- children's games, adult games, athletics, storytelling, etc.
VII. Social Classes -- peasant, citizen, landowner, displaced person, widow, child, slave, nobleman, prophet, priest, king, etc.
VIII. Aesthetics -- human form, scenery, fine art, painting, sculpture, decoration, jewelry, architecture, music, literature, dance, etc.
IX. Warfare -- arms, strategy, tactics, seige, pay, conscription, morale, captives, spoil, etc.
X.   Axiology -- Prestige, sexual distinctions, wealth, family size, occupations, inheritance, ethics, etc.
XI. Religion -- beliefs, rites, associations, priest/clergy Scripture, etc.

Second, one should take note when reading his Bible of any information he finds about any of these categories, filing them away under the proper cultural category. It would create a continually growing and increasingly important file for him. For instance, the Bible student is reading in Isaiah chapter five, verses one and two. Here he gains important insights into how to farm grapes. One notes that the farmer 1) plows the land, 2) removes the stones, 3) builds a tower, 4) hews out a winepress in the bedrock, 5) builds a wall around the vineyard, 6) prunes the vines.

Now, using the set of categories on the previous page, see what you can make of Proverbs 31:10-39; pay special attention to axiology.

Above all, avoid the "gimmick approach" which pins some eccentric custom on some specific strange verse. Rather, seek to comprehend the whole, especially the value system, what gives status, what supplies one's life goals, etc. They are much harder to discover, but far more rewarding.

LESSON 20

THE EXTERNAL CONTEXT:
HISTORY

Add time to geography and culture, and you get history. And the Bible is essentially a history book, a book of *genuine* history. Even the New Testament letters and the Old Testament prophecies were historical events written or proclaimed to meet particular historical needs. The Jews didn't distinguish between their history books and their prophetic books; they called the former, "the Early Prophets," and the latter, "the Latter Prophets."

THE BIBLE IS
HISTORY

The Bible is God's textbook on the history and nature of redemption. Its history is not a self-contained history of its own, unrelated to the history of the ancient Mediterranean. Rather, it is locked in to that Mediterranean history, sharing names and events with it, and assuming its reader has an antecedent understanding of the larger historical context of those names and events.

Without such an understanding, many of the biblical events are misunderstood.

I mean people such as Shishak, So, Tirhakah, Necho, Hophra, Tiglath-pileser III, Shalmaneser V, Sargon II, Sennacherib, Adrammelech, Sharezer, Esarhaddon, Ashur-banipal, Ben-Hadad I, Hazael, Ben-Hadad II, Rezin, Merodach-baladan, Nebuchadnezzar, Evil-Merodach, Nergal-sharezer, Belshazzar, Darius, Cyrus, Ahasuerus, Artaxerxes, Mordecai, Sanballat, Tobiah, Geshem, Tattenai, Johohanan, Augustus, Tiberius, Claudius, Nero, Quirinius, Lysanias, Pilate, Felix, Festus, Sergius Paulus, Gallio, Herod, Antipas, Herodias, Philip, Agrippa I and II, Drusilla, Bernice, Aretas, etc.

I mean events such as the battles of Megiddo, Qarqar, Kadesh, Issus, the campaigns of Amenhotep II, Seti I, Ramses II, Merneptah, Shishak, Shalmaneser I and II, Tiglath-pileser, Sargon II, Sennacherib, Esarhaddon, Necho, Nebuchadnezzar, and such things as the invasion and expulsion of the Hyksos (so-called), the migrations of the sea-peoples, the fall of Nineveh, the journey of Wen-Amon, the archives at Amarna.

And, of course, it goes without saying that we must
include an understanding of the Egyptian, Mesopotamian,
Greek, Roman and Parthian empires and the other
Levantine buffer states like Syria, Phoenicia, Philistia,
Ammon, Moab, Edom, Midian, etc.

This history of the ancient Mediterranean
would furthermore build a bridge between the Old and
New Testaments and yield understandings for the
rather different scene and flavor in the New Testament gospels from the scene and flavor found in the
final Old Testament books: Ezra, Nehemiah and Malachi.

So you can see that the exegete must exegete the
external context of his text at the same time he
exegetes its internal context.

EXEGESIS AND HISTORY

However, the exegete is infected with an
occupational myopia. He assumes that know-how in
grammatical "nitty-gritty" qualifies him to be an
exegete because, to borrow Robert Browning's words:
"He settled *Hoti's* business--let it be!--
        Properly based *oun*--
Gave us the doctrine of the enclitic *de*."
The tragedy is that altogether too often, his exegesis ends here. Doing external exegesis in geography, culture, and history ought to occupy a
major part of his research effort.

New Testament exegesis will take one giant step
forward when it is taken out of the Greek department
and given to the history department.

By saying this, I am not at this late stage
belittling a knowledge of Greek and Hebrew. They are
very important. And every historian, worthy of his
salt, is at ease in the languages of his special area
and period of expertise. So it isn't either/or, either
a knowledge of the languages or of the history, it is
both/and.

SOURCES

How does one go about qualifying himself in the
history of the ancient Mediterranean and Near East?
I think that a college course on this subject is so
important that it *must* be secured even if one has to
get it by correspondence.

The study of encyclopedia articles of people
and events as they appear both in the Biblical text
and in history should be done without a second
thought. Again, this will slow up your reading, but
you will get instant help this way in that particular
text you are interested in at that moment. However,
you will find it frustrating because the full
historical context will not be explained.

Always keep a handy chronological chart by your side when you are studying your Bible. It will aid you significantly. An 8½x11 set of four cards is available which I use a lot. They are called: "Study Graph," done by James L. Boyer and John C. Whitcomb, and published by Moody Press. They include the whole Bible, and even the time between the Old and New Testaments. Though principally a chronology of the Bible, they include the prinicpal dates of Egyptian, Mesopotamian, Greek and Roman history.

Two up-to-date Bible histories are available, both of which integrate biblical history with the surrounding countries. They are:

John Bright. *A History of Israel*. The Westminster Press, 1952, 500 pages.

Charles F. Pfeiffer. *Old Testament History*. Baker Book House, 1973, 640 pages.

There are a number of other books of great help:

D. J. Wiseman, ed. *Peoples of Old Testament Times*. Oxford, 1973, 402 pages. This book treats systematically and separately the history of the surrounding countries which affected the history of ancient Israel.

Jack P. Lewis. *Historical Backgrounds of Bible History*. Baker Book House, 1971, 199 pages, paperback. Dr. Lewis assembled all of the extra-biblical data he could find about Biblical characters.

The Cambridge Ancient History. Cambridge, 12 volumes. This is the definitive work on ancient history. It is in the slow process of being revised.

K. A. Kitchen. *The Third Intermediate Period in Egypt*. Aris and Phillips, Ltd., 1973, 525 pages. I can't resist the temptation to mention this definitive Egyptian history during the time of the Israelitic kings (1,100 to 650 BC). It carefully coordinates this period with Biblical history. A glance at the Biblical index in the back of the book will show how carefully he has done his work. It is a parade ground example of the kind of ancient history book the serious Bible student could use with profit.

The better Bible commentaries are always alluding to events of ancient history. However, they presume a knowledge of the subject few people today now possess. Here are some others that may help:

F. F. Bruce. *Israel and the Nations*. Paternoster, 1963, 242 pages. This is an elementary book strongly weighted toward the latter times, especially New Testament times.

F. F. Bruce. *New Testament History*. Doubleday, 1969, 242 pages. This is a definitive work on the history of the New Testament.

Emil Schurer. *The History of the Jewish People in the Age of Jesus Christ*. It is in the process of complete revision under Matthew Black; the first two volumes are now available. It is being done by T. & T. Clark, Ltd., Edinburgh, and is very expensive.

A painless way to absorb both history and customs is to read well-researched novels. Unfortunately, not all have been that well researched. I am sure that there are many more, but I will mention only four which are very reliable:

Paul L. Maier. *Pontius Pilate*. Tyndale House.

Robert Graves. *I, Claudius* and *Claudius, the God.* Harrison Smith and Robert Haas.

James A. Michener. *The Source*. Random House.

William H. Stephens. *The Mantle*. Tyndale House.

HIS HUMILITY

Whether or not one's faith says that God wrote the Bible, it is still true when a student reads any distance into it, he becomes so awed in the presence of such spiritual giants that he gets quite tractable - so much so that he develops the strong suspicion that the confusion, the inscrutabilities, the apparent contradictions are traceable to his own spiritual ineptitudes. That is, if he is not some insufferable arrogant snob.

He is a true novice exegete, indeed, who has not yet discovered that he is by no means a literary critic evaluating the work done by members of his peer-group. And, he has no more stomach for offering improvements on Isaiah or Nahum or Paul than he has aspirations to produce a twentieth century replacement for the least of them. Humbly he seeks only to understand what he reads and, as best he can, to explain what he does understand to others (see page 13:6).

HIS SCOPE

If we had been raised in the language and culture of the Bible, we would have needed an exegete about as badly as the cowboy needs a lawyer to interpret what the cook means when he calls out, "Come and get it!"

When we who exegete find that we have worked ourselves into such a ridiculous frame as to believe that the Church in Philippi needed one of us before it could get the gist of the letter Paul wrote to it, we know we have fallen into an insane conceit.

Our job is to recover the language and culture loss, period. The rest is up to anybody who has the maturity to conceive and apply spiritual truth. We must work hard at our mundane craft and not take on airs.

But whose role is it to synthesize Scripture? What about this formidable task of coordinating and integrating a text with the whole of the Bible? Whose preserve is this? That of the trained exegete or of the devout Bible student?

I have been thinking a good deal about this
lately. My contradictory, even ambivalent, experience is of little help.

What is left over after correcting for all of
the historical and linguistic loss (if you grant it
is not to be just an intelligence contest) is as
much the hunting ground of the devout student as
it is of anybody else. And to the degree he is
devout, a little more the former's.

The catch comes from the fact that it is only
in the model created in our mind that Biblical content
and historical-linguistic contributions are distinct
categories. This is never so in real life. You
can't really say when one leaves off and the other
begins.

So, the devout Bible student--and to the degree
he is devout, he adds prestige to his calling--
busies himself in historical-linguistic pursuits even
occasionally at the cost of pure Bible reading. And
the historical-linguistic expert, when approaching
his Bible, comes humbly aware that his only advantage
lies in this historical-linguistic knowledge, which
very well might not outweigh the advantage of spiritual comprehensions which an intimate walk with the
Author has given the devout student.

An exegete contributes only historical-linguistic
matters; a Christian exegete seeks to excel in both
these matters and the spiritual insights.

A man who so lives with it all, Genesis through
Revelation, perhaps unconsciously has more success-
fully gathered from the whole of it the mind of God.

HIS TEMPTATION

If you are in search of some kind of high pul-
pit, an unassailable bastion from which you may pon-
tificate, if you are looking for some kind of gas to
make people tractable, if you are gathering paraphernalia to embellish your Christian priestcraft, I can
think of nothing more effective than the generous
application of Greek and Hebrew technical terms.

The skillful parading of your new-found language
skills will net you some very interesting results:

1. It will accent the clergy-layman dichotomy and will
   keep the layman in his place.

2. It is a great ego-trip.

3. It surrounds you with the aura of esoteric, hidden
   knowledge.

4. It helps you settle arguments. I don't know anything
   that will quicker silence opposition than the statement, "It says so in the Greek."

5. It gives your pontifications about Biblical themes a
   stamp of authority.

6. It gives you prestige among the brethren. A Greek or
   Hebrew scholar is a chicken that can peck almost
   anybody.

In order for you to accomplish these goals you must
adopt the following procedures and practice the following
skills:

1. Be sure to parse the words. For example, you say, "In
   John 3:16, the Greek word for 'loved' is ἠγάπησεν.
   It is the third person, singular, punctiliar, active,
   indicative, past form." It won't tell people anything,
   but they will be profoundly impressed.

2. Use exotic Greek and Hebrew terms. For instance, to
   say "present tense" won't impress people very much,
   but to say "aorist" is sheer magic. The most awesome
   expression I know is "the accentuation of disyllabic
   enclitics." Memorize it and repeat it over and over
   again until it rolls off your tongue effortlessly.
   The only problem is that it's awfully hard to work
   into a sermon.

3. Always pronounce every Hebrew and Greek word.

4. Always point out where the English translation is wrong;
   never praise it when it is right. Your aim is to create
   distrust in translations; for to the degree that you
   succeed, you make your own priestcraft more indispensable.

5. Speak, if not disparagingly, at least condescendingly of
   ministers who are not Greek and Hebrew scholars.

6. Don't let laypeople get their hands on this syllabus!
   What they don't know won't hurt them.

Perhaps you are worrying about the person in your
congregation who has studied Greek or Hebrew. Have no
fear. He will be your strongest ally, smiling and nod-
ding every time you refer to the original languages.
For you see, he wants in on the action.

And about the intelligent person; you need not be
concerned here either. For he has already left you
months ago and is worshiping elsewhere, or, thanks to
you, nowhere.

But on the other hand, if your goal is to please
the Lord, then the only reason for your pursuit of
Hebrew and Greek and the development of skill in their
tools is to gain a better understanding of God's Word,

to believe, to do and to teach. Then you must come
up with adequate spiritual resources to resist such
a temptation.

It's awfully hard to impress both God and man
at the same time. Decide which now!

You've got to pray real hard, just as hard as
the minister, the missionary or the martyr. The de-
mands for integrity, the temptations to pride, the
satanic assaults, the requisites for Divine enable-
ment for effective work are the same, and humility
and spirituality just as difficult to attain.

What the priest did in the Holy Place and what
happened to the men who inadvertently touched the
Ark of the Covenant are examples of the awesomeness
and the dangers of the man who presumes to mediate
sacred truth to men.

I have mentioned idioms before (5:4-5 and 12:2).
Now we want to take a good look at them. What is an
idiom? How do you interpret an idiom? And, how do
you recognize one when you see one?

DEFINITION

An idiom is an expression which has a meaning
all its own, a meaning you cannot get at by the normal
processes we have been working on throughout this book.
That is, you can't construct the meaning of an idiom
by syntactically and lexically analyzing its parts.
As I said before, it is marching to the tune of another
band, if I may use an idiom to describe an idiom.

EXAMPLES

Take, for instance, the sentence, "There is a
spider, step on it." The meaning of the expression,
"step on it" yields to the normal processes that we
have been practicing throughout this book. However,
take the sentence, "I'm late, step on it." Now if
you should approach the same words in this manner, you
would come up with a total blank, for it is an idiom.
You don't have to know how this idiom got to mean
what it does; you only have to know that it means,
"Hurry!"

There are many Biblical idioms, such as:

"wind of the day"

"horn of salvation"

"close up one's bowels"

"shake the dust off one's feet"

"to lift up a face"

I have picked obvious ones. Many more are subtle
and difficult to recognize.

IMPORTANCE

I don't think I have to labor the question (an
idiom) that it is important for you to understand
idioms. For if you don't recognize that you are working with one and proceed with it as if it were not,
you will be committing an horrendous blunder and you

will wind up (an idiom) with egg all over your face (an idiom).

EXTENT

What percent of the Bible are we talking about? How much of it is idiomatic? I wish I knew. The obvious kind, like the little list I gave you, I suppose could be counted up and learned. But the semi-idioms, if that is the correct name for them, number far more.

We say that a man writes in an idiomatic, rather than a stilted style. Here, "stilted" becomes an antonym to "idiomatic." We mean by this that his language is as comfortable as a pair of old shoes (idiom), while the man using "stilted" language reminds you of a person breaking in a pair of new shoes.

Unless we are using "idiomatic" in a different sense, and I don't think we are, this kind of writing, so pervasively seasoned (idiom) with idiomatic ex-pressions, must be recognized for what it is (idiom) and interpreted by the canons of idiom.

I suspect that the Bible is far more idiomatic than the pedantic scholarship which is committed to its care is prepared to recognize. If what might possibly be its most popular portion is any indica-tion, there is a whale of a lot (idiom). I will underline the idiomatic parts.

> The Lord is my shepherd.
> I shall not want _____ .
> He maketh me to lie down in green pastures.
> He leadeth me beside the still waters.
> He restoreth my soul.
> He leadeth me in the paths of righteouness
> For His name's sake.
> Though I walk through the valley of the shadow of death
> I will fear no evil.
> For Thou art with me.
> Thy rod and Thy staff they comfort me.
> Thou preparest a table before me in the presence of my
>   enemies.
> Thou anointest my head with oil,
> My cup runneth over.
> Surely goodness and mercy shall follow me all the days
>   of my life.
> And I will dwell in the house of the Lord, forever.

The best book on the subject which I can lay my hands on is *Figures of Speech Used in the Bible*, by E. W. Bullinger, published by Baker. It has an index of some 5,000 separate appearances.

Only a contrived neatness will meticulously file under their proper grammatical genres all expressions which adhere strictly to grammatical law and order (idiom), and then toss (idiom) the rest into a bin (idioms) called "idioms." For idioms differ radically among themselves as to kind and as to the degree that they deviate from grammatical norms.

The Greeks were far more tidy than this. They organized this "Fibber Magee's closet" (idiom) into more than 200 separate categories of idioms.

I suspect that a more accurate representation of the situation as it actually exists would be to see all linguistic entities strung out on a string with that which is most precisely disciplined by grammatical law at one extreme, and the most atrocious idioms at the other. The predicate position of the demonstrative pronoun might well be to the former extreme, while "gird up the loins of your mind" would be toward the latter. Then, the many indetectable booby-traps (idiom) would be distributed in the middle somewhere. These are like:

εἰ = a negative particle so strong that it is accompanied by an oath. It is shorthand (idiom) for the oath, "God do so (looking at a slaughtered animal) to me and more also, if..." See Hebrews 3:11.

When the accusative singular for "grace" (χάριν) is used as a preposition with τοῦτο = "because of this." See Ephesians 3:1.

ἐστι εἰς = "to serve as." See I Corinthians 6:16.

HOW TO RECOGNIZE AN IDIOM

This is the sixty-four-dollar question (idiom). I wish I knew, myself. And I must confess that idiom study is a Johnny-come-lately (idiom) in my Bible study pilgrimage (idiom).

Single word idioms are not so bad (idiom). The lexicon will always try (idiom) to identify a word's idiomatic usage by listing it as one of the definitions (usually the last). So, if you are thorough enough in your research, you will come across (idiom) this.

When doing a thorough research on any given (idiom) verse, you would be well advised (idiom) to see if Bullinger identifies any idiom in it. Of course (idiom) the better commentaries seek (idiom) to do this faithfully. Bullinger singles out Bengel's *Gnomen*, published by Kregel as *New Testament Word Studies*, as the best. But Bullinger's work is old, so it would not have anything to say (idiom) about the more recent commentaries.

The multi-worded idioms are harder. But even here the lexicon tries (idiom) valiantly to identify them. But, under which of the several words in the idiom will this information be given?

By far and away (idiom) the best way to detect idioms is to become not merely a "high-roader" (fast becoming an idiom), but to advance so far on that road that you can easily scan your Bible in its original dress (idiom).

You certainly ought to see by now how inadequate it is to laboriously dissect (idiom) and parse and memorize the possible meanings of each word and employ a prodigious memory to keep all these data in mind (idiom) until you get to the end of a sentence, and think you are translating. Rather, you must be able to scan the sentence so well that individual words have faded into the woodwork (idiom) and all that comes out (idiom) is meaning, loud and clear (idiom).

Then, and only until then can you recognize an idiom when you run across it.

If nothing else does it, the problem of the idiom is enough to disqualify (idiom) computerized exegesis, and force one to discard (idiom) the current practice of leaping (idiom) directly from syntax to exegesis in seminary curriculums, without so much as a nod (idiom) in the direction of (idiom) a skill for speed reading.

HOW TO DEFINE
AN IDIOM

Once you isolate an idiom, no matter how many words it takes to say it, treat it (idiom) as a single semantic unit, like you do a single word which needs to be defined.

And, just like the meaning of a single word can not be ferreted out (idiom) by the etymological process of analyzing its parts, neither can an idiom be defined by the normal lexical analysis of each word plus a syntactical analysis of the relationships between these words.

Just as you discover the meaning of a word by its usage, so you do with an idiom.

Your problem (and mine) is to get a listing of the appearances of the idiom. If the lexicon or commentary doesn't do this, we must fall back on (idiom) our general reading, where the meaning of these idioms begins to come through (idiom) inductively

I have made sure (idiom) that the idiom I have selected for you to practice on has its appearances listed in the lexicons. To this extent, I have cheated (idiom) for you.

It will be an extremely difficult exercise. But you must know about idioms. And, I am keenly (idiom) aware that I have sent out a boy to do a man's job (idiom).

THE END OF THE
"LOW ROAD"

You have come to it, the end of the "low road." It has been my secret hope all along the way that some of you may be enticed to embark on the "high road." But if not, what you have learned will be of considerable help to you in your ongoing study of the most important book in all the world. And you will enhance your ministry to the Body if you wear these new skills with grace and humility.

A

absolute construction: The regular or normal form of a Hebrew noun used with subjects, complements and objects of the preposition. It is the antonym of construct construction, 15:3ff.

accent: The syllable of a word which receives special stress, 1:7; 15:6.

accent, acute: In Greek, one of the accent marks (´) indicating the syllable of a word which receives the stress, 1:7.

accusative case: The case of the Greek noun or pronoun used as the direct object, the subject of the infinitive, the object of the preposition expressing motion toward, and as expressing the extent of time and space, 3:3ff.

active voice: The form of the Greek verb in which the subject of the sentence performs the action, 4:2ff.

adjective: The part of speech which modifies the noun or noun phrase. In Greek and Hebrew the adjective usually follows the noun and agrees with it in gender, number and case, 2:2ff; 3:2.

adverb: The part of speech which modifies a verb, an adjective, or another adverb. In Greek, many adverbs are formed from the adjective and often end in -ως, 2:6.

affix: A syllable which is placed at the beginning, end, or in the middle of a word and which varies the meaning of the word. See "inflection."

agreement: See "concord."

Aktionsart: The German term for the aspect of a verb. See "aspect."

analytical lexicon: See "lexicon, analytical."

anarthrous: The use of the Greek noun without the article, 2:5.

antecedent: The noun or noun equivalent for which the pronoun stands. In, "John brought his lunch," "John" is the antecedent of "his," 2:2.

aorist: The aspect (called "tense" in the grammars) of the Greek verb which expresses punctiliar, or point in time, action. In the indicative mood, it expresses past time and punctiliar aspect, 4:5; 21:3.

Apocrypha: Jewish literature written between the Old and New Testaments which is accepted as canonical by the Roman Catholic Church, but rejected by Protestants and Jews.

apodosis: The main clause in a conditional sentence. In English, we call it the "consequence."

Aramaic: One of the Semitic languages and a close cognate of Hebrew. It was the diplomatic language of Assyria, Chaldea and Persia. Some portions of the Old Testament were written in Aramaic. Aramaic was the common language of Palestine during the time of Christ, Int. 3; 1:3; 17:3.

article: The adjectives "a," "an," and "the." The first two are called "indefinite articles," while the latter is the "definite article." In Greek and Hebrew, only the definite article occurs. The Greek article must agree with its subject in gender, number and case. In Hebrew, the article is attached to the noun, 2:4f; 16:2.

aspect: The form of a verb which indicates the type and duration of action. The aspect can be either punctiliar, linear or combined, 4:4ff.

atlas, Bible: A reference work containing maps and geographical information on Bible lands, Int. 8; Lesson 18.

attributive use of the Greek adjective: The adjective which modifies a substantive and which has an article before it. "The man *the good*," is in this construction and means "the good man," 5:3.

augment: An addition to the verb stem which indicates past action. It consists of either the prefix, "ε," when the word begins with a consonant, or the lengthening of the initial vowel, ε to η, α to η, ο to ω, when the word begins with such a vowel, 4:12.

B

Biblical languages: Those languages in which the original manuscripts were written: Greek, Hebrew and Aramaic, Int. 3.

breathing mark: In Greek, the mark placed over the vowel, diphthong, or at the beginning of a word, which indicates either the absence (᾽) or presence (῾) of the "h" sound. (᾽) is called "smooth breathing," and (῾) is called "rough breathing," 1:6f.

C

canon: In Biblical usage, it is those books which belong in the Bible.

case: The form taken by a noun, pronoun, or adjective to show its use in a sentence and its relation to neighboring words, Lesson 3.

circumflex accent: In Greek, one of the accent marks (~ or ^) indicating the stressed syllable of a word. The circumflex occurs only over long vowels or diphthongs, 1:7.

circumlocution: The use of many words to express what might be expressed by one or a few words. In translation, it is the use of several words to express what was expressed in one word.

Classical Greek: Our term for the Greek spoken or written during the Classical period (see following definition), 1:1.

Classical period: The period of Greek history and culture prior to the time of Alexander the Great (4th century B.C.) which witnessed great accomplishments in literature, drama, sculpture and architecture. Compare "Hellenistic," 1:1.

clause: A group of related words which have a subject and a predicate, 5:1ff.

cognate: A word or words which are related to each other, having in common the same original word or root, 7:4ff; 17:1ff.

combined aspect: A descriptive term for what the grammarians call "perfect tense," the punctiliar (.) combined with the linear (——) to make (·——), a kind of combination of the two, 4:6.

commentary: A book which may explain, interpret, and apply the contents of one or more books of the Bible, Int. 7; Lesson 13.

complement: Any added word or words which complete the predicate, such as a
          direct object, predicate object,   predicate nominative or predi-
          cate adjective.

concord: The agreement which prevails in Greek between nouns and pronouns, in
          gender and number; between adjectives and their nouns, in gender,
          number, and case; and between subjects and verbs, in number and
          person, 2:2ff.

concordance: A reference work which lists the occurrences of the words in the
          Bible. These may be in Hebrew, English or Greek, Int. 6; 6:4ff.

conjugation: The systematic arrangement of a verb form which indicates its
          voices, moods, tenses (i.e., time and aspect), persons and numbers,
          4:8 is an example.

conjunction: A word which connects two independent words, phrases, or clauses,
          like the English, "and," or "but," 2:6; 16:3.

construct construction: A Hebrew substantive which stands in a descriptive or
          possessive relationship to another. In Hebrew, the "of" idea goes
          with the word in construct rather than with the word in the absolute
          state, 15:3ff.

          English: word ofGod
          Hebrew: wordof God

contraction: The shortening of a word by omitting one or more letters or
          sounds, or by reducing two or more vowels or syllables to one, 1:7.

contract verbs: A class of Greek verbs whose stems end in ε, α, or ο. These
          vowels contract with the thematic vowel.

critical commentary: A commentary which seeks to examine the historical, lit-
          erary and textual background and content of the Biblical text, and
          which gives attention to controversial problems, Int. 7; Lesson 13.

crux interpretum: A passage universally recognized as a very difficult one in
          which to understand the author's meaning, 13:7.

D

dative case: The case of the Greek noun or pronoun used for the indirect ob-
          ject and to express many relationships, such as time at which
          something happens, the means by which something happens, or
          motionlessness. It is also a "catch-all" slot for many different
          relationships which would not be as closely implicated in the
          action of the verb as would be the subject or direct object, 3:3ff.

declension: A systematic arrangement of a noun, pronoun, adjective, or parti-
          ciple which indicates its number, gender and case, 3:8 (example).

definite article: See "article."

dental: Consonants which are formed by the tongue touching the teeth or the
          ridge behind the teeth, 1:8.

deponent: Verbs which are active in meaning but middle or passive in form, 4:4.

devotional commentary: A commentary which makes direct application of Biblical
          statements to spiritual needs, Int. 7; Lesson 13.

dictionary, Bible: A book or series of books which deal briefly with the history,
          geography and culture of Bible lands, and with the composition,

formulation and history of the Bible, itself, Int. 8.

direct object: That part of a sentence, usually a noun, which receives the action of the verb. In, "He hit the ball," "ball" is the direct object, 3:1.

diphthong: A combination of two vowels in a single syllable, such as "αι," "ευ," "οι," 1:5f.

E

Englishman's Greek Concordance: A tool which lists in alphabetical order all the New Testament Greek words, and then gives all the appearances and various King James Version translations of each Greek word, 6:4; 10:5ff.

Englishman's Hebrew Concordance: A tool which lists in alphabetical order all the Old Testament Hebrew words, and then gives all the appearances and various King James Version translations of each Hebrew word.

etymology: The origin or derivation of a word as shown by an analysis of its root meaning. This highly critical discipline is a "no-no" to "low-roaders," 7:7; 9:2.

exegesis: A detailed grammatical analysis of a word or passage in the original languages; the resulting interpretation of that word or passage, Less

exegete: The person who engages in exegesis, Lesson 21.

exegetical commentary: A commentary dealing with minute analysis of the Greek or Hebrew texts, Int. 7; Lesson 13.

exposition: A development and analysis of the content of a passage or book.

expositional commentary: A commentary which explains the text with attention to the argument of the passage, Int. 7; Lesson 13.

G

gender: A classification of nouns, pronouns and modifiers according to their endings. The classification may be masculine, feminine or neuter, as in Greek, or just masculine or feminine, as in Hebrew, 2:1; 15:2f

genitive: The case of the Greek noun or pronoun used to express possession, separation, or agency, 3:3.

gerund: A part of speech in which a verb performs the function of a noun, and ends in "-ing," such as, "fishing is fun." It is an English grammatical term, 2:1.

grave accent: In Greek, one of the accent marks (`) indicating the stressed syllable of a word. It occurs in the place of an acute accent on the final syllable of a word when that word is immediately followed by another word, 1:7.

Greek: The language in which all of the New Testament was originally written, 1:1

guttural: A consonant which is formed in the throat, 1:8; 15:2.

H

Hebrew: A North-west Semitic language in which almost all of the Old Testament was originally written, 1:1; Lesson 15.

Hellenistic: That which was characteristic of the Greek culture which spread throughout the Mediterranean world during and after the conquests of Alexander the Great in the 4th century B.C., 1:1.

hermeneutics: The science and art of interpreting the Bible, Lesson 12.

homiletical commentary: A commentary which is devotional in nature, but which also includes illustrations and sermon outlines, Int. 7.

hortatory subjunctive: The use in Greek of the first person plural subjunctive to express exhortation, such as, "Let us...," "We must...," 4:7ff.

hypotactic: A form of sentence construction which is characterized by subordinate clauses. It is characteristic of Greek, 5:2f.

I

idiom: A word or group of words in common use in a language which express a meaning different from the literal word-for-word translation, 5:4; Lesson 22.

imperative mood: The form of the verb which expresses commands and exhortations, such as, "Go!", 4:7ff.

indefinite article: See "article."

indicative mood: The form of the verb which expresses common declarations or objective facts, 4:6ff.

infinitive: A noun which by inflectional change has been converted from a verb, such as, "to swim is fun." It has case, voice and aspect, 2:1; 3:7.

inflection: An affix, usually a suffix, or change in the form of a word to mark distinction of case, gender, number, person, mood, voice, aspect and time, 4:1.

interlinear translation: A book which places the English translation word-for-word under the words of the original language, 6:1f.

introduction, Bible: A book which seems to deal with a few of the more critical problems of the Bible, such as canon, textual criticism, authorship, dating, etc., Int. 7f.

K

Koine: The Greek common to people everywhere in the Hellenistic period, roughly 300 B.C. to 300 A.D., 1:1.

L

labial: A consonant which is formed by the lips, 1:8.

lengthen: To make a short vowel into a long vowel, i.e., ε to η, 4:11.

lexical form: The form of a word agreed upon by writers of dictionaries under which the definition of a word is to be found, 6:1; 7:8; 16:1.

lexicon: A reference work (dictionary) which lists the various meanings for words of the original languages, along with examples and references where this word may be found, Lessons 11; 17.

lexicon, analytical: An alphabetical listing and parsing of every form of every word in the original manuscripts which identifies the lexical form of each, 6:1ff; 7:1ff; 16:4ff.

linear aspect: That aspect of a verb which expresses continuing action, 4:4ff.

liquid: A Greek consonant which is pronounced in such a way that the air is not stopped anywhere in the air passage (λ, μ, ν, ρ), 1:7f.

LXX: The common abbreviation for the Septuagint. It is the number, "seventy," in Roman numerals and is used as representative of the men who made the Septuagint translation, 9:3.

M

Massoretes: Jewish scholars of the eighth century A.D. who introduced vowel markings to preserve Hebrew vowels, and established a text of the Old Testament called the Massoretic text, 14:3f.

middle voice: That form of the Greek verb which either emphasizes the participation of the subject, or shows reflexive action, 4:3f.

mode: See "mood."

modifier: A word or group of words that clarifies or limits the meaning of another word. In, "She sang beautifully," "beautifully" modifies "sang," 2:2.

mood: That form of the verb which expresses the speaker's attitude toward the action or state expressed. They are indicative, imperative, subjunctive and optative. Many grammarians and commentators also include, incorrectly, the participle and the infinitive as moods, 4

morphology: The branch of linguistics which deals with the history and functions of inflections and derivational forms.

movable "ν": A final Greek "ν" without syntactical significance sometimes append to certain third person active verbs. The *Analytical Lexicon* will always omit this letter, see 4:12 (-ε/ει, -σι).

N

nominative case: The case of the Greek noun, pronoun or adjective which is used as a subject or complement, 3:3.

noun: The part of speech which is used as a name for a person, place or thing, 2:1.

number: That which refers to the quantity of a thing. Greek has two numbers, singular and plural; in Hebrew, there are three, singular, plural, and dual, 2:1; 15:2.

O

optative mood: The mood of the Greek verb which expresses something that is unreal, but wished for. It is rare in Koine Greek, 4:8.

P

papyri (1): Writing material made from a reed-like plant on which much of the Old and New Testament was probably written.

Papyri (2): The name given to the body of writing in Hellenistic times which illustrates the Greek of the New Testament. It was named for the material upon which it was written, 9:5f.

parallelism: That which is characteristic of Hebrew poetry; it is saying the same thing twice, but using different wording, 15:5.

paradigm: A chart or diagram which shows the declension of a substantive or the conjugation of a verb, such as on page 4:8.

paraphrase: A translation which is developed meaning-by-meaning rather than word-for-word, and has no qualms about using circumlocution.

paratactic: A form of sentence construction which is characterized by coordinate clauses, and is joined by "and" or "but." It is characteristic of Hebrew writing, 5:2f.

parse: The identification of the inflections of a word. For example, πιστεύω is first person, singular, active, linear, indicative, present. We have asked and answered the six questions one always puts to a verb, 4:13.

participle: A word which by inflectional change has been converted from a verb. In Greek, the participle has the regular endings and functions of the adjective, and yet preserves the aspect and voice of the verb. It is used frequently in Greek, 2:2ff; 3:7.

particle: The little words which are left over after the rest have been classified into the various parts of speech. They do not radically alter the meaning of a sentence, but are inserted for their nuance value and are more often used or omitted because of the writer's stylistic preference, 2:6.

passive voice: The form of the verb in which the subject receives the action of the verb, 4:3f.

Patristic: The early Christian church fathers, their writings, or doctrines, 9:4f.

perfective aspect: See "combined."

periphrastic: In Greek grammar, the combination of a form of "to be" (εἰμί) and a participle. It tends to emphasize the duration of the action, 4:13.

person: A part of the verb form that tells whether the subject is "I," "you," or "he," 4:2.

phrase: A group of related words which conveys a thought, but does not contain a subject and a predicate.

post-positive: A name for certain Greek words which cannot stand first in their clause. They usually are placed as the second or third word, 5:3.

potential moods: Subjunctive, imperative, optative, 4:8.

predicate: The verb or verb phrase of a sentence; that which makes a statement about the subject, Lesson 4.

predicate use of the adjective: The use of the Greek adjective in which the adjective does not immediately follow the article, but rather follows the noun or precedes the article. "The man *good*," or "*good* the man" in this construction means, "the man *is* good," 5:3.

prefix: One or more letters are placed at the beginning of a word. In Greek, these change the meaning of the word; in Hebrew, they may be separate words in themselves, 4:12; 16:1ff.

preposition: A part of speech which shows spacial or time relationship between two objects, such as, "above," "during," 2:5; 16:2f.

present tense: Means linear aspect, and also present time if the verb is in the indicative mood, 4:4-6.

prohibition: A negative imperative, 4:9.

pronoun: A part of speech which stands in place of a noun. In Greek, the pronoun must agree with its antecedent in gender and number. In Hebrew, the pronoun can stand independently or may suffix itself to the word it modifies, 2:2; 16:3f.

protosis: The "if" clause in a conditional sentence. In English, we call it the "antecedent."

Pseudepigrapha: Jewish writings which were included in neither the Old Testament canon nor in the Apocrypha, 9:5.

punctiliar aspect: That aspect of the Greek verb which emphasized the action itself without regard to its duration. Most reference works call it "aorist," 4:4ff.

R

reference Bible: Any Bible with special cross-references in a column next to the text, Int. 8.

rhetorical question: A question which neither expects nor deserves an answer. It is an idiom common to many languages.

root: Same as "stem."

S

Semitic: The designation of a family of languages belonging to the people of the Middle East area. Because so many of these people were descendants of Shem, one of Noah's sons, the entire group is called "Semitic," 1:3ff.

sentence: A word or group of words which expresses a complete thought and contains a subject and verb (written or implied), 3:1ff.

Septuagint: See "LXX."

sibilant: A consonant which is produced by making a hissing sound, such as the Greek "σ," 1:7f.

stem (1): The part of a word to which inflectional forms are added or in which changes are made to vary the meaning of the word, 4:1ff.

stem (2): That form of the Hebrew verb which emphasizes a combination of simple, intensive or caused action, with active, reflexive or passive voice, 15:4.

subjunctive mood: That form of a verb which expresses an unreal, but possible action, 4:7.

substantive: Any word or group of words used as a noun or as a noun equivalent, 3:2.

substantival use of the Greek adjective: The use of the Greek adjective in which the adjective, itself, either with or without the article, is used as a noun, 2:3.

suffix: One or more letters which are placed at the end of a word. In Greek, these change the meaning of the word; in Hebrew, they may be words in and of themselves, 4:12; 16:3f.

syntax: The relationship between words based on grammatical principles, Lesson 5

T

tautological: An apparent redundancy or needless repetition.

taxonomy: The classification of objects according to their natural relationships. Also, the laws and principles involved in such classification.

tense: The form of the verb which indicates the aspect of the verb in all its moods, and also the time of the verb in the indicative mood, 4:4ff.

Textus Receptus: The name of the Greek New Testament used for the translation of the King James Version, 10:5.

thematic vowel: The connecting vowel between a verb stem and its inflectional ending; ο or ε (or lengthened, ω or η), 4:11f.

topical Bible: A Bible which lists verses under topical headings, rather than according to books, Int. 8.

translation: A reproduction of a word or thought into another language, Lesson 8.

U

usus loquendi: The specific or individualistic way in which an author uses a word or phrase, 9:2, 12:2.

V

verb: The part of speech which expresses the action or state of being of the subject, 2:6; Lesson 4.

version of the Bible: The rendering of part or all of the Scriptures into a language other than the original, Int. 8.

vocative case: The case of a noun or pronoun which is used when directly addressing a person or thing, 3:6.

voice: The form of the verb which indicates whether the subject is performing the action, receiving it, or both, 4:2ff.

Name_____

Box_____ Grade_____

WORKSHEET: LESSON 1

PURPOSE AND GOALS

The purpose of this assignment is to help
the student recognize the Greek letters and to
check how much he has really mastered. The goal
of the student is to be able to read the Greek
letters easily and to correctly pronounce the
diphthongs and breathing marks.

TOOLS

1. The notes in Lesson 1.

VALUE: 15

Note: A 15 value worksheet should be completed
in one, two-hour lab period; a 30 value worksheet
in two, two-hour lab periods; and a 45 value
worksheet in three, two-hour lab periods.

1. You now have made an acquaintance with the Greek alphabet. Practice
   your ability to recognize the letters by writing the equivalent
   letters in English to the right of the Greek word. Ex: ιδεα _idea_

   a. δραμα_____   e. ἀσβεστος_____   i. γενεσις_____

   b. στιγμα_____   f. πνευμονια_____   j. διαγνωσις_____

   c. ἀτλας_____   g. πανοραμα_____   k. διπλομα_____

   d. θεσις_____   h. ἐμφασις_____   l. ἀναθεμα_____

2. How about some more practice in pronouncing vowels and diphthongs?
   Again, if you pronounce the word correctly in Greek, you will be
   saying a familiar English word. Say it quietly to yourself and
   then write the English word. Ex: βαικ _bike_

   a. ταιδ_____   g. σουιτ_____   m. γρωψ_____

   b. σλειτ_____   h. ιμευν_____   n. βεζ_____

   c. φοιλ_____   i. βρουμ_____   o. λαξ_____

   d. μαυνδ_____   j. φευ_____   p. ραζ_____

   e. δου_____   k. φρουτ_____   q. δεξ_____

   f. μευσικ_____   l. γρωθ_____   r. δραψ_____

   How is it going? Do you feel as if you know these letters a little
   bit better?

3. To give your eyes a change, put the equivalent English punctuation
   mark and its name next to the Greek mark. Ex: (.) _._ _period_

(,) _____   (˙) _____   _____   (;) _____

4. Just one more practice. Remember how the English h-sound is
   written in Greek? (If you don't, go back and review the section
   under "Breathing.") Complete this exercise as in #2. Watch
   those breathing marks! Ex: αἱτ _height_

a. αὐ_____   e. εἱτ_____   i. αἱζ_____

b. ἐνδ_____   f. εἱτ_____   j. ὠψ_____

c. αὐς_____   g. ἠτ_____   k. ἀψ_____

d. ἠ_____   h. ἐν_____   l. αἱξ_____

Name_____

Box_____ Grade_____

PURPOSE AND GOALS

The purpose of this assignment is to help the student form words by using Greek letters, and to check himself to see if he is able to do it. The goal is to be able to pronounce Greek words easily.

TOOLS

1. The notes in Lessons 1 and 2.

VALUE: 15

A. The following is a little story written with English words but the English words are written in Greek letters. Read it through and then answer the questions at the end of the story.

"ἠ ἰοῦ γαῖς, αἶμ νὰτ γοῖγγ τοῦ τῆκ ἰτ λαίιγγ δαῦν. αἶμ
(Hey you guys, I'm not going to take it lying down.)
γοῖγγ τοῦ δοῦ σάμθιγγ ἀβαῦτ ἰτ. αῦ μένι ὀφ ἰοῦ γαῖς ἀρ υἶθ μί?"

"ἰοῦ ἄρντ ἦβλ τοῦ δοῦ ἔνιθιγγ; φῶν ἰοῦρ κάγγρεσπερσαν."

"αἲ δῶντ νῶ. ἰοῦ γάτα δοῦ σάμθιγγ."

"αῦ ἀβαῦτ ἀ πρώτεστ παρῆδ?"

"ἰοῦ μὰστ μῆκ σὰμ σαῖνς καὶ δέμανστρητ."

"υἱλ σάμβαδι τὲλ αῦ ἀ γρλ ὂτ τοῦ δρὲς φῶρ παρῆζ?"

"αῦ μένι γαῖς καὶ γὰλς ἀρ υἶλιγγ τοῦ δοῦ ἴτ?"

"νὰτ ἂν θέρσδη ἀφτερνοῦν, αἲ γάτα δῆτ τοῦ θὰ βεύτι πάρλωρ."

"ναῦ μάρθα, θὰτ τὲλς θὰτ ἰοῦ ἄρντ καμίτεδ."

"ἠ, αῦ ἀβοῦτ ἂν ἄνδεργραυνδ πῆπερ?"

"αἲ θἰγκ θῆρ ἰς ἀ μίμιωγραφ ἰν θὰ γρλς δῶρμ ἰν θὰ βῆσμεντ."

"ἰοῦ κὺδ σὲλ ἄζ τοῦ μῆκ σὰμ βρέδ."

"ροῦθ κὺδ κὰπ ἴτ καὶ τῆκ ἴτ τοῦ ἔρ ροῦμ καὶ λὲτ ἴτ δαῦν
υἶθ ἀ ρῶπ."

"ἀρ ἰοῦ τόκιγγ ἀβαῦτ ἄζ?"

"νῶ, σίλι, ἀβαῦτ θὰ μίμιωγραφ."

"αἲ υἱλ δοῦ ἴτ. ὠκῆ?"

"μεῖβι υῖ κὐδ τῆκ ἀ πῶλ καὶ πρισὲντ ἴτ τοῦ θὰ σκοῦλ βῶρδ?"

"νῶ, θὰτς τοῦ στρῆτ."

"θὰ τράβλ ἲς, θῆρ ἀρντ ἰνὰφ παρτίσιπητιγγ. γὲτ αλ τοῦ παρτίσιπητ. θὶς ἲς θὰ νῆμ ὰφ θὰ γεῖμ. ἰοῦ γάτα γὲτ μῶρ βράθερς καὶ σίστερς τοῦ παρτίσιπητ!"

"θεῖρς νὰτ ἰνὰφ ἴφεν ἰφ υῖ γὲτ ἀλ θεῖρ ἄρ. θὶς μῆξ θὰ σμάλεστ παρῆδ ἲν θὰ ἴστρι ἀφ στοῦδεντ ριβέλιον! θεῖρς νὰτ ἰνὰφ δίστανς φρὰμ θὰ φρστ τοῦ θὰ λὰστ γαῖ παρῆδιγγ."

"καὶ υἲλς; υῖ γάτα γὲτ σὰμ βὶγ κάμπας βὶγ υἲλς σῶ ἲτ γὲτς σὰμ νῶτις - σεῖ λαῖκ θὰ νοῦς υἲθ κρόγκαιτ."

"λαῖκ οῦ φῶρ ἴνστανς?"

"λαῖκ γρέγ."

"ἰά, καὶ στέφανι; θὶς γὰλδ ρίλι δρὸ θὲμ ἴν."

"ἰά, γρὲγ καὶ στέφανι. αῦρ κὸς ἲς ραίτ."

"κμὰν λὲτς ὂλ σεῖ ἲτ τουγέθρ. αῦρ κὸς ἲς ραίτ."

"αῦρ κὸς ἲς ραίτ."

"ΑΥΡ ΚΟΣ ΙΣ ΡΑΙΤ!"

Now please take the following quiz about this little story:

1. The scene takes place
    ( ) on a campus
    ( ) on the waterfront
    ( ) in the senate
    ( ) on the beach

2. Something that was too traditional to try was
    ( ) a boycott
    ( ) a representation to the grievance committee
    ( ) to take a poll
    ( ) to go on strike

3. A famous person who was mentioned was
    ( ) Roger Staubach
    ( ) Billy Graham
    ( ) George Washington
    ( ) Walter Kronkite

Name_____

Box_____ Grade_____

4. The principal problem in their way was
      ( ) they lacked funds
      ( ) they didn't have influential people with them
      ( ) they lacked transportation
      ( ) they couldn't find a meeting place

5. A plan was devised to steal
      ( ) a mimeograph
      ( ) a silkscreen
      ( ) an armored truck
      ( ) Fort Knox

6. Match:
    a. Stephanie ( ) Would be an influential campus big wheel
    b. Judy   ( ) Wasn't committed enough to serve
    c. Ruth   ( ) Was willing to steal
    d. Martha   ( ) Would be the girl to add glamour to
                      the movement
    e. Greg   ( ) Would ask her father for the car

7. What Greek word was used in this story? _____

   What does that word mean? _____

B. Turn in this workbook to page 6:2. You will find a page reproduced from an *Interlinear Greek New Testament*. Notice how the
Greek lines and their English translations alternate. At the top
of the page is verse 3 of I Peter, chapter 2. How many Greek
words are there in verse 3? _____

I have made enough boxes so that you can copy out each Greek
word and put it in a box. Underneath each Greek word, write the
English translation which this *Interlinear* gives to it. Below
each English word I want you to give its part of speech (noun,
verb, adjective, pronoun, preposition). Above each Greek word I
want you to <u>guess</u> at what part of speech the Greek word is. I
will show you what I want you to do by doing the same thing myself
for the last five words of verse 2. Then do the same for verse 3.

Parts of speech of the Greek words	preposition	(personal) pronoun	verb	preposition	noun
The Greek words	ἐν	αὐτῷ	αὐξηθῆτε	εἰς	σωτηρίαν
The English words	by	it	ye may grow	to	salvation
Parts of speech of the English words	preposition	pronoun	pronoun+ verb	preposition	noun

Parts of speech of the Greek words			
The Greek words			
The English words			
Parts of speech of the English words			

Parts of speech of the Greek words			
The Greek words			
The English words			
Parts of speech of the English words			

Name_____

Box_____ Grade_____

PURPOSE AND GOALS

      The purpose of this worksheet is to help the student learn the Greek articles by means of exercises which are progressive in difficulty. It is also designed to help the student learn the form and function of the Greek case system. A final purpose is to review the Greek letters, diphthongs and breathing marks.

      The goals of the student are to be able to recognize and relate the memorized forms of the article to their proper function in a sentence. This means the student will not only be able to recite the 24 forms, but will also be able to use the correct article in a given sentence by means of his knowledge of the Greek case system. The student should also be able to read the Greek letters and to correctly pronounce the diphthongs and breathing marks with greater facility.

TOOLS

1. The notes in Lessons 1 - 3.

VALUE: 15

1. The following are a series of articles in the order: masculine, feminine and neuter. Each series is either singular or plural, and is in one of the four cases used with the article. One article has been omitted from each series. Fill in the missing article. Ex: ὁ, _ἡ_ , τό

a. τῶν, τῶν, _____

b. _____ , τῆς, τοῦ

c. τῷ, _____ , τῷ

d. τόν, τήν, _____

e. τούς, _____ , τά

f. _____ , ταῖς, τοῖς

2. Now let's see if you can recognize the grammatical description of the article. Remember: Every article has gender, number and case. For the following articles, two of these three parts are given. You must decide the missing part and fill in the blank. (If there is more than one correct answer, write in all the possibilities.) Ex: τό - neu., sing., _nom. or acc._

a. τῇ - fem., sing., _____

b. τά - _____, pl., nom./acc.

c. αἱ - fem., _____, nom.

d. τούς - mas., pl., _____

e. τοῖς - _____, pl., dat.

f. τόν - mas., _____, acc.

3. Let's go one step further. The following are a list of some very simple English sentences with one article underlined in

each sentence. Look at this article and its noun to determine their "sentence slot." This will tell you the case of the article. (If you are not certain, review the notes in Lesson 3.) The gender and number of the article will be obvious (or given). Write the correct Greek article in the blank that follows the underlined English article. Ex: The ___ὁ___ boy hit the ball.

> You know "boy" is masculine and singular, and so is the article by concord. "Boy" also fills the "subject slot" in the sentence and so it is in the nominative case, and so is the article by concord. Therefore the article is ὁ.

a. The _____ boys hit the ball. b. The _____ girls hit the ball.

c. The _____ girl hit the ball. d. The ball hit the _____ boy.

e. The ball hit the _____ girl. f. The ball hit the _____ girls.

g. The notary validated the affidavit for the _____ deputy (M).

h. The notary validated the document for the _____ jury (N).

i. The jury viewed the _____ affidavit (F) of graft for the judge.

j. The deputy of the _____ jury (N) viewed the affidavit of graft.

k. The _____ notary (M) of the court validated the affidavit.

l. The judge heard the plea of the _____ defendants (M).

m. The _____ judge (F) heard the plea of the defendants.

n. The judge viewed the _____ evidence (N) of the prosecution.

4. Can you see the importance of learning the cases and the articles well? For a final practice, fill in all of the blanks in the following sentences.

a. The _____ jury (N) gave the _____ verdict (M) to the _____ judge (F) of the _____ court (M).

b. The _____ judge (F) sentenced the _____ defendants (M) for the _____ good (N) of the _____ public (M).

5. For a quick review of the alphabet, write out the following Greek words in equivalent English letters. Ex: ἔχω ___echo___

a. παθος _____ d. κοσμος _____ g. ἐξοδος _____

b. δογμα _____ e. θερμος _____ h. ἐμφασις _____

c. ἀτλας _____ f. στιγμα _____ i. διλεμμα _____

Name_____

Box_____

6. Remember those breathing marks and diphthongs? Let's practice a bit so you won't forget. Pronounce the Greek word quietly to yourself and then write out the English word the Greek sounds represent. Ex: αἱτ __height__

   a. εἱτ _____   d. ἱλ _____   g. οὑμ _____

   b. εἱτ _____   e. ἱλ _____   h. τοἱλ _____

   c. εὑ _____   f. αἱρ _____   i. κυἱν _____

7. Diagram the sentence we have been working on by assuming all the nouns are in the feminine gender and then placing the proper Greek article in the article slots.

   "The notary of the government validated the affidavit of the graft for the deputy of the grand jury."

8. Diagram the following Greek sentence (using the article as the indicator of the sentence slot of the noun it modifies):

   εὐχαριστεῖ (verb) ὁ ἄνθρωπος τοῦ Θεοῦ τῷ πατρὶ τοῦ ἀποστόλου τὸν δοῦλον

   Some slots will remain blank.

9. Diagram the following Greek sentence as in 8:

   εὐχαριστεῖ (verb) τῷ ἀνθρώπῳ τὸν Θεὸν τοῦ πατρὸς ὁ ἀπόστολος τοῦ δούλου

   Some slots will remain blank.

Name_____

Box_____ Grade_____

WORKSHEET: LESSON 4

PURPOSE AND GOALS

        The purpose of this assignment is to aid the student in his memorization of the prepositions, and to help him relate this knowledge to the correct use of the article. It also provides an exercise where he may transfer into modern terminology the older method of parsing. It also serves as an excellent review of the article and the case system.

        The goal of the student is to be able to identify the correct preposition with its proper case when it is found outside the spacial diagram which he has memorized, to identify the proper sentence slot for articles, and to extrapolate from the older terms found in the reference works the categories which are more linguistically sound.

TOOLS

1. The notes in Lessons 1 - 4.

2. A good memory.

3. Concentration.

VALUE: 15

1. You have been working on the prepositions. Do you think you know them? The following is AN ADVENTURE WITH A LION! First look at the picture to observe the action and then look at the article in the phrase below to observe the case used. Fill in the blank with an appropriate preposition, based on the picture, the meanings and corresponding cases you have learned.

¹Adapted from *Teach Yourself New Testament Greek,* by D. F. Hudson, Association Press, permission given by University of London Press Ltd., London.

2. I trust that your "adventure" was a learning experience! If it was, the following will not be too difficult. Fill in the appropriate prepositions and articles for the following phrases. Be careful to choose the right article according to ⁱts gender, number and case! Ex: <u>κατὰ τοῦ   </u>

                                         down   the (slope - M)

a.<u>   </u>   f.<u>   </u>

    above   the (man)   after   the   (men)

Name_____

Box_____

b._____   g._____
   under   the   (table - F)   over against the (table - F)

c._____   h._____
   behind   the   (girl)   before   the   (women)

d._____   i._____
   with   the   (book - N)   in   the   (house - M)

e._____   j._____
   with   the   (book - N)   into   the   (houses - M)
   (use a different preposition here)

3. How would you translate the following? After each article, state
the gender, number, and case that has been used.
Ex: ἀνὰ τὴν <u>"up the;" feminine, singular, accusative</u>

   a. σὺν τῷ _____

   b. ὑπὲρ τὸν _____

   c. παρὰ τῷ _____

   d. μετὰ τῶν _____

   e. εἰς τοὺς _____

   f. μετὰ τὸ _____

   g. ἐν ταῖς _____

   h. ἀπὸ τῆς _____

4. In the familiar John 3:16, the English word "loved" is a
translation of the Greek word ἠγάπησεν. In the older traditional
terms, this form is the "third, singular, aorist, active,
indicative." Using the chart on page 4:13 and the notes of
Lesson 4, answer the following questions.

   a. What is its person?
     _____ first person
     _____ second person
     _____ third person

   b. What is its number?
     _____ singular
     _____ plural

   c. What is its voice?
     _____ active
     _____ middle
     _____ passive

d. What is its aspect?

_____ punctiliar

_____ linear

_____ combined

e. What is its mood?

_____ indicative

_____ subjunctive

_____ imperative

_____ optative

f. Do you ask this sixth question?_____ What is this
question?_____

(1) If your answer was "yes," check one of the following:

_____ past

_____ present

_____ future

(2) If your answer was "no," explain why:_____

_____

_____

Name_____

Box_____ Grade_____

In the last lesson, we looked at the importance of word order. You learned that the normal
grammatical order for a sentence was subject,
verb and object; or verb, subject and object.
When an author wanted to emphasize a word or
thought, he would do it by:

    (1) placing a word at the beginning of a clause, or
    (2) making a variation from the normal order.

These changes in word order are not obvious
in our English Bibles. However there is a helpful tool which will enable you to observe the
Greek word order, now that you can recognize and
write the Greek letters. *The Interlinear Greek -
English New Testament* has the original Greek
order with a word-for-word translation underneath.

In the following exercise you will observe
some examples of word order changes and then try
to discover the significance of those changes.
As an aid to your memory, write down the two ways
in which an author could emphasize a word or
thought which we have just mentioned above.

(1) _____

(2) _____

PURPOSES AND GOALS

The purposes of this assignment are to:

    1. Introduce you to the *Interlinear New
       Testament*.
    2. Cause you to observe word order.
    3. Cause you to analyze why the author made
       changes.
    4. Give you practice in reading and writing
       Greek words.

The goals are that you might:

    1. Learn to use the *Interlinear* as a study
       tool.
    2. Begin to notice Greek word order.
    3. Discover insights in interpretation not
       noticeable in English.
    4. Gain facility in recognition and writing
       of Greek letters.

TOOLS

1. *Interlinear Greek - English New Testament.*
2. Your own Bible.
3. Your mind.

VALUE: 15

1. An author could emphasize a word by placing it at the _____
   of a clause. You will now work on some examples. Look up the
   reference and study the phrase quoted below in the *Interlinear*.
   Then write out the Greek word that is being emphasized, along
   with its English translation.

                                           (Greek)   (English)

   a. John 1:19 "Who are you?" _____ _____

   b. John 1:21a "Are you Elijah?" _____ _____

   c. John 1:21b "Are you the prophet?" _____ _____

2. Now you have discovered *what* was being stressed, but *why* was it
   emphasized? Read through this passage of Scripture again, noting
   John's answers, and then give your reasons why the priests and
   Levites asked these questions and not others, and why these three
   words were emphasized and not others. (You will want to use the
   cross references in your English Bible for this; especially
   checking the Old Testament references.)

   a. _____

   _____

   _____

   b. _____

   _____

   _____

   c. _____

   _____

   _____

3. Try your hand at another passage. Read Romans 5:1-11 in a good
   English translation. Now, look at verse 6 in the *Interlinear*.
   Which word seems to be out of place?

   _____ (Greek) _____ (English)

4. Reread Romans 5:1-11 in English and state why you think Paul
   emphasized this word.

   _____

   _____

Name_____

Box_____

5. Read Ephesians 2:8-10 in your Bible. Now study verse 10 in the *Interlinear*. What word appears to be out of place (ignoring the Greek word γάρ and its English translation "For") in the phrase, "For we are His workmanship"?

_____ (Greek)   _____(English)

6. Read Ephesians 2:8-10 again in English. Why do you think Paul made this emphasis?

_____

_____

_____

7. There was also another way for an author to emphasize a word. This was to make a _____ from the normal word order. He could do it by:

    (1) placing the direct or indirect object first,
    (2) separating elements of a sentence which naturally belong together, or
    (3) putting the word last in the clause.

Let's see some examples.

8. Read I Corinthians 2:6-13 in English. Now examine verse 10 in the *Interlinear*. Write out the first clause (up to the semi-colon) of verse 10 in Greek and then underneath it in English in the spaces provided. (Note: The English word "for" may not have been placed under the Greek word γάρ in your *Interlinear*, but be sure that *you* place it there!)

_____ ____ _____ __ ____ _____ _____

__ ___ ____ _____ __ ____ _____ _____

What word is emphasized? _____ (Gk) _____ (En)

9. Reread I Corinthians 2:6-13 in English and then explain why you think Paul made this emphasis.

_____

_____

_____

10. Read Hebrews 7:1-10 in your English Bible. Study verse 4 very carefully in the *Interlinear*.

    a. Which word seems to be out of place?

    _____ (Greek)   _____(English)

    b. Where does it come in the Greek sentence? _____

11. Reread Hebrews 7:1-10 in English, looking for the argument of the passage. How do you think the word that is emphasized in verse 4 helps to develop the main thought of this passage?

_____

_____

_____

_____

PURPOSE AND GOALS

The purpose of this exercise is to demonstrate to the student the different methods of discovering the lexical form of the Greek word upon which an English word is based. The goal of the student is to become acquainted with the following tools and to know which of them is/are the most expedient for this purpose. The student should come to exactly the same conclusion at the end of each of the four routes.

TOOLS

1. *Interlinear Greek - English New Testament.*
2. *The Analytical Greek Lexicon.*
3. *Englishman's Greek Concordance.*
4. Strong's *Exhaustive Concordance.*
5. Young's *Analytical Concordance.*

VALUE: 15

"Study to show thyself approved unto God." From the *Concordance* I learn that this verse is found in _____ ____:____ .

PROBLEM: I wonder what the Greek word is for "study?" There are four possible routes to solve this problem. Work on them all to find out which is the best.

ROUTE 1

1. Look up this reference in the *Interlinear Greek - English New Testament.* What English word or words are equivalent to the KJV (King James Version) for the word "study?" _____

2. What is the Greek word above this phrase? _____

3. Look up this word in *The Analytical Greek Lexicon.* According to the column at the right, what is the lexical form for this word? _____ ("id" means "the same as above." Therefore you keep reading up until you come to a Greek word.)

4. Unfortunately, this lexical form is in error and you should note that the CORRECT form is σπουδάζω.

5. In summary of ROUTE 1: The correct lexical form for "study" as found in _____ ___:___ (reference) is _____.

ROUTE 2

1. Look up "study" at the back of *Englishman's Greek Concordance.* You find two Greek words and the pages on which they may be found. They are:

   a. _____ on page _____.

   b. _____ on page _____.

2. Turn to the page number of the first Greek word and find this word on the page. This word appears _____ times in the New Testament.

3. Does one of these times include the verse you are studying? _____ If not, do the same with word "b." _____

4. In summary of ROUTE 2: The correct lexical form for "study" as found in _____ ___:___ (reference) is _____.

ROUTE 3

1. Look up "study" in Strong's *Concordance*. It appears ____ times.

2. Run your finger down the verses until you find the reference you are studying. Notice the number that goes with it. Check the appropriate space below:

   ___ It is a non-italicized number (a Hebrew word).

   ___ It is a number in italics (a Greek word).

   The number is _____.

3. Look up this number in the back of the *Concordance* in the correct section. The original word at that number is _____.

4. In summary of ROUTE 3: The correct lexical form for "study" as found in _____ ___:___ (reference) is _____.

ROUTE 4

1. Look up "study" in Young's *Concordance*.

2. How many different words have been translated "study" in the KJV? _____ How many of these are Hebrew words? _____ How many of these are Greek words? _____

3. Look through the verses for the reference that you are studying. What is the Greek word? _____.

4. In summary of ROUTE 4: The correct lexical form for "study" as found in _____ ___:___ (reference) is _____.

Did you find that some routes were easier than others?_____

Which route was easiest for you? _____

Rank the other routes in order from the easiest to the hardest.

_____

WORKSHEET: LESSON 7

PURPOSE AND GOALS

The purpose of this assignment is to enable the student to identify the form of the Greek word and to compare its cognates.

The following are the student's goals:

1. To gain further ability in the use of *The Analytical Greek Lexicon*.
2. To be able to identify the abbreviations used after a Greek word.
3. To compare the cognates of the given Greek word and distinguish a difference in their use.

TOOLS

1. *Interlinear Greek - English New Testament*.
2. *The Analytical Greek Lexicon*.
3. Your own Bible.

VALUE: 15

I. PROBLEM: What is the form of the Greek word translated "study" in II Timothy 2:15?

1. Look up II Tim. 2:15 in the *Interlinear* and write the Greek word that is translated "study" in the KJV._____

2. Look up this word in the *Analytical Lexicon*. You find it on page _____. Copy out the line, beginning with the word itself, and then the abbreviations that follow it.

_____, _____. _____. _____, _____.

3. Now list the abbreviations only, and write out the full word beside its abbreviation, just like the example in the lesson.

_____ _____ (person: Question #1)

_____ _____ (number: Question #2)

_____ _____ = what aspect_____
                                  (aspect: Question #4)

_____ _____ (mood: Question #5)
                                  Is this the mood that has time?
                                  _____ If so, what is the
                                  time?_____

              _____ (voice: Question #3 - What voice
                                  do you assume if none is given?)

4. In summary, the word "study" _____ (Greek word) from
   II Timothy 2:15 is (parse) _____

   _____

   _____

5. You learned in your last assignment that the lexical form should
   be corrected to σπουδάζω.

II. PROBLEM: What do we learn from the cognates of the word trans-
               lated "study" in II Timothy 2:15.

1. The Greek word for "study" in II Tim. 2:15 is _____.

2. The lexical form given in the *Analytical Lexicon* is _____.

3. Look up this "uncorrected lexical form." It is on page _____.

4. List only the cognates of this given lexical form, their parts
   of speech and the number of times that each cognate appears in
   the New Testament, according to the *Analytical Lexicon*. After
   this, look up each appearance of each cognate which the *Analytical
   Lexicon* gives. Study each cognate in these contexts and write
   down the basic meaning or meanings that they have in the contexts
   in the column entitled "Observations."

	COGNATE	PART OF SPEECH	NUMBER OF APPEARANCES	OBSERVATIONS
a				
b				
c				
d				

6. All the cognates have _____ as a common idea.

7. As you listed the parts of speech, you found one cognate that
   is a verb. The given lexical form is also a verb. How would
   you distinguish meaning between these two verbs? (Be sure to
   specify which you are talking about!)

   _____

   _____

   _____

8. CONCLUSION: Why do you think that the correct lexical form for
   "study" in II Tim. 2:15 should be σπουδάζω rather than σπεύδω?

   _____

   _____

Name_____

Box_____ Grade_____

The purposes of this assignment are to bring particular forms of certain Greek words to the student's attention and to guide him in forming conlusions in the interpretation of the context where these words are found.

The goals of the student are the following:

1. To distinguish differences of form in Greek words.
2. To spell out the specific meaning of a sentence by interpreting the form of one of its words.
3. To explain important Scripture truth readily seen in the Greek which is not obvious in the English.
4. To understand his ability and limitation in the study of word forms.

TOOLS

1. An exhaustive English *Concordance*.
2. *Interlinear Greek - English New Testament*.
3. *The Analytical Greek Lexicon*.
4. Your own English Bible.
5. Lesson notes.

VALUE: 30

PROBLEM: What conclusions may I draw from an understanding of the form of a word?

1. What interpretation can I make from the word "study" in II Tim. 2:15?

   a. Look up II Tim. 2:15 in the *Interlinear* and write out the word translated "study." _____

   b. Look up this word in the *Analytical Lexicon* and place the abbreviations of the word form in the first column below. In the next column, write out what the abbreviation stands for. In the last column, write a brief interpretation concerning each part of the word form as was done in Lesson 8. You may have to go back over your notes of Lesson 4 in order to interpret all the abbreviations.

	ABBREVIATION	UNABBREVIATED FORM	DESCRIBE WHAT THIS ADDS TO THE VERSE
1			
2			
3			

(continued on next page)

ABBREVIATION   UNABBREVIATED WORD   DESCRIBE WHAT THIS ADDS TO THE VERSE   (cont.)

4		
5		

Why is there no "6"?_____

Which of the 5 other verb elements was missing (no abbreviation given)?_____   And what should you do about it?

_____

As in the case of "taste" in the notes for Lesson 8, there is nothing really unusual in this particular word form which does not come through into the English translation. However, the purpose is to give you some basic practice so that you can do some interpretation in the following problems.

2. How can looking at the word form help me interpret the controversial passage in Hebrews chapter 6?

   a. Read Hebrews 6:1-6. What three things are tasted?

      (1)_____ (2)_____ (3)_____

   b. What are the two Greek words for "taste"?

      (1)_____ (2)_____

      (3) Are these two words for "taste" different in any way?

      _____

   c. Look at the direct objects of "taste" and fill in the columns below. You will need to look up the Greek word for each direct object.

	ENGLISH	GREEK	CASE*	NUMBER
vs. 4				
vs. 5				
vs. 5				

   d. What is the only difference in case between them?_____

      _____

   e. Some people say this passage refers to Christians, while others believe it refers to non-Christians who are well acquainted with the Gospel. How could the study of these particular cases help you interpret this controversial passage? (You may need

   *One of these words will have two possibilities given for its case. Be sure to choose the one which functions as a direct object!

Name_____

Box_____

to refer back to the last part of Lesson 3.)   _____

_____

_____

_____

3. How can a word form clarify an otherwise obscure and debatable
   verse?

   a. Where do you find the verse, "Touch me not, for I am not yet
      ascended"? _____ What tool did you use?_____

   b. What is the Greek word for "touch" in this verse?_____
      What tool did you use?_____

   c. Write out (parse) the word forms of that Greek word. (Write
      the full words, not just the abbreviations.)

      1_____   2_____   3_____

      4_____   5_____   6_____

      Did you fill out #6?_____   Why?_____

      _____

      What is the lexical form?_____

      When you parsed the verb, did you use the more modern termi-
      nology or the old? If you used the old, go back and do it
      over again, using the new.

   d. Lesson 4 on the Greek verb made a distinction between two kinds
      of prohibitions based upon two different aspects. What is the
      difference in meaning between the two aspects when applied to
      prohibitions?_____

      _____

   e. Based upon that difference, how can this negative command be
      interpreted?_____

      _____

   f. From the context, what do you think was in Mary's mind?_____

      _____

4. Matthew 26:27 (KJV) reads, "Drink ye all of it." Does the "all"
   refer to how much they were to drink, or to the fact that all of
   of them were to drink it?

a. If the verse means that all of them should drink it, what sentence slot does the "all" fill?_____ Diagram the sentence that way.

_____

b. If the verse means that they should drink all of it, what sentence slot does the "all" fill?_____ Diagram the sentence that way.

_____

c. If the first possibility, "a," is correct, in what case does the Greek word for "all" have to be?_____

d. If the second possibility, "b," is correct, in what case does the Greek word for "all" have to be?_____

e. What Greek word does "all" translate in Matthew 26:27?_____

f. What is the case of this word in this context?_____

g. Therefore the correct interpretation is:_____

_____

5. I Corinthians 15:3-5 is a very significant passage which expresses the four facts of the Gospel. There are four verbs whose verb forms appear to be the same if you only have the English to go by.

a. Look up I Corinthians 15:3-5. What are the four English verbs that deal with Christ?

(1)_____   (2)_____

(3)_____   (4)_____

b. Look up the passage in the *Interlinear*. What are the four Greek verbs which are translated by these English verbs?

(1)_____   (2)_____

(3)_____ * (4)_____

c. Look up all four verbs in the *Analytical Lexicon*. Then fill in the blanks in the chart on the next page. Remember to use the new terms for time and aspect, and not the old terms for "tense!"

*The final letter of this word is a movable "ν."

Name_____

Box_____

	(1)	(2)	(3)	(4)
PERSON				
NUMBER				
ASPECT				
VOICE				
MOOD				
TIME				

d. As far as the forms of these four verbs are concerned, exactly where are they different?_____

_____

_____

e. Why do you think these distinctions were made? Select the distinction you think was the most significant theologically and explain it in detail.

_____

_____

_____

_____

_____

_____

_____

_____

_____

_____

WORKSHEET: LESSON 10

PURPOSE AND GOALS

The purpose of this exercise is to show the student the value and methods of studying a given word in all its appearances.

The goals of the student are the following:

1. To be able to identify the books to use for this study and to know how to use them.
2. To be able to list all the appearances of a given word in the New Testament.
3. To be able to distinguish between the various meanings of the word.
4. To be able to select and write synonyms which might fit each context.

TOOLS

1. *The Englishman's Greek Concordance*.
2. An English Bible.

VALUE: 15

PROBLEM: Is the Greek word translated "study" in II Timothy 2:15 used anywhere else in the New Testament? If so, how is it used?

1. What is the Greek word for "study" in II Tim. 2:15?_____

2. What is the CORRECT lexical form (Lesson 6)?_____

3. Look up the CORRECT lexical form in *The Englishman's Greek Concordance*. How many times is it used in the New Testament?_____

4. Into how many different English words is it translated in KJV?____

5. Excluding II Timothy 2:15, list all the appearances of this word, together with the KJV translation in each appearance. Then, pick up the flow of thought to, into, through, out of and beyond each appearance of this word. Keep your cranial television set going! Use "X" for the word in italics. In each case, suggest another English translation, using a different word from the one used in the KJV. (Do this even when you have concluded that the KJV selection was the best one.)

	REFERENCE	KING JAMES WORD	MY SUGGESTION
1			
2			
3			
4			

(continued on next page)

	REFERENCE	KING JAMES WORD	MY SUGGESTION
5			
6			
7			
8			
9			
10			

6. Excluding II Timothy 2:15, pick the three occasions where you think the KJV most needs correction and write out your suggestion for the improvement. After you have completed this, then enter the word used in each of these instances by a modern translation. (Use only one version, either RSV, NASV, New International or Jerusalem Bible.) Do not alter your suggestion from #5.

	REFERENCE	KJV WORD	MY SUGGESTION	MODERN VERSION TITLE_____
1				
2				
3				

In comparison, are you pleased with yourself or mad at the modern version?   Pleased with self_____   Mad at modern version _____

7. Review all the information you have gathered thus far in the study of this word. In the light of this information, what word (or words) would you use in the place of "study" in II Timothy 2:15?_____

Why?_____

_____

_____

_____

_____

_____

_____

_____

Name_____

Box_____ Grade_____

The purpose of this exercise is to give the student practice in using the *Lexicon* by Arndt and Gingrich, by showing him how it is used in conjunction with the other study books he has been using.

The goals of the student are the following:

1. To find a word in Arndt and Gingrich's *Lexicon*, and interpret the abbreviations into useful information.
2. To be able to distinguish which of the various study tools will give him the information he needs.
3. To construct his own definition of a word from context study and compare this definition with that of Arndt and Gingrich.

TOOLS

1. Your own English Bible.
2. *Interlinear Greek-English New Testament.*
3. *The Analytical Greek Lexicon.*
4. The *Greek-English Lexicon* by Arndt and Gingrich.
5. *The Englishman's Greek Concordance.*

VALUE: 30

PROBLEM: According to Arndt and Gingrich's *Greek-English Lexicon,* what does the word "study" in II Timothy 2:15 mean?

1. What is the CORRECT lexical form for "study" in II Timothy 2:15?

_____

2. Look up this word in Arndt and Gingrich's *Lexicon.* What part of speech is it?_____

3. a. Who was the first known Greek writer to use this word? (abbreviated) _____; (unabbreviated) _____

   b. In what century did he live? _____

   c. Who were two other famous Greek writers that used the word? (abbreviated)_____ and _____; (unabbreviated) _____ and _____

4. In what four Jewish writings is the word found?

   a. _____   b. _____

   c. _____   d. _____

5. How many meanings does this word have? _____

6. From your own study of this word in the previous assignments, which of Arndt and Gingrich's definitions do YOU think best fits II Timothy 2:15? _____

7. a. Which meaning do Arndt and Gingrich choose for II Timothy 2:15? _____

   b. How does your definition differ from theirs? _____ _____

   c. After reading their definition, in what way (if at all) are you influenced? _____

8. Which three patristic writers also used the word with this same meaning? (Put abbreviations in the first blank, then write out the unabbreviated form in the second.)

   a. _____ = _____

   b. _____ = _____

   c. _____ = _____

9. a. How many times does this meaning of the word appear in all of Christian literature (New Testament and patristics)? _____

   b. How many times do the two meanings appear in the New Testament only? _____

   c. How many times does the word occur in the New Testament according to the *Englishman's Greek Concordance*? _____

10. If you wanted to learn about the word in more detail, in what three books would you look?

AUTHOR(S)	TITLE	PAGE OR SECTION
a.		
b.		
c.		

11. At the very end of the entry, there is an asterisk (*). What does this mean? _____

PROBLEM: What does the phrase "rightly dividing" mean in II Timothy 2:15?

1. Look up II Timothy 2:15 in the *Interlinear*. What is the Greek word for "rightly dividing"? _____

2. Which book will you use to "parse" this word? _____

   a. What part of speech does this book tell you this word is? (abbreviated) _____; (unabbreviated) _____

Name_____

Box_____

b. According to page 8:3, how many questions do you ask this part of speech? _____

c. Use as many blanks below as you need to ask and answer these:

(1) What is its _____? _____(Answer)

(2) What is its _____? _____

(3) What is its _____? _____

(4) What is its _____? _____

(5) What is its _____? _____

(6) What is its _____? _____

d. What is its lexical form? _____

3. How many times is it used in the New Testament? _____

4. Look it up in Arndt and Gingrich. DO NOT READ THE DEFINITION GIVEN!! Only read enough to find out where it is used in the LXX. What are the references? _____

5. Look up these two references and study their contexts. In both cases, the word is used in connection with the word "path" or "way." How would you define or explain the meaning of this word in the Old Testament? _____

_____

_____

6. Remember, etymology is a _____. However, sometimes you *have* to use it. (See page 7:7.)

a. When do you *have* to use etymology? _____

b. Does the word for "rightly dividing" qualify as such an exception? _____

c. The word is composed of two stems. Write out the Greek word and place a hyphen where you think the word is divided.
_____-_____

d. Try to find a word spelled somewhat like this first stem in Arndt and Gingrich. What did you find? _____
What is its definition?_____

e. Try this for the second stem. What word did you find?_____
What is its meaning?_____

f. What would you guess that the etymology would suggest the word means?_____

7. Read all of the context (all of II Timothy 2). Try to get the
   flow of thought clearly in mind. Paul is using several vocations,
   one of Shakespeare's "seven stages of man" (*As You Like It,* Act 2,
   Scene 7, Lines 139-166), and a common household article in simile
   and metaphor to illustrate for Timothy some aspects of the Christian
   life. Omitting verse 15, list all of these, and then describe
   briefly what each admonishes Timothy to do. (One will make two
   applications.)

VERSE	"FIGURE"	APPLICATION

8. From the flow of the passage, think of the kind of vocation that
   would go along with the others and that would require "rightly
   dividing" something. _____

9. "The road-builder 'X' the road." From your cranial television,
   what does the "X" stand for? _____

   "The _____ (supply your answer from #8) 'X' the true
   word." From your cranial television, what does the "X" stand
   for? _____

10. Now read Arndt and Gingrich's definition of the Greek word for
    "rightly dividing." How does your definition agree or disagree
    with theirs? _____

    _____

    _____

    _____

Name_____

Box_____ Grade_____

     The purposes of this exercise are to ac-
quaint the student with various commentaries and
to lead him in a study of a given passage.

     The goals of the student are the following:

    1. To distinguish the quality of various com-
      mentaries.
    2. To compare the various commentaries on a
      given phrase and write out their consen-
      sus.
    3. To interpret a given phrase based upon
      information gleaned from the commentaries.

TOOLS

     Various commentaries selected from the
library.

VALUE: 15

PROBLEM: What can a commentary tell me about II Timothy 2:15?
        (Before you begin to read the various commentaries, you may
        want to read the questions under #10 and make notes as you go.)

1. What commentaries support the translation of the word "study" in
   II Timothy 2:15? _____

2. What commentaries openly and explicitly reject this translation?
   _____

3. How do the majority of commentaries think the word "study" in the
   KJV should be translated? _____

4. What is the consensus of opinion of what Timothy should not be
   ashamed? _____

5. What is the consensus of what "rightly dividing" does *not* mean?
   _____
   _____

6. What is the consensus of what "rightly dividing" does mean?
   _____
   _____

7. What is the consensus of the meaning of "approved"? _____
   _____

8. The phrase "rightly dividing the Word of truth" is sometimes used
   as a "proof text" for teaching the division of the Bible into various "dispensations." Either support or criticize this use of the
   text. _____

(8) _____
    _____

9. According to the majority of commentaries, which part of the
   verse is the most difficult to interpret? _____
   _____

10. Which of the commentaries: (If you cannot answer any of the
                                    following questions, explain why.)

    a. was the most helpful? _____

    b. was least helpful to you? _____

    c. changed your mind the most, or gave you the most to think
       about?_____

    d. was addressed to the lowest level of reader? _____

    e. was addressed to the highest level of reader? _____

    f. was most careful to consider the views of others? ____
       _____

    g. best related the text to the context? _____

    h. seemed to be the most logical? _____

    i. made the best spiritual applications? _____

    j. was the most liberal? _____

    k. was the most fundamental? _____

    l. would be the first one you would buy? _____

Name_____

Box_____ Grade_____

PURPOSE AND GOALS

The purposes of this assignment are to help the student in his choice of commentaries by means of a guided study, and to give him practice in the use of the various study tools.

The student's goals are the following:

1. To know and correctly use the right tools to answer the questions.
2. To become selective in choosing commentaries.
3. To gain insight into the passage by searching for and writing out the answers to the various questions.
4. To learn to recognize different meanings to a word and to determine which meaning is to be preferred in a given context.

TOOLS

1. *Interlinear Greek-English New Testament.*
2. *The Analytical Greek Lexicon.*
3. *Greek-English Lexicon,* by Arndt and Gingrich.
4. *The Englishman's Greek Concordance.*
5. At least five commentaries each on Romans and Colossians.

VALUE: 30

I. PROBLEM: What does the word "commendeth" mean in Romans 5:8 (KJV)?

1. Read Romans 5:8. What is the Greek word for "commendeth" (KJV)? _____ (Note: this Greek word has as a final letter a "movable ν," which means that it may be spelled with or without that ν, yet still mean the same thing.)

2. Now, ask and answer the five or six questions you ask of this part of speech in order to parse it:

a. What is its _____? _____ (Answer)

b. What is its _____? _____

c. What is its _____? _____

d. What is its _____? _____

e. What is its _____? _____

f. What is its _____? _____

g. What is its lexical form? _____

3. How many times does the word occur in the New Testament? _____

4. As a "transitive verb," how many different meanings does the word have in Arndt and Gingrich's *Lexicon*? (Count only the arabic numerals, such as 1, 2, etc.) _____ As an "intransitive verb," how many different meanings do they give? _____

5. What meaning do they give this word in the Romans 5:8 context? _____

6. What are parallel New Testament passages that use this word with the same meaning? _____ _____ _____

7. Why do you think that this particular time and aspect was used of the verb in this particular context? (You may need to review parts of Lesson 4.) _____

_____

8. Now study five good commentaries on this passage, after reading the following questions, so that you can answer these questions while you go. Also read the final question of this worksheet so you can get the necessary information as you use each commentary.

9. Go back to your English Bible and read the larger context several times. Where, in your judgment, does the paragraph begin and end in which Romans 5:8 is found?_____ What title would you give to this paragraph?_____

10. What subject or theme is emphasized in verse 8? _____

_____

11. How would you translate the word "commendeth" in verse 8?

_____

12. What are four good parallel passages that correspond to the thought of Romans 5:8? (They do not have to have the word "commendeth" in them.) _____

II. PROBLEM: What does "consist" mean in Colossians 1:17 (KJV), and what significant truths are brought out in this verse?

1. Read Colossians 1:17. What is the Greek word for "consist" (KJV) in this verse? _____ (Note the "movable ν.")

2. Parse this word:

   a. What is its _____? _____

   b. What is its _____? _____

   c. What is its _____? _____

   d. What is its _____? _____

   e. What is its _____? _____

Name_____

Box _____

    f. What is its _____? _____

    g. What is its lexical form? _____

3. What meanings do Arndt and Gingrich give to this word in this
   context?_(Careful!)_____

4. What is the parallel New Testament passage that uses this word
   with the same meaning? _____

5. Why do you think that this particular time and aspect was used
   of this verb in this context? _____

   _____

6. After looking ahead at the following questions, read over five
   good commentaries on this passage.

7. Go back to your English Bible and read the larger context several
   times. Where, in your judgment, does the paragraph in which
   Colossians 1:17 is found begin and end? _____
   What title would you give to this paragraph?

   _____

8. Should this verse read "<u>was</u> before all things," or "<u>is</u> before all
   things? _____ Why? _____

   _____

9. What title or name did Christ use for Himself which conveys the
   same truth? _____

10. According to the consensus of the commentaries, does πρό mean
    "above" or "before"? _____

11. What does τὰ πάντα in verse 17 mean in this context? (You may
    need to read comments on verses 15-17 to find the answer.)

    _____

    _____

12. What is the lexical form of the word πάντα? _____

13. Where else in Colossians does τὰ πάντα have the same meaning it
    does in 1:17? (By the way, be sure you are using a book you can
    depend on for meanings! Look until you find this exact phrase
    listed. You will know it is correct if you also find Col. 1:17
    listed.) _____ Where else in the
    New Testament is this expression used with the same meaning?

    _____

    _____

    Where did you get this information? _____, page___

14. How would you translate the word "consist" in Colossians 1:17?

    _____

15. How does Colossians 1:17 fit into the paragraph in which it is found? _____

16. What are some good parallel passages that correspond with the thought of verse 17? _____

III. SUMMARY:

1. What was the lexical form of "commendeth" in Romans 5:8 (KJV)?
   _____

2. What was the lexical form of "consist" in Colossians 1:17 (KJV)?
   _____

3. What did you discover the word meant in Romans 5:8? _____
   _____

4. What did you discover the word meant in Colossians 1:17? _____
   _____

5. Etymologically, this word means "to stand together." Can you relate this basic meaning to the meanings of the word in these two verses? _____
   _____
   _____
   _____

6. Below, list the author(s), title, publisher and date of the ten best commentaries you used (five for Romans and five for Colossians).

   a. _____

   b. _____

   c. _____

   d. _____

   e. _____

   f. _____

   g. _____

   h. _____

   i. _____

   j. _____

Name_____

Box_____ Grade_____

PURPOSES AND GOALS

The purposes of this assignment are to introduce the student to the Hebrew language and to acquaint him with a few of the basic tools used in its study.

The goals of the student are the following:

1. To recognize and identify Hebrew letters.
2. To gain facility in using Hebrew study tools.
3. To attempt to solve a question through the comparative study of two Hebrew words.

TOOLS

1. Strong's *Exhaustive Concordance.*
2. *The Englishman's Hebrew Concordance.*
3. *Hebrew Analytical Lexicon.*
4. *Hebrew and English Lexicon,* by Brown, Driver and Briggs.

VALUE: 15

PROBLEM: In Genesis 1:3, God said, "Let there be light," and there was light. On the fourth day, Genesis 1:14f, God said, "Let there be lights in the firmament of the heaven...to give light upon the earth." If God created light on the first day, why did He need to create it on the fourth day? What was it that He made on the first day? Did it differ from what He made on the fourth day? If so, what is that difference?

1. Look up the word "light" in Strong's *Concordance.* What is the number for the word "light" in Genesis 1:3? _____

2. Look up this number in the back of Strong's. (Be sure you are in the right section!) To what Hebrew word does this number refer? [On the writing of Hebrew letters, don't try to copy exactly the shapes of printed script of these letters with all the shading and "serifs" — the fancy flairs at the ends of the letters, like שׁ for שׁ. Be contented to get all the basic lines correct, making sure to include the characteristics that distinguish ד and ר, ה and ח, ו and ז, etc.] _____

3. What is the number for "light" in Genesis 1:14? _____

4. To what Hebrew word does this number refer? (Since there are four possibilities of spelling, write only the first.) _____

5. Look up the Hebrew word used in Genesis 1:3 in the *Englishman's Hebrew Concordance.*

   a. How many times does it appear? (Count each occurrence of the word, not just the number of verses.) _____

   b. To what does the literal use of the word basically refer?

(Be explicit!) _____

_____

6. Look up the Hebrew word used in Genesis 1:14 in the *Englishman's Hebrew Concordance*.

   a. How many times does it appear? _____

   b. Read this list of references. Does this word seem to be more specific? _____ If so, in what way? _____

   _____

7. How would you distinguish between these two Hebrew words?

   _____

   _____

   _____

8. Look up the Hebrew word used in Genesis 1:14 in the *Analytical Hebrew Lexicon*. What is its lexical form?

   _____

9. Look up the Hebrew word in Genesis 1:3 in the *Lexicon* by Brown, Driver, and Briggs. Make sure you are reading the correct definition by looking to see if Genesis 1:3 is mentioned. What meaning do they give for the word used in Genesis 1:3? _____

   _____

10. Look up the definition of the word in Genesis 1:14 by tracing down the entries under its lexical form (question 8) until you find the word spelled the same way as in the back of Strong's *Concordance*. You may have to look for a page or two until you find it spelled this way. What meaning do Brown, Driver and Briggs give to the Hebrew word in Genesis 1:14? _____

    _____

11. In what way, if at all, did your way of distinguishing these two words vary from that of Brown, Driver and Briggs? _____

    _____

    _____

12. Since there were no sun, moon or stars until the fourth day, what possible explanation could you give regarding the light that God created on the first day? _____

    _____

    _____

    _____

Name_____

Box_____ Grade_____

WORKSHEET: LESSON 17

PURPOSES AND GOALS

The purposes of this exercise are to guide the student in an understanding of an English word found in both the Old and New Testaments, and to teach him what tools are necessary in this type of study.

The following are the goals of the student:

1. To use the study tools with greater facility.
2. To identify given Hebrew words in the study books.
3. To compare the various uses or meanings of the given words.
4. To make some observations concerning the meaning of the words.
5. To compare the way the word is used in the Old and New Testament.

TOOLS

1. Your own English Bible.
2. Strong's *Concordance*.
3. *Englishman's Greek Concordance*.
4. *The Hebrew Analytical Lexicon*.
5. *Hebrew and English Lexicon*, Brown, Driver and Briggs.

VALUE: 15

PROBLEM: In Exodus 25:17ff, God gives instructions to Moses about a "mercy seat" which was to be made and placed in the tabernacle. It was there that God met Moses. Because of its name, it is natural that you form a mental image of some type of seat or chair where mercy was shown. But, is that really true? What was the "mercy seat"? What was it for? What would be a more accurate name for it? What was its symbolic meaning? These are the questions you will seek to answer in this assignment. So that you can keep an open mind as you study, the "mercy seat" will be referred to as, "X," in this worksheet.

1. Look up "X" in Strong's *Concordance*. Since "X" is two words, you will have to search for the complete phrase among all the references listed under "mercy." What is the number for the Hebrew word, "X"? _____

2. Look up this number in the back of Strong's. What is the Hebrew word for "X"? _____

3. Look up this Hebrew word in the *Hebrew Analytical Lexicon*. What is its root?_____

4. Look up this root in the same book. Not counting the lexical form, how many cognates does this form have?_____
Is "X" one of these cognates?_____

5. a. List the root and all of its cognates in the following chart. After studying the contexts in which they appear,

try to give one English word which you use in everyday
conversation which could define each Hebrew word. If you
need more than one word for any cognate, number these as
distinct definitions.

HEBREW	ENGLISH	HEBREW	ENGLISH
1. :		5. :	
2. :		6. :	
3. :		7. :	
4. :		8. :	

b. Did you find any words with more than one definition?_____
How many?_____ These *may* be from distinct roots,
although they are spelled the same way (Lesson 16:7).

c. Use the following chart to categorize and relate each of the
cognates into root categories. List the same spelling more
than once if you think it is from a distinct root.

ROOT I	ROOT II	ROOT III	ROOT IV

d. It would be of interest and value to check your guesswork
with both Koehler-Baumgartner *and* Brown, Driver and Briggs.
Your worksheet only requires using the latter. Do the other
if you have time.

6. Look up the root in the *Hebrew-English Lexicon* by Brown,
Driver and Briggs.
a. How many *large-print* roots are there for this spelling?____
b. Which root (I, II, etc.) is "X" a cognate of?_____
c. What basic meaning do the root and "X" have in common?
_____

7. Look at your cognate guesswork in question 5. c.
a. Do you have as many roots as Brown, Driver and Briggs?_____

Name_____

Box_____

b. How many distinct words (do *not* count the roots themselves) do they list?_____

c. Rework your chart (use arrows to move words into their "proper" columns) to reflect the arrangement of BDB.

8. a. According to Exodus 25:17-22, with what piece of tabernacle furniture was "X" associated?_____

b. What was "X" made of?_____

c. What was formed on each end of "X"?_____

d. Describe as simply as you can what "X" looked like._____

_____

e. Using modern English, what would be a good name for "X"?

_____

9. Read Exodus 25:21.

a. Based on this verse and the simple meaning of the Hebrew word, what did "X" cover?_____

b. What was inside the ark that was being covered? (See verse 21 and Exodus 31:18.) _____

10. Look up the word "X" in Strong's again. (This time it is spelled as one word.) What is the Greek word for "X"?_____

11. Look up this Greek word in *Englishman's Greek Concordance*.

a. How many times is it used in the New Testament?_____

b. Look up these references in your English Bible. According to one of these verses, "X" was a picture or type of whom?

_____

12. In what way or ways do you think He could be an "X"? (Think of the purpose "X" served in the Old Testament.)

_____

_____

_____

_____

Name_____

Box_____ Grade_____

PURPOSES AND GOALS

The purposes of this exercise are to show the student how his tools can help him do a geographic study and to give him practice in using his tools.

The goals of the student are the following:

1. To increase ability to look up Hebrew words in the study tools.
2. To identify geographic locations by means of this study.
3. To interpret correctly the meanings of given Hebrew words.
4. To form personal opinions based upon his study of the Hebrew.

TOOLS

1. A Hebrew (or Hebrew-English) Bible.
2. *Englishman's Hebrew Concordance*.
3. Strong's *Concordance*.
4. *Hebrew Analytical Lexicon*.
5. *Hebrew and English Lexicon*, Brown, Driver and Briggs.
6. *Septuagint*.
7. *Interlinear Greek - English New Testament*.
8. *Natural History*, Pliny (reproduced, page W18:3).
9. Selected atlases.
10. Selected Bible dictionaries.

VALUE: 30

PROBLEM: The Red Sea plays an important part in Bible geography. Its name becomes so familiar that perhaps you have never thought of its meaning. Why is it called *Red* Sea? Is that really its color? Where did that name come from? How much territory did the Sea cover in the minds of the Bible writers?

1. In the back of the *Englishman's Hebrew Concordance* is an English index to the Hebrew words. Look up "Red Sea."

   a. What is the Hebrew word for "Red" in "Red Sea"? _____

   b. In the same index, what is the first Hebrew word for "Sea"? _____

2. Look up this phrase in the concordance section of this book. In what reference is "Red Sea" first mentioned? _____

3. Look up this verse in a Hebrew Bible. Find these two words in the verse and write them exactly as they appear. _____ Did you notice that one word is a little different in spelling than the form you found in the back of the *Englishman's Hebrew Concordance*? _____ That is because the word in this verse is not in its lexical form. Look up this non-lexical form in the *Hebrew Analytical Lexicon*.

    a. What part of speech is it? _____

    b. Ask and answer the three questions which will parse this part of speech (see page 16:6).

       (1) What is its _____ ? _____ (Answer)

       (2) What is its _____ ? _____

       (3) What is its _____ ? _____

    c. What is the explanation of the suffixed letter? (This is not significant to us at this point.) _____

4. Look up the Hebrew word for "Red" in the *Englishman's Hebrew Concordance*.

    a. How many times does it appear? _____

    b. How many times does the word appear when it is *not* linked with the word, "Sea"? _____

    c. What does it seem to mean in those references? _____
    _____

    d. How many times does it appear with the word, "Sea"? _____

5. Look up each of the references to "Red Sea" in the Bible. Using the context of each reference, plus some atlases, locate each reference on the map supplied on page W18:4. Show the approximate location of where the author understood the Red Sea to be by writing that reference in that place on the map. Some verses will be vague and you may have to guess a little, but all the references from question 4.d. should be written on the map.

6. Look up the word for "Red" in Brown, Driver and Briggs' *Lexicon*. (Be sure you are looking at the correct part of speech!) According to them, what does this word mean? _____
_____

7. Look up "Red Sea" in a few Bible atlases and read the *text*, not the map, concerning it.

8. Now, look up "Red Sea" in a few Bible dictionaries or encyclopedias and read their articles on the subject.

9. Translate *literally* into English the name that the Hebrews used for this body of water. _____

10. If that was the Hebrew name, where did the name "*Red* Sea" come from? How and when did the name become changed? Read the section from Pliny's (c. 23-79 A.D.) *Natural History* which is printed on the next page. Although the Hebrews had their own name for this body of water, the Greeks had another name. According to Pliny, what name did the Greeks (by Pliny's countrymen) use for this body of water? _____

Name_____

Box_____

11. The Septuagint (LXX) is a translation of the Hebrew Old Testament into what language? _____ Since the Greeks used one name and the Hebrews used another name for the same body of water, which do you think the translators of the LXX chose? _____ To find out, use Strong's to discover the Greek words for:

a. "sea" _____   b. "reed" _____

c. "red" _____ (Strong misprinted #2281 here when he really meant to print #2063. Don't you blow it, too!)

12. a. If the men had translated it into "Reed Sea," how would they have written it in Greek? _____

   b. If they had translated it, "Red Sea," how would they have written it in Greek? _____

   c. Look up Exodus 10:19 in the LXX. Which of these Greek names is used for this body of water? _____

   d. Look up Hebrews 11:29 in the *Interlinear*. Which Greek name did the writer of Hebrews choose? _____

13. How and when do you think the name of the "Sea" was changed?

_____

_____

14. Use a felt pen or colored pencil to color in all the area that you think was included in the "Red Sea" on the map supplied.

_____

BOOK VI, Section xxviii.

XXVIII. Moreover in this region the sea then makes a double inroad *a* into the land; the name given to it by our countrymen is the Red Sea, while the Greeks call it Erythrum, from King Erythras, or, according to others, in the belief that the water is given a red colour by the reflexion of the sun, while others say that the name comes from the sand and the soil, and others that it is due to the actual water being naturally of such a character. However, this sea is divided into two bays. The one to the east is called the Persian Gulf, and according to the report of Eratosthenes measures 2500 miles round. Opposite is Arabia, with a coastline 1500 miles in length, and on its other side Arabia is encompassed by the second bay, named the Arabian Gulf; the ocean flowing into this is called the Azanian Sea. The width of the Persian Gulf at its entrance some make five and others four miles; the distance in a straight line from the entrance to the innermost part of the Gulf has been ascertained to be nearly 1125 miles, and its outline has been found to be in the likeness of a human head. Onesicritus and Nearchus write that from the river Indus to the Persian Gulf and from there to Babylon by the marshes of the Euphrates is a voyage of 1700 miles.

In an angle of Carmania are the Turtle-eaters, *The Red Sea and Persian Gulf.* who roof their houses with the shells and live on the flesh of turtles. These people inhabit the promontory that is reached next after leaving the river Arabis. They are covered all over, except their heads, with shaggy hair, and they wear clothes made of the skins of fishes. After the district belonging to these people, in the direction of India there is said to be an uninhabited island, Cascandrus, 50 miles out at sea, and next to it, with a strait flowing between, Stoidis, with a valuable pearl-fishery. After the promontory the Carmanians are adjoined by the Harmozaei, though some authorities place the Arbii between them, stretching all along the coast for 421 miles. Here are the Port of the Macedonians and the Altars of Alexander situated on a promontory; the rivers are Siccanas and then the Dratinus and the Salsum. After the Salsum is Cape Themisteas, and the inhabited island of Aphrodisias. Here is the beginning of Farsistan, at the river Tab, which separates Farsistan from Elymais. Off the coast of Farsistan lie the islands of Psilos, Cassandra and Aracha, the last with an extremely lofty mountain, and consecrated to Neptune. Farsistan itself occupies 550 miles of coast, facing west. It is wealthy even to the point of luxury. It has long ago changed its name to Parthia.

Taken from Pliny's *Natural History*, translated for the Loeb Classical Library by H. Rackham, published by Harvard University Press, and used by permission.

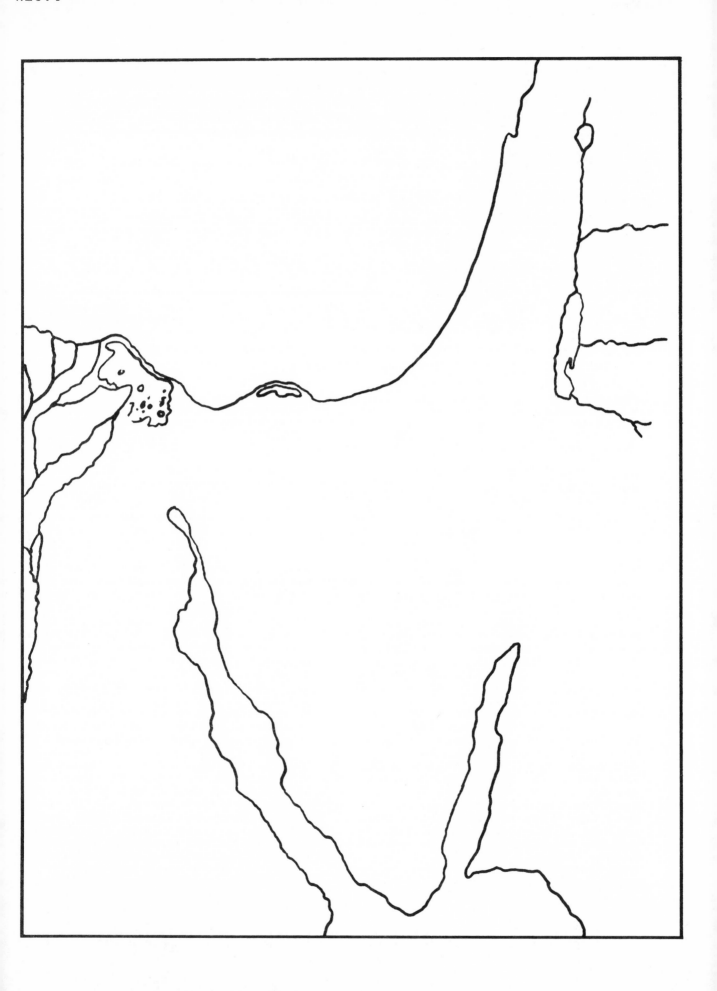

Name_____

Box_____ Grade_____

PURPOSES AND GOALS

The purposes of this exercise are to guide the student in the study of a well-known passage and to see it in its historical context, as well as its future fulfillment.

The goals of the student are the following:

1. To use the Hebrew and Greek study tools with increasing facility.
2. To identify the historical background of a given passage of Scripture.
3. To identify specific countries and movements on a map (provided in this lesson).
4. To learn to distinguish between the immediate and future meanings of a given passage.
5. To choose and write his own definition of a given word after a study of the Hebrew and Greek usages.

TOOLS

1. Your own English Bible.
2. Septuagint.
3. *Englishman's Hebrew Concordance.*
4. *Hebrew Analytical Lexicon* and *Greek Analytical Lexicon.*
5. *Hebrew and English Lexicon,* Brown, Driver and Briggs.
6. *Englishman's Greek Concordance.*
7. *Greek - English Lexicon,* Arndt and Gingrich.
8. Selected atlases and/or Bible dictionaries.
9. Selected commentaries (on Isaiah).
10. *Interlinear Greek - English New Testament.*

VALUE: 45

PROBLEM: Many evangelicals rejected the Revised Standard Version of the Bible because of the translation of Isaiah 7:14. The KJV says, "Behold, a *virgin* shall conceive..." whereas the RSV has, "Behold, a *young maiden* shall conceive...." Many evangelicals say that the RSV has destroyed and is denying the prophecy of the virgin birth of Christ. What is the word in Hebrew? Did the translators of the RSV have any grounds for changing the translation? What is the basic or primary meaning of this passage? Could this verse have more than one fulfillment?

1. Look up "virgin" in the English index in the back of *Englishman's Hebrew Concordance.*

   a. What is the first Hebrew word for "virgin"? _____

   b. What is the second Hebrew word for "virgin"? _____

2. Look up the first word in the concordance part of *Englishman's.*

   a. How many times does the word appear? _____

b. How is it *usually* translated? _____

c. How many times is it translated this way? _____

d. How else is it translated? _____

e. How many times does it appear this way? _____

3. The Hebrew word that immediately follows it in this concordance section is its only cognate.

   a. What is that Hebrew word? _____

   b. How many times does it appear in the Old Testament? _____

   c. How is it *usually* translated? _____

   d. How else is this cognate translated? _____

4. Look up each appearance of the word in question 1.a. There are five columns in the chart below. Place each reference in the column that best fits it. (In some cases you may need to list the references in both C and D.) When the verse speaks of the girl as:

   A. someone who is *NOT* a virgin, put it in column A.

   B. someone who is a young girl, but it is *unknown* if she is a virgin or not, but she could be, write it in column B.

   C. someone who is definitely a *virgin*, put it in column C.

   D. someone whose virginity is a *critical factor* in the context, write this in column D.

   E. something other than a human being, i.e., "virgin" is used *figuratively*, write it in column E.

A	B	C	D	E

Name_____

Box_____

5. a. Using modern, everyday English, how would you translate this
      Hebrew word? _____

   b. Look up this word in Brown, Driver and Briggs. What is their
      definition of it? _____

   c. How, if at all, does your definition differ from their's?
      _____

      _____

6. Look up the word of question 1.b. in the *Englishman's Hebrew
   Concordance.*

   a. How many times does it appear in the Old Testament? _____

   b. How is it usually translated in the KJV? _____

   c. How many times is it translated this way? _____

   d. How else is it translated? _____

7. Using the same basis as in question 4, list each appearance of
   this word in the appropriate columns of the chart below.

A	B	C	D	E

8. a. Using modern, everyday English, how would you translate this
      Hebrew word? _____

   b. Look up this word in Brown, Driver and Briggs. (You will find
      it listed as a cognate of II. עלם.) According to them, what
      does this word mean? _____

   c. How, if at all, does your definition differ from theirs?
      _____

      _____

9. If you were writing about a young girl and the fact of her virginity was a critical factor, which Hebrew word would you choose to
   describe her? _____ Why? _____

   _____

   Which word did Isaiah choose? _____

10. Before you study Isaiah 7:14 in more detail, but based upon your
    Hebrew word study thus far, how would you translate עַלְמָה in this
    verse? _____

11. Read Isaiah 7:1-25 very carefully. Then, answer the following:

a. Who is making the prophecy? _____

b. Who is listening to him? _____

c. Where is the prophecy being given (be specific)? _____

d. With what verses does the specific promised sign begin and end? _____

e. What is this specific promised sign? _____

f. Who is Ahaz? _____

g. Who is Rezin? _____

h. Who is Pekah? _____

i. Who or what is "the house of David"? _____

12. a. In order to understand the passage a little better, you will need to read about the historical situation. You will find it in the historical books of II Kings 16:3-9 and II Chronicles 28:2-6. Was Ahaz a godly or an evil king? _____

b. At that time, the nation of Assyria was gaining power. Both Israel (Northern Kingdom) and Syria (country to Israel's north) were afraid, and desired to enter a mutual defense pact with Judah (Southern Kingdom) for the protection of everyone. However, Judah refused. So, Israel and Syria decided to make war against Judah in order to depose Ahaz and set up a puppet king in his place who would join them. According to the verses above, to whom did Ahaz turn for help? _____

c. At this time, God sends Isaiah to give Ahaz some advice. This is where Isaiah 7:1ff fits in. What is Isaiah's advice (mark one)?

( ) Unite with Rezin and Pekah to fight against Egypt.

( ) Unite with Rezin and Pekah to fight against Assyria.

( ) Unite with Tiglath-Pilezer to fight against Rezin and Pekah.

( ) Unite with Sennacherib to fight against Rezin and Pekah.

( ) Stay aloof and trust in Yahweh.

13. On the map printed on the following page, write in the countries, alliances, and movements. Explain the situation on the map.

14. Study Isaiah 7:14 and its context in a few good commentaries, such as Lange's, Keil and Delitzsch's, Young's, etc. Which did you select? _____
(After reading these, you may go back and change any answer, if you are genuinely convinced that it needs changing.)

15. a. Does the word for "virgin" in Isaiah 7:14 have an article? _____

b. What is the significance of its presence or absence? _____
_____

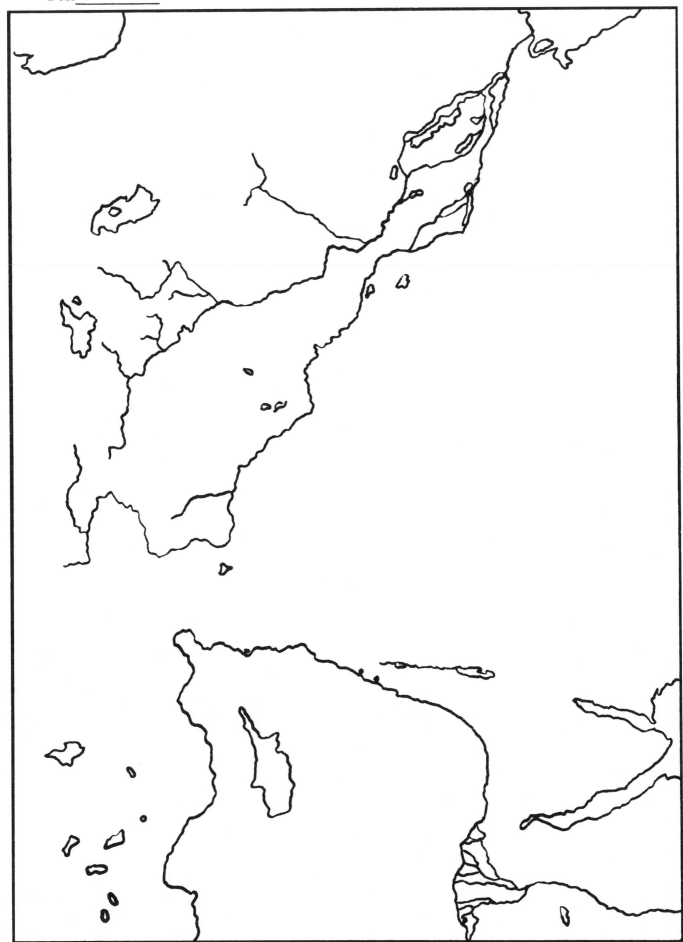

Name_____

Box_____

16. a. What did Ahaz do that caused Isaiah to make this prophecy?
_____

   b. Was God giving this sign as an evidence of His pleasure or His displeasure? _____

17. a. List a few parallel passages that speak of both butter and honey. _____

   b. Under what conditions might people eat butter and honey?
_____

18. Approximately how old would the child be when the prophecy of verse 16 would take place? _____

19. In good Biblical studies of the Old Testament, it is essential to try and understand exactly what the passage meant to its first hearers. After seeing the first meaning intended, it is possible to find "double" meaning from New Testament verses. After your historical study, and before you study the New Testament, how would you now translate עַלְמָה in Isaiah 7:14?
_____

20. From your study of the chapter, of whom do you think Isaiah 7:14 is speaking? (Use the number, 1, to indicate immediate or primary fulfillment, and, 2, for secondary or future fulfillment.)

   ( ) The wife of Isaiah.

   ( ) The wife of Ahaz.

   ( ) A woman of that time - perhaps a member of the court.

   ( ) A woman completely unknown (at that time) as to her person or date of life.

   ( ) Mary.

21. Look up the Greek word for "virgin" in the English index in the back of the *Englishman's Greek Concordance*.

   a. How many Greek words are there for the word, "virgin"? _____

   b. List the word(s). _____

   c. Look up the first in the concordance section of this book. How many times is it used in the New Testament? _____

   d. Look up all of these references. Do the contexts imply the person referred to is definitely a virgin? _____

   e. Look up this word in Arndt and Gingrich. What is their definition? _____

22. Look up Isaiah 7:14 in the LXX. What Greek word is used for עַלְמָה? _____

23. a. What New Testament verses or contexts could you use to support the doctrine of the virgin birth of Christ in addition to

Name_____

Box_____

      Isaiah 7:14 and its quotation in Matthew 1:23? _____
_____

b. Regardless of how Isaiah 7:14 is translated, in view of the context of Matthew 1, and the lexical definition of the Greek word for "virgin," how must you translate this word in Matthew 1:23? _____

c. In Matthew 1:23, deliberately replace "virgin" with "young woman." Now read the context. Does the chapter still teach the virgin birth?_____

d. Before investigating the Greek, read in English the genealogy in chapter 1:1-16.

    (1) Through what gender of person (male or female) is this genealogy traced? _____

    (2) To whom, then, would you assume the "whom" of verse 16 refers? _____

    (3) What gender, then, would you assume this word is in the Greek? _____

    (4) Look at this verse in the *Interlinear*. What is the Greek word which is translated, "whom"? _____

    (5) What gender is it? _____

    (6) What does this have to do with the virgin birth? _____
_____
_____

It is so easy to simply accept what everyone says without think-ing through the facts for yourself. The following are questions to make you think. They are not to be graded, but rather are to stimulate your thinking process. Answer them as accurately as you can.

1. If you were translating Isaiah 7:14 and were thinking only of the immediate context, what English word(s) would you use for עַלְמָה? _____ Why? _____
_____

2. If you were thinking of both present and future meanings, would you change your translation? _____ If so, how? _____
_____ Why? _____

3. If you chose to translate the word עַלְמָה by "virgin," how many virgin births would there be in history? Explain: _____
_____
_____

4. a. If the virgin birth was the sign, who is the one person who would be positive it really was a *virgin* birth? _____

   b. For whom, then, would the birth most serve as a sign? _____

    c. For whom was the sign given in Isaiah 7:14? _____

    d. Why was the sign given? _____

    _____

    e. Would the birth of Christ fulfill this immediate purpose?

    _____

5. a. Isaiah 7:14 speaks of a sign being given. Was there a sign
    given? _____

    b. What do you think the sign was? _____

    _____

    c. How did it serve as a sign? _____

    _____

    _____

Name_____

Box_____ Grade_____

PURPOSES AND GOALS

        The purposes of this assignment are to
demonstrate to the student how he can now use
his tools in a study to determine the meaning
of an idiom which involves both the Old and
New Testaments, and to give him practice for
doing further studies of his own.

        The goals of the student are the following:

1. To identify an idiom that is used in both
   Testaments.
2. To compare the idiom in all of its Biblical
   usages in order to understand its meaning.
3. To write out the meaning of the idiom and
   spell out its significance in a specific
   New Testament passage.
4. To use all the study tools with facility.

TOOLS

1. Your own English Bible.
2. An exhaustive Bible concordance.
3. *Interlinear Greek - English New Testament.*
4. *Analytical Greek Lexicon.*
5. *Greek - English Lexicon,* Arndt and Gingrich.
6. *Analytical Hebrew Lexicon.*
7. *Hebrew and English Lexicon,* Brown, Driver and Briggs.

VALUE: 30

PROBLEM: In the Gospels, we have the account where Mary approaches
         Jesus and asks Him to perform a miracle. He turns to her
         and says, "Woman, what have I to do with thee?" This phrase
         sounds very harsh and disrespectful. Why would Jesus answer
         His mother in this way? What did He mean by this phrase?

1. a. Where is the question, "Woman, what have I to do with thee?"
      found? _____

   b. Not counting the word, "woman," write out the Greek words of
      this question. _____ _____ _____ _____

   c. List each word in order in the columns below. Parse each word
      (when it can be parsed), state its part of speech, give its
      lexical form and give its English translation.

GREEK	PARSED	PART OF SPEECH	LEXICAL FORM	TRANSLATION
	(first ref.)			
	(first ref.)			

d. Translate the expression literally. _____

2. This expression is an idiom. (Reread 5:4-5.) In order to understand its meaning, you must study the appearance of the idiom in
   its contexts. This phrase is included in the meaning of the
   Greek word for "I," in Arndt and Gingrich. Look up this word
   (its lexical form should be in the last line of the chart in 1.c.)
   and glance down the information until you find the idiom of 1.b.
   Read carefully what they say about it. If you don't understand,
   read it again. How many New Testament references do they cite
   for this idiom, and the idiom that is very similar? _____
   List them. _____

3. a. According to Arndt and Gingrich, where does this idiom come
      from? _____

   b. Write out the idiom in this language. _____ _____ - _____

   c. Now, fill out the chart below as you did in 1.c. (You may
      need to reread 16:1-4.) NOTE: The first word will be listed
      in the *Analytical* with a "kamets" instead of the vowel given.

HEBREW	INDIVIDUAL WORD*	PARSED	PART OF SPEECH	LEXICAL FORM	TRANSLATION

				---	

   *That is, separate the letter cluster and deal with each individual word.

   d. Translate the expression literally. _____

4. Compare the Hebrew with the Greek.

   a. When this Hebrew idiom was translated, did the Greeks choose
      their own way of expression, or did they translate the Hebrew
      word-for-word from the original? _____

   b. As far as meaning is concerned, then, which of the two languages
      would be your first authority? _____ Why? _____
      _____

5. Look up the first word of this idiom in Brown, Driver and Briggs.
   Glance through the material until you find the idiom written out.
   Beginning with "(c)," read what they have to say about the idiom.
   How many Old Testament references do they cite? (Include the two
   listed after "cf.") _____ List these. _____
   _____

Name_____

Box_____

6. Study each of the Old and New Testament appearances of
   this idiom. List them in order (from Genesis to Revelation) on the chart supplied on the next page. Different
   references which describe the same event should be listed
   together on the same line! List all the verses on the
   chart before you begin the study. The specific verse
   you are studying in this worksheet should be in the last
   line.

   It will be best for you to work across the page, answering one reference at a time. Briefly describe the historical background or setting in column B (i.e., time and
   place in Biblical history and main people involved).
   In order for the question of this study to be asked,
   there must be two sides. One side wants the situation
   to remain as is and resists any change. The other side
   wants to introduce a change as an intruder. List the
   name of the former, the "resister," in column C. List
   the "intruder" in column D. Observe in each case whether
   the "resister," who is asking the question, expects an
   answer, or if this idiom is only intended as a statement.
   Write "yes" in column E if you think an answer is expected.
   What is the situation before the "intruder" comes, or which
   causes him to come? Write this in column F. Finally, in
   column G, list the change which the "intruder" wants to
   make, or is thought to have made.

7. After you have completely finished the chart, answer all
   of the following questions.

   a. When was the last time Christ had seen his mother
      prior to John 2? _____

   b. Where? _____

   c. What significant events had occurred in the life of
      Christ between that time and the present situation of
      the text? _____

      _____

      _____

   d. What major change did these events bring about in the
      life of Christ? _____

      _____

   e. What did Jesus mean by, "What have I to do with thee?"

      _____

   f. Why did He say it to His mother? _____

      _____

      _____

A VERSE REF.	B HISTORICAL BACKGROUND	C RESI STER	D INTR UDER	E ?	F SITUATION BEFORE INTRUDER ARRIVES	G CHANGE INTRUDER DESIRES

ANSWER KEY

This answer key contains answers only to the statistical and lexical type of information. The opinion type of answers and thought questions are your responsibility.

WORKSHEET 1: 1a. drama 1b. stigma 1c. atlas 1d. thesis 1e. asbestos 1f. pneumonia 1g. panorama 1h. emphasis 1i. genesis 1j. diagnosis 1k. diploma 1l. anathema 2a. tied 2b. slate 2c. foil 2d. mound 2e. dew 2f. music 2g. sweet 2h. immune 2i. broom 2j. few 2k. fruit 2l. growth 2m. gropes 2n. beds 2o. locks 2p. rods 2q. decks 2r. drops 3(,) , comma (') : colon ; semi-colon (;) ? question mark 4a. how 4b. end 4c. house 4d. hay 4e. ate 4f. hate 4g. hate 4h. hen 4i. hides 4j. hopes 4k. hops 4l. hikes

WORKSHEET 2: 1. campus 2. poll 3. Kronkite 4. influential people 5. mimeograph 6a. glamour 6b. no 6c. steal 6d. not committed 6e. big wheel 7. καὶ = "and"

B. 6

particle	verb	conjunction	adjective	article	noun
εἰ	ἐγεύσασθε	ὅτι	χρηστὸς	ὁ	κύριος
if	ye tasted	that	good	the	Lord [is]
conjunction	pronoun+verb	conjunction	adjective	article	noun+verb

WORKSHEET 3: 1a. τῶν 1b. τοῦ 1c. τῇ 1d. τὸ 1e. τὰς 1f. τοῖς 2a. dat. 2b. neu. 2c. pl. 2d. acc. 2e. mas. or neu. 2f. sing. 3a. οἱ 3b. αἱ 3c. ἡ 3d. τὸν 3e. τὴν 3f. τὰς 3g. τῷ 3h. τῷ 3i. τὴν 3j. τοῦ 3k. ὁ 3l. τῶν 3m. ἡ 3n. τὸ 4a. τὸ - τὸν - τῇ - τοῦ 4b. ἡ - τοὺς - τῷ - τοῦ 5a. pathos 5b. dogma 5c. atlas 5d. cosmos 5e. thermos 5f. stigma 5g. exodus 5h. emphasis 5i. dilemma 6a. ate 6b. hate 6c. hue 6d. ill or eel 6e. hill or heel 6f. hire or higher 6g. whom 6h. toil 6i. queen 7. see page 3:3

8. ἄνθρωπος | εὐχαριστεῖ | δοῦλον / πατρὶ   9. ἀπόστολος | εὐχαριστεῖ | θεὸν / ἀνθρώπῳ
         ὁ   τὸν   τῷ   ὁ   τὸν   τῷ
       θεοῦ   ἀποστόλου   δούλου   πατρὸς
        τοῦ   τοῦ   τοῦ   τοῦ

WORKSHEET 4: 1.1 πρὸς 1.2 πρὸ 1.3 περὶ 1.4 μετὰ - παρὰ 1.5 ἀνὰ 1.6 ὑπὲρ 1.7 εἰς 1.8 ἐν 1.9 ἐκ 1.10 ἐπὶ 1.11 κατὰ 1.12 ὑπὸ 1.13 ἀπὸ 2a. ὑπὲρ τὸν 2b. ὑπὸ τὴν 2c. ὀπίσω τῆς 2d. σὺν τῷ 2e. μετὰ τοῦ 2f. μετὰ τοὺς 2g. ἀντὶ τῆς 2h. πρὸ τῶν 2i. ἐν τῷ 2j. εἰς τοὺς 3a. "with the"; masc./neu., sing., dat. 3b. "above the"; mas., sing., acc. 3c. "beside the"; mas./neu., sing., dat. 3d. "with the"; mas./fem./neu., pl., gen. 3e. "into the"; mas., pl., acc. 3f. "after the"; neu., sing., acc. 3g. "in the"; fem., pl., dat. 3h. "away from the"; fem., sing., gen. 4a. third 4b. singular 4c. active 4d. punctiliar 4e. indicative 4f. yes; What time? 4f(1) past 4f(2) *No answer*

WORKSHEET 5: 1. beginning 1a. Σὺ - Thou 1b. Ἠλίας - Elijah 1c. προφήτης - prophet 2a. "you" is emphasized - the religious leaders wanted John himself to explain who he was 2b. "Elijah" was to precede the Messiah (Mal. 4:5,6) and thus would be the indication of his coming 2c. The "Prophet" was another Messianic character for whom Israel was looking (Dt. 18:15). 3. Χριστὸς - Christ 4. The emphasis is on the free and unmerited work of *Christ* to whom our attention should be focused in this section. 5. αὐτοῦ - his 6. The emphasis on salvation is not on us, but on God; also on who we are as Christians: *His* work, created for *His* purpose 7. variation 8. ἡμῖν - to us 9. Things never before known or revealed are now in *our* possession because it was revealed to *us* by the Spirit (in context, "us" refers to the apostles). 10a. πατριάρχης - patriarch 10b. at the end 11. The emphasis is on the superiority of Melchizedek to Abraham, even though he was the *patriarch*, he gave a tenth to Melchizedek recognizing that he was greater.

WORKSHEET 6: R1: 1. be diligent 2. σπούδασον 3. σπεύδω 5. II Tim. 2:15 - σπουδάζω R2: 1a. σπουδάζω - 696 1b. φιλοτιμέομαι - 787 2. 11 3. yes 4. II Tim. 2:15 - σπουδάζω R3: 1. 3 2. italics - 4704 3. σπουδάζω 4. II Tim. 2:15 - σπουδάζω R4: 2. 4 - 2 - 2 3. σπουδάζω 4. II Tim. 2:15 - σπουδάζω

WORKSHEET 7: 1.1 σπούδασον 1.2 374 - σπούδασον, 2 pers. sing. aor. 1, imper. 1.3 2 pers. second person; sing. - singular; aor. 1 - aorist 1 = punctiliar; imper. - imperative, no; active 1.4 σπούδασον is second person, singular number, punctiliar aspect, imperative mood, active voice 2.1 σπούδασον 2.2 σπεύδω 2.3 373 2.4a σπουδή - noun - 6 2.4b σπουδάζω -

verb - 2 2.4c σπουδαῖος - adjective - 3 2.4d σπουδαίως - adverb - 3 2.5 "earnest effort" 2.6 σπεύδω emphasises haste, speed; σπουδάζω emphasises diligence 2.7 σπουδάζω, "to be diligent," far better fits the context of craftsmanship and care in the use of God's Word than does the idea of "making haste"

WORKSHEET 8: 1a. σπούδασον 1b.1 2 pers. - second person, Paul is directly addressing the person he is talking about 1b.2 sing. - singular, Paul is talking to one person 1b.3 aor. 1 - aorist (punctiliar aspect), there is no emphasis on the duration of the action; it is simply conceived of as an event 1b.4 imper. - imperative, the action of the verb is commanded to take place 1b.5 no abbr. - no abbreviation; no "6" as imperative mood has no time; missing element is "voice" - assume "active" 2a(1) gift (2) word (3) powers 2b(1) γευσαμένους (2) same (3) no 2c. vs. 4 gift - δωρεᾶς - gen. - sing. 2c. vs. 5 word - ῥῆμα - acc. - sing. 2c. vs. 5 powers - δυνάμεις - acc. - pl. 2d. δωρεᾶς = gen., others = acc. 2e. As the "word" and "powers" are accusative, they may have been sampled more fully than "gift" which is genitive. This could mean that the people referred to participated in Christian activities without receiving the "gift" of eternal life. 3a. Jn. 20:17 3b. ἅπτου 3c.1 second person 3c.2 singular 3c.3 present = linear aspect 3c.4 imperative 3c.5 middle 3c.6 no time in imperative; lexical form = ἅπτω 3d. punct. = "Don't start"; linear = "Quit" 3e. "Stop handling me!" rather than "Do not (begin to) touch me!" 3f. She probably wanted a physical indication that it was really Jesus and not a spirit, or simply wanted to express affection. 4a. subject slot - ye - all | drink | it 4b. object slot - ye | drink | it - all 4c. nominative 4d. accusative 4e. πάντες 4f. nom. 4g. All of you drink some of it 5a.(1) died (2) buried (3) raised (4) seen 5b.(1) ἀπέθανεν (2) ἐτάφη (3) ἐγήγερται (4) ὤφθη 5c.(1) ἀπέθανεν - third, sing., punc., act., ind., past (2) ἐτάφη - third, sing., punc., pass., ind., past (3) ἐγήγερται - third, sing., combined, pass., ind., present (4) ὤφθη - third, sing., punc., pass., ind., past 5d. ἀπέθανεν is active in voice; ἐγήγερται is combined in aspect and present in time 5e. The combined present indicates Jesus is still risen.

WORKSHEET 10: 1. σπούδασον 2. σπουδάζω 3. 11 4. 5 5(1) Gal. 2:10 - was forward 5(2) Eph. 4:3 - endeavouring 5(3) I Th. 2:17 - endeavoured 5(4) 2 Tim. 4:9 - do diligence 5(5) 2 Tim. 4:21 - do diligence 5(6) Titus 3:12 - be diligent 5(7) Heb. 4:11 - labour 5(8) 2 Pet. 1:10 - give diligence 5(9) 2 Pet. 1:15 - will endeavour 5(10) 2 Pet. 3:14 - diligent 6.(1) Gal. 2:10; was forward; I desired; I was eager (2) 2 Tim. 4:9 or 21; do diligence; try hard; do your best (3) Heb. 4:11; labour; try hard; make every effort 7. "do your best" or "be diligent;" The idea of "speed" is out. "Study" in older English meant "work hard" not "hit the books." But today "do your best" or "be diligent" best communicates the idea of earnest and dedicated striving as a craftsman to treat God's Word in a manner He would approve.

WORKSHEET 11: Problem 1: 1. σπουδάζω 2. verb 3a. Soph. - Sophocles 3b. fifth century B.C. 3c. X. and Pla. - Xenophon and Plato 4a. Septuagint 4b. Philo 4c. Josephus 4d. Testaments of the 12 Patriarchs 5. 2 6. "make every effort" 7a. "be zealous or eager, take pains, make every effort" 8a. 2 Cl. = 2 Clement 8b. B. = Barnabas 8c. IEph., IMg., IPhld = Ignatius 9a. 20 9b. 11 9c. 11 10a. Blass-DeBrunner, Grammatik d. ntl. Griechisch, sec. 392, 1a 10b. Robertson, A Grammar of the Greek NT in the Light of Historical Research, p. 1077f. 10c. Moulton-Milligan, The Vocabulary of the Greek NT 11. Every appearance in Christian lit. cited Problem 2: 1. ὀρθοτομοῦντα 2. Analytical Lexicon 2a. part. = participle 2b. 5 2c.(1) case - accus. (2) number - singular (3) gender - masculine (4) voice - active (5) aspect - linear 2d. ὀρθοτομέω 3. 1 4. Proverbs 3:6; 11:5 5. "to make a straight (path)" 6. no-no 6a. when a word appears only once or twice 6b. yes 6c. ὀρθο-τομέω 6d. ὀρθός - straight 6e. τομος - cutting 6f. "to cut straight" 7. vs. 1 - son - be strong in Christ and copy me, your "father"; vss. 3-4 - soldier - (1) endure hardship (2) work only for your commander; vs. 5 - athlete - compete according to the rules in order to win; vs. 6 - farmer - share in the crops; vs. 21 - vessel/instrument -

be clean and usable for noble purposes; vs. 24 - servant - not quarrelsome, but a gentle teacher

WORKSHEET 13: *No answers will be given here.*

WORKSHEET 14: 1.1 συνίστησι(ν) 1.2a person - third 1.2b number - singular 1.2c voice - active 1.2d aspect - linear 1.2e mood - indicative 1.2f time - present 1.2g συνίστημι 1.3 13 1.4 2 1.5 "demonstrate, show, bring out" 1.6 Ro. 3:5; 2 Cor. 7:11; Gal. 2:18 1.7 Proof of God's love is now continually evident in the fact of the cross. 1.9 Rom. 5:1-11; "Peace with God through His undeserved work in Christ" 1.10 The undeserved character of God's love and the unlikely timing of its demonstration 1.11 "demonstrates" 1.12 Eph. 2:8; Jn. 3:16; I Jn. 4:10; Rom. 6:23 2.1 συνέστηκε(ν) 2.2a person - third 2.2b number - singular 2.2c voice - active 2.2d aspect - combined 2.2e mood - indicative 2.2f time - present 2.2g συνίστημι 2.3 "continue, endure, exist and be composed or compounded, consist" 2.4 2 Pt. 3:5; 2.5 All things came into being and continue to exist in the present because of Christ - this is the idea of present-combined. 2.7 1:15-20; "The Supremacy of Christ." 2.8 "is"; emphasis is on now, continuing to be before/above 2.9 "I am"; Jn. 8:58; Rev. 1:8 2.10 above 2.11 the creation 2.12 παν 2.13 Col. 1:16; Ro. 11:36; I Cor. 8:6a,b; 15:28a,b; Eph. 3:9; 4:10; Phil. 3:21; Hb. 1:3; 2:10a,b; Rev. 4:11; 2.13 BAGD, page 633 2.14 "hold together" 2.15 describes Jesus' relation to the universe as Creator and Sustainer 2.16 Jn. 1:1ff; Heb. 1:1-4 3.1 συνίστημι 3.2 συνίστημι 3.3 "demonstrate" 3.4 "hold together" 3.5 not without forcing a meaning unnatural to the Rom. 5:8 context 3.6 If you did not encounter these, do some reading in: Romans: Murray (Eerdmans), Cranfield (T & T Clark), Barrett (Harper); Colossians: Bruce (Eerdmans), Lightfoot (Zondervan), C.F.D. Moule (Cambridge)

WORKSHEET 16: 1. 216 2. אוֹר 3. 3974 4. מָאוֹר 5a. 123 5b. light as opposed to darkness 6a. 19 6b. yes; the source of light 7. אוֹר is light itself; מָאוֹר is the thing light comes from 8. אוֹר 9. "light as diffused in nature, light of day" 10. "light, light-bearer, luminary, lamp" 11. none 12. The light could have been the expression of God's glory with Him as the source; later He created other sources for the light He had called into being.

WORKSHEET 17: 1. 3727 2. כַּפֹּרֶת 3. כפר 4. 7; yes 5a.1 כָּפַר 1. cover 2. atone 5a.2 כָּפָר village 5a.3 כְּפַר הָעַמּוֹנִי village of the Ammonites 5a.4 כְּפוֹר 1. cup 2. hoar-frost 5a.5 כְּפִיר 1. lion 2. village 5a.6 כְּפָר 1. village 2. pitch 3. flower 4. ransom 5a.7 כְּפָרִים atonement 5a.8 כַּפֹּרֶת covering 5.b yes - 4 5.c In the following chart, the asterisked (*) words are from BDB, the bracketed words [ ] are from K-B. They agree on words with no marks.

ROOT I	ROOT II	ROOT III	ROOT IV
כפר 4	כֹּפֶר 2 *	כְּפִיר 1.2. *	כְּפוֹר 1.2. *
כָּפַר 2 (+1)	כָּפָר 1 *	כֹּפֶר 3 *	
כְּפָרִים		כְּפָר	
כַּפֹּרֶת		כֹּפֶר 1	
כפור 2.] [		כְּפַר הָעַמּוֹנִי	
כפיר 1.2.] [			

Words not related to a root in K-B כפר 2.3.

6a. 4 6b. I 6c. "cover" 7a. You probably guessed wrong, but I wanted you to think about it. 7b. 14 7c. see 5c. 8a. Ark of the Covenant 8b. gold 8c. cherubim 9a. Ark of the Covenant 9b. Tablets of the testimony 10. ἱλαστήριον 11a. 2 11b. Christ

WORKSHEET 18: 1a. סוּף 1b. יָם 2. Ex. 10:19 3. יָמָּה סּוּף; yes 3a. noun 3b. (1) number - singular (2) state - absolute (3) gender - masculine 3c. local ה 4a. 29 4b. 4 4c. water

plants 4d. 25 6. "reeds, rushes" 9. Sea of Reeds 10. Erythrum 11. Greek 11a. θάλασσα
11b. κάλαμος 11c. ἐρυθρά 12a. κάλαμος θάλασσα 12b. ἐρυθρος θάλασσα 12c. ἐρυθρὰν θάλασσαν
12d. ἐρυθρὰν θάλασσαν 13. During the intertestamental period, the Greek name became the
more characteristic designation. The Greek name got into the LXX as the Greek translation of "Reed Sea" and into the NT from the LXX. 14. You should have colored all of the
Gulfs of Akaba and Suez.

WORKSHEET 20: 1a. בְּתוּלָה 1b. עַלְמָה 2a. 50 2b. virgin 2c. 38 2d. maiden 2e. 12
3a. בְּתוּלִים 3b. 10 3c. virginity 3d. maid 4. Because of the subjective nature of these
classifications, we will not give this chart. But few, if any, of your answers should be
in D. 5a. virgin 5b. "virgin" 5c. none 6a. 7 6b. virgin 6c. 4 6d. damsel, maid 8a. young
woman 8b. "young woman (ripe sexually; maid or newly married)" 8c. none 9. בְּתוּלָה - used
more often without doubt to refer to virginity 10. young woman 11a. Isaiah 11b. Ahaz
11c. see vs. 3 11d. 7:14-25 11e. The devastation of the land in the infancy/childhood of
the promised child 11f. king of Judah 11g. king of Syria 11h. king of Israel 11.i king or
he and his court 12a. evil 12b. king of Assyria 12c. stay aloof 15a. yes 15b. If present,
a specific person known to the hearers is intended. 16a. refused God's proposal 16b. displeasure 17a. 2 Sam. 17:29; Job 20:17 17b. prosperity or depopulation 18. within his
first 12 years 20. (1) woman of that time (2) no other possibility in context 21a. 1
21b. παρθένος 21c. 14 21d. yes 21e. "virgin" 22. παρθένος 23a. Lk. 1:26-35 23b. virgin
23c. yes 23d. (1) male (2) Joseph (3) masculine (4) ἧς (5) feminine (6) It shows Joseph
was not biologically connected with Jesus' birth, only Mary.

WORKSHEET 22: 1a. Jn 2:4 1b. τί ἐμοὶ καὶ σοί 1c. τί - nom., sing., neu. - interrogative -
τίς; ἐμοῦ - dat., sing., - pronoun - ἐγώ; καὶ - no parsing - conjunction - καί; σοῦ - dat., sing., -
pronoun - σύ 1d. "What to me and to you" 2. 6: Jo. 2:4; Mk. 5:7; Lk. 8:28; Mt. 8:29; Mk. 1:24;

מַה	..	no parsing	interr. מָה
לִי	לְ	no parsing	prepos. לְ
	י.	first, sing.	pronoun -
וְלָךְ	וְ	no parsing	conjun. וְ
	לְ	no parsing	prepos. לְ
	ךְ	2nd, sing., fem.	pronoun -

Lk. 4:34; 3a. Hebrew 3b. מַה־לִּי וָלָךְ 3c. see included chart 3d. "What to me and to you" 4a. word-
for-word 4b. Hebrew; it was the language originally 5. 8: Ju. 11:12; 2 Sm. 16:10; 19:23; I Kn.
17:18; 2 Kn. 3:13; 2 Ch. 35:21; Jos. 22:24; 2 Kn.
9:18,19 6. We will not provide these answers.
7a. Sometime before His baptism. 7b. in Galilee
7c. His baptism beginning His ministry, as witnessed by John. 7d. New role - Messiah - directly
answering only to His heavenly Father. 7e. "What
have I to do with you?" i.e. "Who are you to involve me?" 7f. "Do not exert any longer your
authority over me."